HEALTH IMPACT OF PARTICIPATION IN THE LIBERATION STRUGGLE OF ZIMBABWE BY ZANLA WOMEN EX-COMBATANTS IN THE ZANLA OPERATIONAL AREAS

Dr. Kalister Christine Manyame-Tazarurwa

authorHOUSE®

AuthorHouse™ UK Ltd.
500 Avebury Boulevard
Central Milton Keynes, MK9 2BE
www.authorhouse.co.uk
Phone: 08001974150

First published by AuthorHouse   06/16/2011

ISBN: 978-1-4567-7728-9

This book is derived from the author's Ph.D. thesis (2009)

ABSTRACT

These are accounts of what happened during the liberation struggle of Zimbabwe, what life was really like for those who fought. How they suffered, their bravery, and their hardships. What happened to the women who fought beside the men lies behind the women's stories in a universal theme showing that women everywhere recognize the fight for independence, and then the isolation and disregard and suppression all accumulating to the trauma that follows.

Until women can talk about their war experiences and make a connection with their grief and anger, they will each still be unconsciously trying to get out of their own personal camps. The experiences are unique, but they are examples of the broader experience of cultural assumptions and attitudes towards women, how these permeate lives, and how each woman, attempts to survive them. Talking about war experiences is talking about trauma and suffering, it is about understanding the long-term health consequences but it is also about women's resilience and strength.

Dedication

This thesis is dedicated to God Almighty

For making it possible to write this piece of work in Memory of a dearly loved brother and son - Martin - who perished at Mavhonde, Mozambique while liberating Zimbabwe.

Contents

Section 1

CHAPTER ONE: INTRODUCTION   **3**

1.1 About the thesis   3
1.2 The author's interest on healing and objectives of the study   3
1.3 Interest on healing from other organisations   4
1.4 Women and War   4
1.5 Academic contribution from other studies   8
1.6 Background of the armed struggle in Zimbabwe   9
    1.6.1 The Unilateral Declaration of Independence (UDI)   11
    1.6.2 The guerrilla war   11
    1.6.3 Racism   12
    1.6.4 Women and the guerrilla war   12
    1.6.5 The involvement of the church   13
    1.6.6 Communism and the guerrilla movement   14
    1.6.7 My bones shall rise again   14
    1.6.8 Lessons from FRELIMO (*the Frente de Libertacao de Mozambique –
    Front for the liberation of Mozambique*)   15
    1.6.9 Power versus Powerlessness   15
    1.6.10 Power and peasantry resistance   16
    1.6.11 The involvement of women in liberation struggles   16
    1.6.12 The Chimbwidos   17
1.7 Activities of the state machinery   18
    1.7.1 Selous Scouts   18
    1.7.2 Central Intelligent Officers (CIO)   18
    1.7.3 Regular Army   19
    1.7.4 Call up   19
    1.7.5 The Police   19
    1.7.6 Government officials   19
1.8 Conclusion   20

CHAPTER TWO: METHODOLOGY   **21**

2.1 Introduction   21
2.2 Ethical considerations   21
2.3 Qualitative approach   22
2.4 Literature survey   24
2.5 Pilot study   25
    2.5.1 Access to documentation   26

2.5.2 People's reactions 26
2.6 The major study 28
    2.6.1 Focus groups. 29
    2.6.2 Face to face interviews 29
    2.6.3 Sociological and Historical Accounts 32
    2.6.4 Narrative inquiry 32
    2.6.5 Recollection of events 34
    2.6.6 Power relations in an interview 34
    2.6.8 Criteria for inclusion 36
    2.6.9 Challenges 36
    2.6.10 Data analysis 37
    2.6.11 Data reduction 38
    2.6.12 The researcher experience 38
    2.6.13 Phenomenological interpretation 39
    2.6.14 Constant comparative analysis 40
    2.6.15 Data validation 41
    2.6.16 Data analysis theory 42

CHAPTER THREE: ZANLA WOMEN IN THE LIBERATION STRUGGLE AND EQUALITY   **44**
3.1 Introduction 44
3.2 Reasons for joining the liberation struggle 44
3.3 The early women recruits – the peasants and roles they played 46
    3.3.1 Burying the dead 47
3.4 The elite women's perception of the liberation struggle 48
3.5 The elite and roles they played 48
    3.5.1 Administration and caring 48
    3.5.2 Keeping of security documents 49
3.6 Anxiety of not being trained to fight 50
3.7 Class differences and women's rebellion 50
3.8 The Chimoio attack 52
    3.8.1 Deaths at Chimoio 54
3.9 Training and deployment: equality with men on the battlefield 55
    3.9.1 No excess baggage 56
    3.9.2 Women's determination 56

CHAPTER FOUR: TRAUMAS OF THE CAMPS AND HEALTH ISSUES   **58**
4.1 Introduction 58
4.2 Diseases and illnesses in the camps 58
    4.2.1 Hurricanes 59
    4.2.2 Hiccups 60
    4.2.3 Migraine 60
    4.2.4 Matekenya 60
    4.2.5 Madef (menses) and fertility during the struggle 61
4. 3 Factors that contributed to the women's health 62
    4.3.1 The journey to Mozambique 62
    4.3.2 Conditions in the camps 62
    4.3.3 Feelings of hopelessness 64

4.3.4 Displacement   64
4.4 Food shortages   66
     4.4.1 Food shortages and training   66
     4.4.2 Food shortages and death   67
     4.4.3 Sexual favours   69
4.5 Bioethics and War   69
4.6 Sleep depletion   71
4.7 rapes in the camps.   71
     4.7.1 Gender power   77
     4.7.2 Physical and psychological injuries of rapes   77
     4.7.3 Rights to reproduction   77
4.8 Torture of women   78
4.9 Biological and chemical warfare   78
     4.9.1 Food poisoning   79
     4.9.2 Spirit mediums, poisoning and witchcraft accusations   79
4.10 Personal care   80
4.11 Pregnant women and Osibisa   80
     4. 11.1 Children dying in the bush   81
     4.11.2 Recording of the babies   81
     4.11.3 Experiences of children in the camps   82
4.12 Meaning of war   82
4.13 Trying times in the struggle   83

Section 2

CHAPTER FIVE: HEALTH ISSUES OF WOMEN EX-COMBATANTS POST 1980.   **85**
5.1 Introduction   85
5.2 Post traumatic stress disorders   85
     5.2.1 Hurt and anger   86
     5.2.2 Witnessing   86
     5.2.3 Loss of loved ones   89
5.3 Women – ex-combatants' perception of their health post 1980   90
     5.3.1 Stomach problems   90
     5.3.2 Trauma of rape and torture   91
     5.3.3 Difficulty in documentation   92
5.4 Fertility issues   93
5.5 Life chances   94
     5.5.1 Women ex-combatants and marriage   95
     5.5.2 Parenting   98
     5.5.3 Integration of women ex-combatants in to civilian life   98
     5.5.3 Women and the freedom of movement   101
     5.5.4 Gender violence and development   103
     5.5.5 Difficulties of obtaining birth certificates for children born during the
         liberation struggle   103

5. 6 Response of health institutions to the needs of ex-combatants 104
5.7 A table showing some traumas of the Zimbabwe liberation struggle 106
5.8 Betrayal 107
    5.8.1 Land distribution 108
    5.8.2 Betrayal as sources of strengths 108
5.9 Going back to war 109

Section 3

CHAPTER SIX: HEALING -TRADITIONAL, CHRISTIAN AND BIOMEDICINE **113**
6.1 Introduction 113
6.2 Healing approaches 113
    6.2.1 African religion 114
    6.2.2 African religion and the liberation struggle 114
    6.2.3 Honouring spirits and the work of the Mafela Trust 117
6.3 African Religion, Guerrillas and Christianity 118
6.4 Healing needs 119
6.5 Illnesses 119
6.6 African Religion and causes of illnesses 120
    6.6.1 The ngozi phenomena 120
    6.6.2 Witchcraft 121
6. 7 Women and Witchcraft Accusations 122
6.8 Seeking help 123
6.9 Healing approaches 123
6.10 Challenges women face in seeking healing 125
    6.10.1 Power versus powerlessness 125
    6.10.2 Economic hardships 127
6.11 Healing processes 127
    6.11.1 Compensation 128
    6.11.2 Acceptance of compensation 128
    6.11.3 Distancing from the perpetrator 129
    6.11.4 Rituals on a family level 129
    6.11.5 Rituals on a national level 131
    6.11.6 The burial rituals 133
    6.11.7 ZINATHA (Zimbabwe National Traditional Healers Association) 133
6.12 Christianity 134
    6.12.1 Christian healing questioned 136
6.13 Biomedicine 136
    6.13.1 Commemoration 137
6.14 Findings 138
    6.14.1 Effectiveness of the healing approaches 138
    6.14.2 Children of traumatised parents 138
6.15 Challenges facing health providers in meeting women's health needs 139
    6.15.1 Western medicine 139

6.15.2 Discriminatory policies   140

6.15.3 Health concepts   140

6.15.4 Traditional healing   140

6.15.5 Colonial reinterpretation of the work of traditional healers   141

6.16.Traditional Religion and limitations   141

6.17 Coping strategies   142

6.19.Contribution of the study to healing   143

CHAPTER SEVEN: CONCLUSION   **144**

7.1 Introduction   144

7.2 The liberation struggle.   144

7.3 Rape and fertility   145

7.3.1 Rape and impunity   146

7.3.2 Women's voices   146

7.4 Witchcraft accusations and the impact on the health of women   146

7.5 The Long term physical and psychological wounds   147

7.5.1Traumas of displacement and loss   147

7. 5.2 Traumatic events and sense of control   148

7.6 Women ex-combatants and integration   148

7.7 Healing processes   150

7.7.1 African religion   150

7.7.2 Biomedicine   150

7.7.3 Christianity   150

7.8 Contribution of the study to the understanding of war trauma   151

BIBLIOGRAPHY   **153**

Map of Zimbabwe

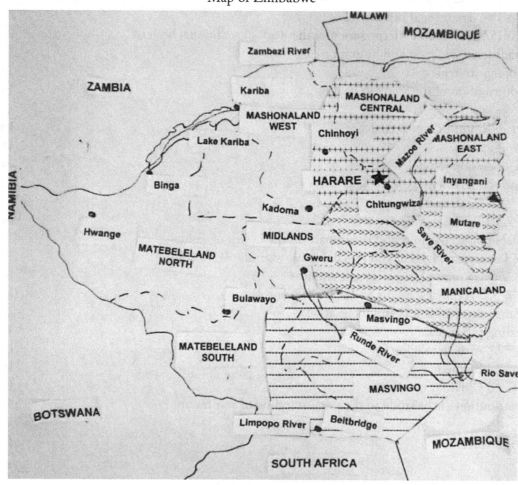

Key

Fig. 1. ZANLA operational areas

ZANLA operational areas	Adopted from Nhongo-Simbanegavi (2000)
+++++++++++++++++	Tete Province
>>>>>>>>>>>>>>>>>>>	Manica Province
-----------------------------	Gaza Province

Glossary of Acronyms and Abbreviations

BSA	British South Africa
BSAP	**The British South African Police**
CCPJZ	Catholic Commission for Peace and Justice in Zimbabwe
CIO	Central Intelligent Officer
Chimbwidos	girl war collaborators
Chimurenga	The liberation Struggle
Chiremba	Traditional doctor or medicine man
Chivanhu	Traditional
Comrade	A combatant of the liberation struggle
ECOSOC	Economic and Social Council of the United Nations
FRELIMO	Frente de Libertacao de Mozambique
ICRC	**International Committee of the Red Cross**
Masvikiro	**Avenging spirits moving about**
Mhuri	***Family***
Mudzimayi	***Mother or wife***
Midzimu	Ancestral spirit
Mukoma	trained male combatant
mutengesi	sell out
Mwari	God
Mweya	Spirit of the dead
NAZI	Short for National Socialist German Workers' Party (NSDAP)
NGO	Non Governmental Organisation
Ngozi	The avenging spirits
N'anga	***Traditional doctor or witch doctor***
OMM	*Organizacao de la Mulher Mocambicana -* Women's wing of FRELIMO
OVT	Organised violence and torture
Pungwe	***All night***
(PTSD)	Post Traumatic Stress Disorder
Selous Scouts	Government special security group
TRC	Truth and Reconciliation Committee
UDI	Unilateral Declaration of Independence
UNICEF	United Nations Children's Fund
UNIFEM	United Nations Development Fund for Women
varoyi	Witches
WHO	**World Health Organisation**
ZANLA	**Zimbabwe National Liberation Army**
ZANU	**Zimbabwe African National Union**

ZANU PF	Zimbabwe African National Union Patriotic
Front	
ZAPU	**Zimbabwe African People's Union**
ZIANA	Zimbabwe Inter-Africa News Agency
ZINATHA	Zimbabwe National Traditional Healers Association
ZIPRA	Zimbabwe People's Revolution Army

Photographs 2-11: Courtesy of Male medical doctor and ex-combatant F

Acknowledgements

My heartfelt gratitude goes to my director of studies Professor Angus Duncan who undertook the supervisory role at a very difficult time. His encouragement and assurance that with hard work there is light at the end of the tunnel kept me going. Thank you Sir.

Professor Ian Bridgeman, I would have been lost without the 'historical' guidance. Your patience with me when one could and would have given up is greatly appreciated.

Professor Gurch Randhawa, thank you for reading my methodology chapter over and over again and pointing out areas that needed attention. I have kept notes and will find them of use some day. Thank you very much.

I am indebted to my external supervisor, Professor Terence Ranger, who kept a sinking ship on course! I shall not attempt to imagine what would have happened had I not been fortunate enough to have you as one of my supervisors. My appreciation for all your support is immeasurable.

I would not have written this thesis, if the ex-combatants, male and female, who shared their experiences with me had not done so. To all the women, you are not forgotten. You will always be remembered and thank you. Your contributions to the liberation struggle will always be part of the history about women and war. Those who did not know what you went through will learn from your experiences what courageous women you are.

To my family, I am because we are and since we are, I am. To my mother - thank you for believing in me. Your words of wisdom and love kept me warm and hopeful. You always knew what I was going through as I traveled on this emotional unpredictable academic journey. You always told me that today will be gone someday! The cups of tea and the comforting little chats we had were sources of strength. Thank you mummy for being my friend. To my sisters, maiguru "Boss" and mainini mai Munya, thank you for walking the road with me. Many times I fell down, but you picked me up and wiped away the tears. My sisters you are dearly cherished and loved. The books you bought, your company as I went around researching, your encouragement, all these are the gifts you gave me and will be kept in my heart. To my nieces and nephews, I do not have space to mention you all but you know who you are and thank you for standing by me. And Tari, I won't forget your support. Thank you. To my brother in law – Mr. C.Jokonya, for all that you have done for me, I can only say may you be blessed abundantly. To my children, Simba and Tapiwa, thank you for comforting me when I was weary. I love you so dearly. To sekuru Martin, thank you for the spiritual support. To my brother Gilbert, thank you for everything.

I want to thank professionals and friends in both the United Kingdom and Zimbabwe who encouraged me to work on this thesis. Thank you Professor Michael Preston-Shoot - Dean of Faculty of Health and Social Sciences - Professor Sandra Jowett, Professor David Barrett, Barbara Burden, Doctor Louise Newport, Professor C. Mararike, Professor Gordon Chavunduka, Doctor Felix Muchemwa,

Angelas Dube, Baba wa Taru, Pamela and Vuli Major, Ms. P. Gumbo, Ms. O. Jirira, Ms. Mlambo, Cathy Mareya, Mary Mugabe, Hilary Gomwe, Tendai Bare, Pastor and Mrs Bernard and many others.

To the computer technical support team – Simba, thank you my son, Bobby Sibiya, thank you my nephew.

Last but not least, I want to thank St. Margaret's Methodist Church in Luton for standing with me in prayers.

Thank you all very much

Section 1

This section describes what the thesis is about and uses the literature on women and war to put it in to context. The methodology applied in the study is followed by a chapter on women combatants in the field looking at the traumas of the camps.

Chapter One: Introduction

1.1 About the thesis

The Zimbabwe liberation struggle or *Chimurenga* of the 1960s to 1980 was fought by ZANLA (Zimbabwe African National Liberation Army) and ZAPU (Zimbabwe African People's Union). Women fought alongside men in this liberation struggle. This thesis is about the long-term physical and psychological traumas suffered by ZANLA Shona women in the period 1975 to 1990. The period of focus was chosen because more women than before started joining the liberation struggle in 1975 and after 1990, too many other factors such as poverty, lack of employment and Aids begin to have adverse impact on women's health to be able to identify the impact of war clearly. Although women of the Ndebele culture participated in the liberation struggle as well, the language barrier and limited financial resources to engage an interpreter prevented the author, who is Shona herself, from focusing on them.

The research was carried out in 2003 at a time when life expectancy for women in Zimbabwe was pegged at 34 years (The Independent, 26 November 2006). The women who joined the liberation struggle at 16 in 1975 were 44 at the time of the study and had already exceeded the life expectancy. In this regard the information obtained was valuable because the study was undertaken when chances of learning about the long-term physical and psychological war traumas suffered by the women were diminishing.

The Independent (26 November 2006) notes that issues that have contributed to the low life expectancy of 34 among women in Zimbabwe include Aids pandemic, food crisis and an economic meltdown that is killing an estimated 3,500 people every week. That figure is more than that dying in Iraq, Darfur or Lebanon. In war-torn Afghanistan, where women's plight has received global attention, life expectancy is still above 40 (The Independent, 26 November 2006). In this respect the information obtained about the Zimbabwean women's war experiences while it was still available is valuable.

To this end, Bhebe and Ranger (1995, p.1) have noted that ''Zimbabwe needs to remember and to understand the war: to understand it at the level of high analysis and to understand it at the level of suffering and trauma. We need to understand it for reviewing policy, for making the record more complete, for healing memories''. These are reflections that epitomise the widespread violations of human rights brought by the liberation struggle.

1.2 The author's interest on healing and objectives of the study

The author's interest was drawn by the realisation that health is an important factor towards development of a nation. While women have fought in wars for economic, social, political and other developments, the author argues that health remains a paramount phenomenon, without which there is no meaningful development to talk about.

Meaningful development of a nation largely depends on the physical and mental well being of its people. The health of a people in turn depends on the existence of social infrastructure which is accessible to the majority of the people particularly women and children (World Health Organisation - WHO - Report on Health and Development Issues, October 1994). Thus gender and health are crosscutting themes that cannot be dealt with in isolation (University of Zimbabwe: Paper on Health and Gender Development in Zimbabwe, 1991).

To this extent, the aims of this thesis are;
- to examine the long term health impacts of participation in the liberation struggle in the period 1975 to 1990 by women in general and specifically by ZANLA women ex-combatants in the ZANLA operational areas which are predominantly Shona culture areas.
- to look at the Post Conflict attempts that have been made to heal the trauma, physical wounds and the illnesses that women have suffered as a result of their war experiences.

1.3 Interest on healing from other organisations

Recently there has been an increasing interest from the government authorities of post-conflict countries in Africa to assess the psychosocial consequences of armed conflicts, and to find desirable culturally congruent local therapies to help the people cope with them (WHO, 1997). This call comes at a time when studies done on healing in many parts of Africa and Southern Africa in particular, indicate that there is still much pain in the communities as a result of what happened during wars and conflicts (WHO, 1997). The wars and conflicts affect not only the bodies but also the 'hearts' and 'minds' of those who suffered as they were physically and psychologically afflicted and affected by the violence that wars bring.

1.4 Women and War

For centuries women all over the world have fought private and public battles, to make the world safer for themselves and for those with whom they live (Mcfadden, 2001). The United Nations Children's Fund (1986) noted that the continued existence of political conflict and violence has had the effect of reducing interest in other economic and social issues including many of the areas which have the greatest impact on women.

The literature on women and war from the First World War to the Sudan conflict demonstrates that conflicts expose both men and women to the dangers of combat but women are particularly affected because of their biology. The United Nations Development Fund for Women (Unifem, 2000), notes that both the experience of conflict itself and the impact of conflict on access to health care determine the physical health and the psychological well-being of women and girls in particular ways. Women are not only victims of the general violence and lack of health care, they also face issues specific to their biology and to their social status. To add to the complexity of the picture, women also carry the burden of caring for others, including those who are sick, injured, elderly or traumatised. This in itself is stressful and often contributes to illness.

Events in Bosnia and Herzegovina, Kosovo, Israel, Liberia, the occupied Palestinian territories, Rwanda, Sierra Leone and Somalia show how violence shatters women's lives during and after conflict. In Congo many people including women and children have suffered and died.

Marwick (1977) in his studies about women in the First World War observes that the shortage of soldiers led to the conscription of more men in to the war leaving women to work in industries that previously were the domain of men. Pugh (1992) notes that with 2 million out of 10.6 million working men enlisted by January 1915, the labour market needed women to work in production, transport, and services. The great demand for munitions led to health effects associated with working in poor conditions and hazardous environments. The Home Office allowed night work, long hours, long overtime, Sunday work, shorter breaks, and hazardous working conditions for women, all of which had been prohibited or controlled before the war (Woollacott, 1994).

The women's Trade Union League complained of exploitation, particularly where women were working with such dangerous substances as aircraft dope or TNT (Braybon, 1981). Findings about TNT showed that the symptoms were nasal discomfort, nose bleeds, smarting eyes, headaches, sore throat, tight chest, coughs, pains in the stomach, nausea, constipation alternating with diarrhoea and skin rashes, anorexia, giddiness, the swelling of hands and feet, drowsiness and finally death (Braybon, 1981).

In general people expressed concern about the effect of industrial work upon women's physical capacity to bear and raise children and upon their moral fitness to be wives and mothers. Indeed, in 1918 the chairman of the Health of Munition Workers Committee noted that women labour involved a physiological and a social problem and raised problems of maternity, infant welfare and home building (Braybon, 1981).

In addition to the health effects of working in the war industries, women suffered loss and bereavement. To this extent, Winter (1995) notes that the one experience shared by survivors regardless of socio-economic status, educational attainment, or political tendency, was that of bereavement. There was scarcely anyone on the home front who had not lost a close relative. Kitchen (2000) suggests that of the 60 million European soldiers, who were mobilised for World War1 about 8 million were killed, 7 million were permanently disabled, and 15 million were seriously injured. Marwick (1977) argues that while many people died and suffered, the war opened economic and political opportunities for women.

However, the gains brought by the First World War were short-lived as some advances women had made were greatly reduced when the soldiers returned from fighting abroad. The women who had found alternate employment lost their jobs. The returning soldiers had to be found jobs and many wanted society to return to its pre-war position. In this regard, as pointed out by Summerfield (1989), by 1939 many young girls found employment in domestic service and the women who had found employment in the Civil Service, in teaching and in medicine had to leave when they got married. Women who applied for jobs with the London Transport in November 1939 were turned down. Employers preferred to employ and promote men and reduce the number of women who had been employed during the First World War. These changes arguably had an impact on the well being of women whose standards of living changed due to the loss of their jobs.

With signs that the outbreak of the Second World War was imminent, Summerfield (1989) notes that Britain whose policy towards women's employment was laissez –fare, as it was in the First World War and in the inter war years, was facing a dilemma of deciding whether women's labour was more needed by the war or home demands. In the end policy makers decided to gradually place women's labour in both the home and industry. As the Second World War progressed, the need for extra labour increased and as a result by 1943 women represented 33 percent of the total labour force in industries as compared to 14 per cent in 1939 (Braybon and Summerfield, 1987). To this extent, the Second World War gave more women jobs and at the same time exposed them to the dangers of working in industry especially munitions factories.

Since World War 1 and World War 2, the world has continued to experience women's involvement in wars. The wars have had an impact on the health of women. In patriarchal societies they have been considered the spoils of wars under collateral damage (Mashall, 2004). Violence was central in the formation of the states that emerged from the former Yugoslavia, ripping apart the very fabric of community life as neighbour fought against neighbour, as families were divided and uprooted, and as hatred spiralled through torture, rape and killing (On Line: www.amnestyusa.org/stopviolence/factsheets/armedconflict.html 5th August, 2005). Here, the women were both the victims of rape and gendered violence, but also the mothers, wives and daughters of soldiers (On Line: www.amnestyusa.org/stopviolence/factsheets/armedconflict.html 5th August, 2005).

The Bosnian Muslim and Bosnian Croat women in the former Yugoslavia, were detained by Bosnian Serb forces in the town of Foca in August 1992 where they were taken every night to be raped and were denied medical care for injuries sustained from sexual abuse and beatings (On Line: www.amnestyusa.org/stopviolence/factsheets/armedconflict.html). To this extent, a twelve year old girl detained for ten days in August 1992, was taken from the centre to be raped; her mother was taken twice (On Line: www.amnestyusa.org/stopviolence/factsheets/armedconflict.html 5th August, 2005). More than 20 000 Muslim women were raped as part of an ethnic cleansing campaign in Bosnia (Mashall, 2004).

In Rwanda, at least 250 000 women were raped in the 1994 genocide; in 2003, thousands of women and girls were raped during fighting in the Democratic Republic of Congo.Gang rape was so widespread and brutal that doctors began classifying physical destruction of private parts as combat-related crime (Mashall, 2004). Violence and the threat of violence against females represent features in patriarchal societies that deny that a woman's body is her own property and that no one should have access to it without her consent (O'Toole and Schffman, 1997).

It appears that a particular feature of conflicts is the frequency of rape. Allcock et al. (1998) point out that rape is a regular feature of human communities throughout the world and across history, particularly during times of war where the claims about its scale, organisation and status as an item of policy have marked out the recent experience of Yugoslavia . Sometimes the Muslim women and children were forced to cross the dangerous frontline on foot and they would reach their destiny in a state of shock and exhaustion (Rogel, 1998).

At the time of this thesis, rape is being used as a weapon of war in Darfur, Sudan in the internal conflict currently taking place. Amnesty International writes that some fifteen women and girls were raped in different huts in the Darfur village. The Janjawid broke the limbs of some women and girls to prevent them from escaping. The Janjawid remain in the village six to seven days where women and girls are being attacked, not only to dehumanise the women themselves but also to humiliate, punish, control, inflict fear and displace women and persecute the community to which they belong (On line: Amnesty International-Sudan: rape as a weapon of war in Darfur). A woman in Darfur described her experience, 'Five to six men would rape us, one after the other, for hours during six days every night, My husband could not forgive me after this, he disowned me'

(On line: www.amnestyusa.org/stopviolence/factsheets/armedconflict.html 5th August, 2005).

Work done by the World Health Organisation (WHO, 2001), the International Committee of the Red Cross (ICRC, 2003), the United Nations programme for Women (Unifem, 2000) and research papers on Conflict Women and Health point out that conflicts have devastating impact on the health and well being of women. The impact generally arises from physical as well as psychological injuries. The International Conference of the Red Cross further highlights that in wartime women may face grave risks to their security; they may lose loved ones, they may suffer from reduced access to the means of survival, they may face increased risk of sexual violence and injury and they may be forcibly displaced from their homes (ICRC, 2003). Other studies have also highlighted that many types of violence against women are exacerbated by wars including indirect violence against civilian populations in post-conflict situations. These include rape/sexual assault and sexual harassment both within the groups of warring factions and perpetrated on civilian populations (Langan and Day, 1992).

In this regard, the United Nations Security Council has expressed deep concern that despite its repeated demands for an immediate end to violence against women caught in armed conflicts, rape and other forms of sexual abuse, as well as all other forms of violence have become systematic, and have reached high levels of atrocity (The International Herald Tribune, 2007).

A variety of resources on the health effects of war on women, indicate that war represents one of the most ancient forms of man-made violence in terms of the magnitude of its effects (McFarlane and de Girolamo, 1996). While certain trends are prevalent across conflicts and regions, and while most women suffer the impacts of war in similar multiple ways, leading to severe physical and psychological hardships, it is important to note that armed conflict affects women in a number of forms that are region and culture-specific. To this extent, some studies suggest that what can be widely conceived as a traumatic experience is not always transferable from one culture to another (Igreja et al, 2001).

Other studies on women and war have shown that while women contribute to the victory of their nations and suffer various forms of violence, they rarely receive recognition and their efforts are soon forgotten when the conflicts end (Staunton, 1990; Omaar and de Waal, 1995; Nhongo, 2000). This lack of recognition has led to feelings of low esteem in many women as they feel used and exploited. Although the experiences of women and war are parallel in many countries, the cultural differences in ideas of health and healing in Zimbabwe will be explored.

1.5 Academic contribution from other studies

Whilst the debate on women and war has generated a very considerable volume of literature, there has been a relatively limited amount of investigation which has focused on the experiences of women as it relates to their health. Honwana's (1997) study looks at trauma healing in Mozambique after the civil war of 1975 to 1992, but there is less focus on trauma as it affects women.

The studies on the liberation struggle of Zimbabwe point towards an understanding of history and the different analyses of the positions of women (Kriger, 1992). Kriger argues that masses were coerced to support the guerrillas and women were either coerced or they supported the liberation struggle in an effort to address their own gender agendas. Josephine Nhongo -Simbanegavi (2000) in her book ' For better or Worse? Women and Zanla In The Liberation Struggle' a book which is derived from her PhD thesis (1997) 'Zimbabwean Women In the Liberation Struggle: ZANLA And Its Legacy, 1972-1985' challenges the claim that women's roles in the liberation war earned them equality and esteem; she shows that women were marginalized and continued to experience discrimination. Lyons in her PhD thesis (1999) titled 'Guns and Guerrilla Girls: Zimbabwean Women in the National Liberation War', focused on the ideological perceptions and representations of women. Although Lyons' work, like much of the literature about the experiences of women in the liberation struggle, is based on the voices of the women themselves mainly through interviews, it can be argued that it is important to let the woman ex-freedom fighters speak again and again as the meaning of experience may change over time.

Other scholars such as David Mark Lan (1985) and Eleanor O'Gorman (1999), in their studies 'Guns and Rain Guerrillas and Spirit Mediums – a book derived from Lan's PhD thesis (1983) 'Making history: Spirit Mediums and the Guerrilla War in Dande Area of Zimbabwe' and 'A Study of Women and Local Resistance In The Zimbabwean Liberation War' respectively, shed some insight on the historical accounts of ZANU and ZANLA Liberation Wars. Lan (1985) gives spirit mediums a pivotal role in mobilising the peasants to support the guerrillas a process that gave the guerrillas legitimacy. Bourdillon (1984) observes that it is possible that mediums worked hand in hand with guerrillas either out of fear or because of the power and legitimacy that would come to both from such a co-operation. O'Gorman (1999) discusses the agency of women and resistance as they get involved in the liberation struggle and the attitudes of reintegration they faced in postwar Zimbabwe.

These earlier studies provide some background against which changes that occurred in the position of female freedom fighters and civilians during and after the liberation struggle can be measured. The changes may be due to failing memory as time lapses or the prevailing political climate. Werbner (1991) in his study of 100 years of family history in Zimbabwe from the colonial period to the present shows how people through memory use narratives to portray their personal image or sense of self and their place in a community. The gap that the study under investigation hopes to fill is the women's perception of the impact of war on their health from the time they were in the camps to the time they were in post-war Zimbabwe.

It is hoped that the present research will contribute to the wider debate of the war experiences of the women and how these have impacted on their health looking at historical, social, economical and political factors. It is further hoped that the present research will deepen the institutional approach to the health needs of women affected by sharing best practices and lessons learned from the research. In addition, It is hoped that the present research will contribute to a deeper understanding of women in armed conflicts and women's potential role in preventing wars. Assuming that women are more peace oriented because of maternal family instincts, their increased participation in politics and in decision making should be given more weight.

With no end in sight to wars and conflicts in many countries such as Sudan, and Iraq, it is important to recognise the effects of wars on women and the need to heal. The need to heal comes from the recognition that not only can healing improve the lives of the individuals but that the development and the well being of the future generations must be secured by the present, taking the right actions. Using the WHO definition of health as 'a state of complete physical, mental and social well-being and not merely the absence of disease or infirmity' (World International Health Conference, 1948), the study supports WHO's view that the impact of war and violence must be measured not only by death and injuries due to weaponry, but by often the greater longer-term suffering linked with damage to essential infra structure. During conflicts, the universal values pertaining to mental, physical and social well being of humans, are violated against and healing everywhere depends on the social and cultural context.

1.6 Background of the armed struggle in Zimbabwe

The reasons for going to war by the indigenous population of Zimbabwe can be understood by looking at the political environment that existed in the colony.

Since the middle of the nineteenth century white hunters and later on white missionaries were arriving in increasing numbers in Southern Africa in the region that is now the country of Zimbabwe (Aranha, 2002). Attracted by gold and other mineral deposits in the area, the numbers of European (primarily British) traders, mining prospectors and hunters grew rapidly. In 1890, the region known as Mashonaland was occupied by the British South Africa (BSA) Company and the town of Salisbury - now Harare - was established (Aranha, 2002). Three years later in 1893, the BSA under the leadership of Cecil Rhodes defeated an uprising of the Ndebele King Lobengula who had ruled the southern part of Zimbabwe, known as Matebeleland (Blake, 1978). Rhodes' great plan was to establish the Cape to Cairo railway so that the gold and other riches of the African continent could be easily transported to the shores of the southern Mediterranean and then across to Europe (Blake, 1978). With this end in mind, Rhodes set about expanding European settlement northwards from South.

With the expansion of Europeans northwards, the land of Zimbabwe was settled by the British in 1890 and named Rhodesia after its founder, Cecil John Rhodes, who believed that the English had an inherent right to imperial rule because they were the first race in the world and therefore the more of the world (they) inhabited, the better it would be for the human race (Nyangoni,1978).

When they colonised Zimbabwe in 1890, they not only committed acts of repression and dispossession, they also destroyed pre-colonial power structures, African religion and values. It was this sense of dignity that had been gradually stolen by imperialism and eroded by settlers that the indigenous Zimbabweans sought to restore. Through the first *Chimurenga* (liberation struggle) of 1896 to 1897 two spirit mediums, Nehanda (Female) and Chaminuka (male), fought to resist white domination (Shoko, 2006). They were charged and executed in 1897 for insurgency (Shoko, 2006).

The following years saw Africans demanding change only within the limitations of the imperial constitution, calling for equal access to jobs and the right to participate in their government (Gann,

1981). But from the 1960's, the nationalists' vision of freedom became more radical; they now demanded an overthrow of the minority rule if their rights were to be fully recognised (Gann, 1981).

Following the demands of the African people in Southern Rhodesia (now Zimbabwe) a royal commission from Britain toured Northen Rhodesia (Zambia), Nyasaland (Malawi) and Southern Rhodesia (Windrich,1978). In its 1960 report, the commission recommended that the territories be allowed to withdraw from the federation under black majority governments but white British settlers, especially those in Southern Rhodesia, were terrified of the prospect of domination by a black run government (Windrich,1978). Northern Rhodesia and Nyasaland withdrew from the federation in 1963 and became the independent countries of Zambia and Malawi within a year (Windrich,1978). The Southern Rhodesian whites refused to accept a multiracial government in their country.

The Africans of Rhodesia were then ruled by an all-white government in which they were not allowed to participate. Nyangoni (1978) notes that only whites were granted the right to vote and elect the leaders governing their land. To this extent laws were passed which prohibited the presence of Africans in many public places. Chung (1989) points out that ordinances allowed for inequitable distribution of the land that provided Zimbabwe's large population of farmers with sustenance. Under these ordinances, 6000 whites seized the best half of the land while the worst half was left to the 600,000 black peasant farmers (Chung, 1989). The ideology of innate British superiority served as justification for their discriminatory colonial policies which led to much civil unrest among the Africans (Nyangoni, 1978).

Indeed the British settlers believed, like the Afrikaaners, that a black man was born to hew wood and carry water and nothing more but they were too civilised to admit this even to themselves (Raeburn, 1978). It was their behaviour that proved it, the way the British talked down to Africans, called them boys and girls, the way they were horrified at the idea of touching them and the discriminatory laws they passed. But they always left the odd loophole in the law to keep their consciences clear: There was the occasional multi-racial hotel or theatre where the small African elite could go (Raeburn, 1978).

Some white families also experienced the discriminatory practices. A white farmer's son remarked how his father treated blacks. "Many times I was witness to outright disintegration of innocent black workers at my father's hands. I did not think a man like my father should be allowed to live. I changed my name because I did not want to be associated with him. I hated the image that people would have of me, the identity they would give me simply because I was white" (Richards et al., 2003).

To this extent, the European colonisers' perceptions, manipulations, and oppressive actions shaped the identity of the indigenous population (Young, 1990). The colonisers granted different degrees of privilege to the people they colonised based on phenotypes, as a result divisions and mistrust were created between "racial" groups that kept them from developing a collective identity as oppressed persons or as Africans (Young, 1990).

In this regard the identity of men and women of Zimbabwe in the colonial era was a political concept connected to the idea that blacks as a group of people who share the same origins and cultural characteristics such as religion was oppressed. Young (1990) further observes that oppression makes a group, as was the case with the Zimbabwean indigenous population, peculiarly vulnerable to cultural imperialism, violence, exploitation, marginalisation and powerlessness.

1.6.1 The Unilateral Declaration of Independence (UDI)

The white minority government of Ian Smith and the Rhodesian Front party challenged moves by the United Kingdom towards black majority rule in the then British colony by declaring self rule-UDI (Unilateral Declaration of Independence). Although Ian Smith declared UDI, his government will be referred to as colonial because the author feels that it represented colonial aspirations.

When Prime Minister Ian Smith of Rhodesia declared the UDI from Britain on December 11, 1965, little did he know that this political act of defiance convinced the colonised blacks that the only way to attain black majority rule was through 'the barrel of the gun'. "Not in a thousand years would the blacks of Rhodesia rule themselves", declared Ian Smith (Chingono, 1999). Thus, the stage was now set for the next round of the political game. This time, it was politics with violence as the blacks argued that if they were not to remain forever victims, there was no option but to fight back against what they represented to be an inhuman system perpetuated by the colonial government (Hays, 1977).

Although the International world imposed sanctions against Rhodesia in response to UDI, Britain under the Tory government of Mr. Heath went on to trade with Rhodesia ignoring the inevitable future consequences this was to bring out (Humberacci et Nuchnik, 1974). America too went on to import chrome from Rhodesia in 1971 in defiance of the UN Security Council sanctions against the illegal regime of Salisbury (Humberacci et Nuchnik, 1974). While dockers went on strike in protest against the arrival of the first shipload of the Rhodesian chrome, Senator Edward Kennedy said that the ship would be unloading ' a tremendous cargo of American discredit' (Humberacci et Nuchnik, 1974). In this regard, America's Foreign policy is viewed with suspicion wherever popular movements run counter to vested economic interests (Taber, 1970). In the meantime, the nationalists' vision of freedom become more radical after UDI, they now demanded an overthrow of the minority rule if their rights were to be fully recognized (Nyangoni, 1978).

The first officially acknowledged military engagement following UDI occurred at the end of April 1966 when seven members of a ZANU group were killed near Sinoia (now Chinhoyi), and in May another ZANU group shot dead a white farmer and his wife at their farm near Hartley (now Chegutu) (Raeburn, 1978). The objective of the guerrillas seems to have been to strike at the white agricultural sector by frightening the farmers off their farms and creating labour shortages by encouraging alien workers (Mozambicans and Malawians) to go to their own countries thereby creating room for easier penetration that would undermine the security of the whites (Raeburn, 1978).

1.6.2 The guerrilla war

In human history, including women's history, revolutions are the peaks (Cliff, 1984). The colonial era was when ideas of liberation from colonial oppression blossomed. Each and every revolutionary movement is the result of the historical development of the struggle of a people to achieve liberty and justice (Cliff, 1984).

Many have suggested that when people decide to take up arms, they do so because they believe that there is no other way to rectify injustice (Zimbabwe women writers, 2000). They often do so because they have ideals and dreams. They are prepared to make sacrifices. In this regard the early resistors Mbuya Nehanda and Chaminuka died because of their love to save Zimbabwe from the settlers. Des Pres (1976) has provided some insight in to how some people resolve conflicts – they do so by dying and through death ensure that the spirit they spoke or fought for shall not perish. Similarly the execution of Mbuya Nehanda and Chaminuka would inspire the children of Zimbabwe to regain the country taken by the colonial settlers by fighting and dying for the liberation of Zimbabwe.

To this extent, the independence of Zimbabwe was secured in 1980 after a fierce liberation struggle between Ian Smith's Rhodesian Front (RF), and a coalition made up of two armies from opposition political parties: the Zimbabwe African National Liberation Army (ZANLA) the fighting wing of ZANU (Zimbabwe African National Union) based in Mozambique, and the Zimbabwe People's Revolution Army (ZIPRA) the fighting wing of ZAPU (Zimbabwe African People's Union) based in Zambia (Nhongo, 2000).

Through violence, the settlers and the nationalists exercised power over each other to retain what each believed was rightfully theirs. The liberation struggle turned out to be a bloody war that left many civilians and ex-combatants dead, maimed, wounded, tortured and scarred for life. It brought untold suffering to many. The consequences of the liberation struggle have no doubt left a legacy of wounds and scars of war that need healing.

1.6.3 Racism

The irrevocable struggle between colonialism, neo-colonialism and imperialism were the driving forces for the need for a change (Martin and Johnson, 1981). This explains why the indigenous group of black men and women, took up arms to fight as a race belonging to the oppressed. The young Rhodesians sent to fight were told that 'the war was a glorious adventure, an easy test of manhood, a war that was right and always honourable, a war where the good were white and the evil were black, a war as simple as that' (Moore-King, 1988, p. 3). In this sense, it can be argued that the fundamental antagonism in the colony was that between races, not sexes.

In this regard, women's oppression can only be understood in the context of the wider relations of class exploitation. It was the oppressive system leading to feelings of hopelessness and powerlessness that women alongside men sought to escape by taking up arms to fight the colonial government.

If these young women had any political ideology at all when they joined the struggle, their motive was to defeat the enemy and liberate the country; the 'enemy to most of them, was simply the white man, who had imposed the white rule on their country. They were not thinking of a war against male domination, for to most that was God given (Nhongo, 2000).

1.6.4 Women and the guerrilla war

With the progression of war, the Zimbabwe African National Liberation Army (ZANLA) and the Zimbabwe People's Revolution Army (ZIPRA) soon realised that they needed women in the armies. Josephine Nhongo (2000, p.41) puts it 'Once full-scale war developed, ZANLA soon grasped the fact that it needed the masses and it needed women'. It deliberately recruited women, but not for combat duties. ZANLA leaders allocated women roles as cooks, nurses, and, above all, as porters and carriers. Thus in the early days of the struggle, there were women in the ZANLA forces but they were custom bound. They did the cooking, they carried arms over the border so that the men could fight.

Women of different age groups and from different backgrounds fought in the 1966 to 1980 liberation war in order to escape the oppressive system.

An estimated 250,000 women joined the liberation struggle (UNICEF Report, 1994). Girls as young as thirteen, sometimes younger, had roles that they played. Women, single, married, widowed, or divorced; all had roles in the struggle that won Zimbabwe independence in 1980 (Staunton, 1990). The desire to liberate Zimbabwe was accelerated from 1974 to 1975 by the attainment of independence in Mozambique where the Portuguese bowed down to the indigenous' resistance (Nhongo, 2000).

When the women arrived in Mozambique, they found out that they had to wait in refugee camps not knowing when they would be trained because male guerrillas got trained first. These women who were not trained were required to do domestic duties including walking long distances on foot and on rough terrain, carrying loads of heavy ammunition.

In response to the armed struggle engaged by the indigenous people, the colonial government of Ian Smith fought back with all its might to defend what it termed 'Christian civilisation' but in reality Ian Smith was defending the economic prosperity that was being enjoyed by the white minority at the expense of the black majority (CCPJZ, 1999).

1.6.5 The involvement of the church

When we bear in mind the imperialistic nature of Western, European civilisation motivated and justified by the Christian religion, we can appreciate its global as well as national influence (Rai and Lievesley, 1996). Once this basis of a society is fully understood the critique can be rigorous and far-reaching (Rai and Lievesley, 1996).

In this regard it is not surprising that African nationalism became more aggressive and hostile to Christianity which was seen to support the status quo. Trade unions too criticised the churches because they allegedly softened the people into acquiescence to the settler government. The suspicion of the church also reflected the fact that the church had supported the colonial government after it defeated an uprising of king Lobengula and the Ndebele people in 1893. Father Prestage had declared ''If ever there was a just war, the Matabele was a just war. I am delighted that such a tyrannical and hateful rule has been smashed up. The Chartered Company's forces deserve sound praise, they have done their work well'' (McLaughlin, 1996, p. 10).

To this extent combatants used to lament about religion. 'Yes, the bible and the sword. That's why it all started. The days of prayers are gone. We have prayed long enough and it's time we give them back their bible and we claim back our land. The land of our ancestors. Forward with the People's revolution. We salute you Mbuya Nehanda, we salute you sekuru Kaguvi, and we give back the white man's religion' (Nzenza, 1988, p.54).

Against this background, the churches were to respond by offering support to the liberation movements, but none spoke out so publicly nor so frequently as the Catholic church, nor suffered more casualties both at the hands of the guerrillas and the Rhodesian government's security forces (McLaughlin, 1996). Indeed Bishop Lamont of the Catholic Church was a thorn in the Rhodesian security forces because he was seen as a person who was using the church to support terrorism (Mclaughlin, 1996). The official attitude was that the Roman Catholic Church in particular was actively involved in supporting terrorism in every aspect – from weapons, safe houses, information supply and medicine (McLaughlin, 1996.)

The attitude of Swedish missionaries to the liberation struggle has been documented by Bhebe (1999). The attitude was abstention from participating in Rhodesian politics by first emphasising their differences of nationality from the Rhodesian white settlers and secondly by upholding the Lutheran doctrine which taught that citizens must be obedient to their secular rulers because they represented the will of God. In this light, further notes Bhebe, the Swedish frowned upon church employees who actively participated in nationalist politics as that was regarded as a form of rebelliousness against, if not actual attack upon the secular rulers. As a result, Lutherans knew that African nationalists or White settler politics were not allowed in the church and that political participation was an individual's private affair.

1.6.6 Communism and the guerrilla movement

The Zimbabwe masses were ready for a radical change in the hope that it would bring equality and justice for all. The political environment in Rhodesia then could be likened to that which had existed in essentially agrarian countries of China, Yugoslavia, Vietnam, Cuba, to name just a few. In these countries, the political climate was conducive for the development of a unique radical tradition where the plight of the rural masses, in particular brought about by the acute land shortage and overpopulation, had exalted the peasant in the eyes of the local intelligentsia (Frankel et al., 1992).

Throughout the liberation struggle, the Rhodesian Front Government was to use the fear of communism, whose ideology ZANU had adopted, to win support for its counter-insurgency measures. The civil war was depicted as a battle against atheism and terrorism with nationalist guerrillas referred to as 'communist terrorists' (McLaughlin, 1996).

Indeed guerrillas were called communist terrorists because much of their funding came from Russia and China. Further the nationalists felt that there were similarities between what they were fighting for and what the socialist movements in Russia and China fought for. It is therefore not surprising, that ZANU adopted Marxist-Leninist-Maoist ideology. To win support from all classes of people, ZANU had to modify the Marxist-Leninist-Maoist ideology. Mclaughlin (1996) notes that the new directives read, "While we are still executing the general line of armed struggle against the enemy, it is not possible to effect a socialist revolution. We need to unite with all forces in Zimbabwe that oppose the settler regime. These include businessmen, trade unions, women organisations, student, peasants and intellectuals, despite their ideological beliefs". To this end, the nationalists searched for a religious and cultural base for their movement, through a revival of traditional religion (McLaughlin, 1996).

1.6.7 My bones shall rise again

As nationalism turned into guerrilla war in the later 1960s and 1970s, the old combatant role of African religion which connects the dead to the living was rediscovered as the indigenous population began a struggle for self-determination, democracy, freedom, social justice, human dignity and peace (Ranger and Alexander, 1998). It is the prophetic voice of Chaminuka, one of the fallen heroes, 'My bones shall arise again' that was to influence the liberation struggle of the 1960s to 1980. True to the prophecy, the 1950s African nationalist movements emerged (Ranger, 1967). Nationalist leaders visited Mwari shrines and senior mediums to ask for spiritual power to overthrow white rule; mass nationalist rallies sang hymns to the spirit mediums executed in 1897 (Ranger, 1967). African religion connected modern Zimbabweans to past kings and generals; it laid a profound African claim to the soil and the landscape (Ranger, 1967). The atmosphere of the shrines had a powerful influence on the imagination of cultural nationalists. Joshua Nkomo (1917-1999), widely known as "Father Zimbabwe," who first visited the war shrine in the Matopos in 1953 as a young urban politician, continued to visit the shrines until his death more than forty years later (Ranger and Alexander, 1998).

1.6.8 Lessons from FRELIMO (*the Frente de Libertacao de Mozambique* – Front for the liberation of Mozambique)

When Mozambique was fighting for independence, it was FRELIMO, the main indigenous movement that mobilised the masses to fight against the Portuguese settlers. The Mozambican nationalists knew that they needed the support from everyone in order to win the war. On 25 September 1963, FRELIMO had appealed to the indigenous populations- workers and peasants in plantations, sawmills and concessions, in mines, ports and factories, intellectuals, officials, students, soldiers of Mozambique in the Portuguese army, men, women, young people and patriots for the conquest of the Portuguese colonial government and independence for their country. (Humbaraci and Munhinik, 1974).

The overthrow of Antonio de Oliveira Salazar of Portugal on 25 April 1974 meant that the paralysed government was no longer able to control the Portuguese colonies in Africa (Weisbord, 1974). The African colonies had to be given up with Guinea-Bissau becoming independent on 10 September 1974, Mozambique on 25 June 1975 and Angola on 11 November 1975 as the rebellious African movements took advantage of Lisbon's bankruptcy (Waterhouse, 1996).

Continued military success for Frelimo in 1974, combined with the Portuguese revolution in the same year, led to sudden victory and a negotiated transition to independence in June 1975, when Frelimo became the ruling and only political party in Mozambique. With Frelimo poised to take power, the majority of the 200,000 Portuguese settlers fled, removing or destroying property and infrastructure in their wake and leaving the country virtually devoid of educated and skilled labour (Waterhouse, 1996).

1.6.9 Power versus Powerlessness

The significance of power, as an organizing concept for the study of the liberation struggles in Zimbabwe lies in its implication that there was a greater level of disharmony between individuals and society. Goverde et al. (2000) note that disharmony between individuals and society implies that the very constitution of society itself – its infrastructure, its stability, its mechanisms of continuity and adaptation, adopts the language of the social theorist Michael Foucault that some people are dominated systematically by others. In this context, progress in society derives not from some felicitous virtuous circle or invisible hand but from the continuing struggle of individuals and groups to improve their lot in a context of both continual manifest and deep division between them and others who have less or more power than them.

The armed struggle of Zimbabwe arguably represents different actors who had power to speak and act as well as silencing and rendering others powerless. The claims of truth made by the colonial government of Ian Smith and the liberation movements can be viewed as a strategy of power which enabled those who had truth on their side to speak but rendered mute those who did not. Laclau and Mouffe's (1985) work on hegemony and socialist strategy note that the truth becomes a way of defining the possibilities of debate.

1.6.10 Power and peasantry resistance

The mass exploitation exercised and felt in various ways can be explained in the paradigms of power relations that existed in Rhodesia. Michael Foucault provides indications to what holds society together in its heterogeneity (Foucault, 1994). It is a task accomplished by a multiplicity of force relations extending from indirect domination to relations of direct repression (Foucault, 1994). It is argued that Foucault's analyses make clear that at the same time as relationships of power restrict certain opportunities for engaging in different types of action, they make others possible (Goverde et al., 2000). In this case, the author argues that while the colonial government exerted power over the indigenous people in an effort to stop them from gaining entry into equal economic and political participation, it also made it possible for the indigenous people to seek alternative ways of gaining entry through resistance, violence and the armed struggle.

By the mid – 1970s, the violence of conquest, of forced migration, of state agrarian policies and of political repression had long shaped the indigenous people, giving them an unusually refined understanding of state power, as well as of strategies of resistance, accommodation and adaptation (Alexander et al., 2000). In this regard, Barbalet (1985) argues that Foucault's work not only places the conception of power in central focus but promotes the idea that where ever power has to be found, one would also find resistance. He found power and resistance almost inescapable and dialectically linked. In this regard, the acute land shortage and overpopulation led to feelings of revolting against the colonial government (Ranger, 1967).

Indeed it was poverty and extreme land shortage that made the rural people receptive to radical messages of the nationalists and the guerrillas to the extent that the rural mass was eager to participate and collaborate in the liberation struggle. They were especially driven to such volatile and aggressive moods not just by frustration of meagre existence but also by their extreme consciousness of what appeared like suffering amid plenty. Everywhere around them there was plenty of wealth and abundant resources to which they were denied any direct access (Bhebe and Ranger, 1996). It is this period that the Rhodesian State, arguably, faced its real challenges from ZANU and ZAPU liberation movements (Alexander et al., 2000).

However, Kriger argues that coercion within rural society along with gender, age, wealth and lineage lines, played a more important factor than ideology towards peasant support (Kriger, 1992).

1.6.11 The involvement of women in liberation struggles

It is believed that no revolution will triumph without the participation of women (Davies, 1983). Zimbabwean women contributed a great deal to their nation's fight for independence. At the beginning of the struggle, women were needed as couriers as the late commander, comrade Tongogara put it, " the geographical barrier - the Zambezi - made it very impossible for us to have a continuous flow of supply…particularly weapons, food and other things. The people would go and get engaged for a week and then exhaust all the ammunition…they are carrying on their backs and…when the battle continues you run away because you have no weapons" (Nhongo, 2000, p. 41). By 1974, a Women's Detachment had been created specifically for the courier purposes (Nhongo, 2000).

By carrying supplies of food, ammunition, and medicines, the women had been allocated mothering duties of providing, protecting and caring – domestic duties that have an affinity for nurturing, while men performed 'fierce and war duties of fighting, the author argues.

Later, traditional gender roles were subverted, as many women recruited as freedom fighters were active participants in the guerrilla warfare. They dressed in fatigues and were often indistinguishable from the men (Nhongo, 2000). Gann (1995) points out that the women's duties contributed to the success of the Zimbabwe liberation struggle.

To this extent, it has been pointed out that the actual role and status of women in any society is largely determined by the particular conventions, and prejudices existing about the nature and position of women (Marwick, 1977). In Mozmbique, women were heavily involved in the independence struggle and during this period, travelled long distances, often staying away from home, outside the context of familial authority. In 1973, a women's wing of FRELIMO, the *Organizaçao de la Mulher Moçambicana* (OMM), was established, as the vehicle for women's emancipation (Urdang, 1989).

The participation by African women in the liberation struggles for independence is believed to have been started by Algerian women (Turshen, 2002). During their war for independence from France (1954-1962), thousands of women were active participants, taking deadly missions to fight for independence from France but also political weapons to free women from ignorance and servitude (Turshen, 2002). In this sense the Algerian war set a precedent for African women in liberation movements.

During World War II, both the Soviet Union and resistance movements throughout Europe, prompted by egalitarian ideologies as well as desperate manpower shortages, mobilised women as combatants (Higonnet et al.,1987). The women's Corps of the British Army, set up in 1917, was one of a number of innovations introduced by concerned civilian and military authorities to help solve the persistent problem of providing sufficient manpower for the army (Higonnet et al., 1987). Here, women like men, were mobilised for both civilian and military work and they moved from auxiliary and support roles such as nursing to sabotage and combat (Higonnet et al., 1987).

However, In *Gone With the Wind* we are told that war is men's business not the ladies, but events of the twentieth and twenty first century force us to acknowledge that in many different ways it is women's business too. Higonnet et al. (1987) notes that mass communication and psychological warfare affect all sectors of societies in conflict. In this sense it can be argued that war brings with it the definition of gender, it provides the battleground not only for nations but also for the sexes, it is an event of gender politics.

1.6.12 The Chimbwidos

These were civilian female war collaborators for guerrillas. Their role was oscillating between the soldiers and freedom fighters gathering information for use by the guerrillas. This role carried with it risks, some of which are only emerging now. One young woman took ten years before she could talk of the six weeks she spent in prison. She was eleven years old when soldiers interrogated her as to the whereabouts of her sister, a chimbwido. She was devastated by the experience but told no one. She expressed her distress in a long series of health crises, which were eventually resolved by the intervention of a doctor who gave her physical and psychological attention (Reynolds, 1996).

In Mozmbique, women were heavily involved in the independence struggle and during this period, traveled long distances, often staying away from home, outside the context of familial authority. In 1973, a women's wing of FRELIMO, the *Organizaçao de la Mulher Moçambicana* (OMM), was established, as the vehicle for women's emancipation (Urdang, 1989).

The participation by African women in the liberation struggles for independence is believed to have been started by Algerian women (Turshen, 2002). During their war for independence from France (1954-1962), thousands of women were active participants, taking deadly missions to fight for independence from France but also political weapons to free women from ignorance and servitude (Turshen, 2002). In this sense the Algerian war set a precedent for African women in liberation movements.

1.7 Activities of the state machinery

Realising that the freedom fighters were gaining support from civilians, the Smith government devised ways of removing or minimising this support. This they achieved by giving itself power to kill, burn dwellings and food, making people disappear. These acts instilled confusion and fear in the civilians.

1.7.1 Selous Scouts

A special group called the Selous Scouts was formed and given mandate to carry out atrocities against the civilians. These included blacks and were a special corps. The Selous Scouts pretended to be freedom fighters and collected information about families (Reid-Daly, 2001). The community was placed in a state of confusion, not knowing who told the government securities about the freedom fighters' presence in the village. The community started accusing each other. Spirit mediums and witchdoctors (*n'angas*) were consulted to find out who the *mutengesi* (sell out) was. If the witchdoctor hated so and so, that person would be implicated. Selous Scouts are said to have raped civilians as a way of spreading propaganda against the guerrillas and instilling fear in the civilians so that they stopped supporting them

Through the Selous Scouts, the state achieved several aims, among them confusion and ideological warfare. Because the Selous Scouts could change from being a 'freedom fighter' at one time to being a member of the army at another, the community was subjected to a verbal war. Depending on the role that they were playing at the time, the Scouts looked for support from the villagers or punished them for providing that same support. Punishment came in different ways. One of them was killing the accused, freedom fighters or civilians in front of others as a lesson. Sometimes they would chop body parts like mouths, ears and limbs. Children were subjected to all these torturers' acts. In this way, the Selous Scouts introduced trauma in the community (Reid-Daly, 2001).

At the same time, the author feels that the civilians were placed in a position of conflict within themselves. On one hand they were compelled to feed the guerrillas by the guerrillas themselves and on the other hand they feared for their lives if they fed the guerrillas as they were under close scrutiny from the colonial security agents who were stationed in the protected villages.

1.7.2 Central Intelligent Officers (CIO)

This was a government group that had its own twist arm tactics. The CIO would recruit informers as well as use government employees to carry intelligence work in order to ascertain the movements and plans of the freedom fighters (Staunton, 1992). People became afraid of betraying their families or happy to settle their own scores. For the most part, this arrangement took away trust in the families, caused family discord and community upheaval in the process.

1.7.3 Regular Army

The regular army in its powerful cars, with their clean uniforms could be distinguished from the others. They had distinguished features; they dressed smartly, and they were well armed, as opposed to Selous Scouts who pretended to look like dirty guerrillas (Reynolds, 1996). This army had powers to kill, maim or exert excruciating pain by physical torturing in order to get people to confess. Confession was along the lines dictated by the army. They also destroyed or burnt homes, food and clothes (Reynolds, 1996)

The black members of the army and the police did not stop to consider that by working against fellow blacks, they were working against their own future and that of the African people (Mungazi, 1996). It is a tragic truth that they helped to destroy the African Identity that blacks were seeking for so long. In this regard, the army caused a lot of trauma among people. Many began to betray the comrades.

1.7.4 Call up

In order to beef up their numbers, the Rhodesian regime recruited young men through a process known as call up. Most blacks who were called up were ordinary level school leavers, thus relatively educated (Bhebe, 1999). On hearing of the Smith plans to recruit school children in to the army, guerrillas came to the school at night to denounce the regime and its military plans. Then in the morning, the security forces came and collected some girls and boys to the main camp for interrogation and torture. At night, the same boys and girls would be required by the freedom fighters to report on what they told the soldiers (Bhebe, 1999).

When recruitment was done, divisions were created between the educated blacks in the army and uneducated blacks who were in the village. This was most evident at weekends when the soldiers visited the village where the war was being fought (Reynolds, 1996). Freedom fighters would shoot them purely on envious reasons. The soldiers looked better because they had everything as compared to the comrade who looked poor (Kriger, 1992). Recruiting members meant that it was possible for brother in the army to fight brother who was a freedom fighter. This created conflict of interest to both regular army members and freedom fighters.

1.7.5 The Police

The British South African Police (BSAP) as it was known, did regular policing duties of maintaining law and order as well as military duties (Reynolds, 1996). The BSAP did a lot of damage as they took on duties done by the Selous Scouts (Reynolds, 1996).

1.7.6 Government officials

The government officials came from the District Commissioner's office. They had unparalleled powers to dangle the carrot and stick. If suspected that one was a pro-nationalist, the officials would get extra cows from him. They enriched themselves by robbing communities of cattle and food. They were also informers. The District Administrators did a lot of harm. In addition to looting, they raped victims and had the potential of spreading sexually transmitted diseases including aids (Zimbabwe women writers, 2000).

On the District Commissioner's behalf, dip attendants, agricultural assistants, nurses teachers and technicians (all rural technocrats) got sucked in to the war (Weiss, 1986). Female teachers and nurses especially became targets of torture and rape. Sometimes they were forced into relationships they did not want or they were recruited to be informers. The rural people told of the many atrocities that the security forces committed (Weiss, 1986). The female teachers and nurses got caught in crossfire and conflict of interest. The comrades (freedom fighters) would call them to their bases or *pungwe* nights were political education was being taught and the government officials would want information about the comrades. A lot of women lost their female - hood from both groups (Reynolds, 1996).

The struggle to independence brought a lot of suffering to individuals, communities, groups, families and society at large. The traumas experienced in the liberation struggle need healing for the development of all those affected and that of the nation.

1.8 Conclusion

This chapter has looked at the literature on women and war and the historical background of the colony. Before it was a colony, the people who lived in it, the Shona and the Ndebele people had their own way of governing themselves.

When the missionaries, hunters and gold prospectors came, the hand of friendship that had been extended to them was abused and the land we now call Zimbabwe was colonised. Those who resisted colonisation were killed. Later the indigenous people including women decided to take up arms and fight for the liberation struggle.

Chapter Two: Methodology

2.1 Introduction

The study sets the problem into context by using data available on women and war, and investigates the war experiences of women ex-fighters and civilians in the liberation struggle of Zimbabwe. The study further researches on how the war has impacted on the health of the Zimbabwean women who participated in it and how the war experiences have been dealt with as an attempt to heal the wounds.

The aim for the research is two-fold, firstly to provide deeper understanding of the long term health effects of participation by women in the liberation war and an insight in to how the health issues were addressed during the war, and secondly, to find the healing processes made after independence in order to address health needs of women, as health is an important factor towards development of a nation.

As war is a sensitive subject to talk or write about, any discourse on it, therefore creates problems of perception and presentation (The Herald, Harare, 10th April, 1997). In this regard the methodology provides epistemological complexities and challenges that authors meet in dealing with sensitive topics. It is generally believed that because of the threat they pose, sensitive topics raise difficult methodological and technical problems (Lee and Renzetti, 1993; Lee, 1993). In a study, based on juvenile prostitution, Margaret Melrose (2002) reflects and explores the ways in which the practical constraints, practical difficulties and ethical considerations that are inevitably encountered in a sensitive area of research such as young people who are exploited through prostitution, are intrinsically linked to choice of methods and the process of research.

2.2 Ethical considerations

Based on full information about the sensitive nature of the topic, the research objectives and method, the ethical code adopted required strict confidentiality and ongoing consent from the interviewees to participate in the study. In this respect, coding recorded interviews in order to conceal the names of the participants preserved anonymity and confidentiality of both participants and data.

All participants were given the assurance that the recorded interviews would be destroyed on completion of the study. This is in keeping with the requirements of respecting the mutual rights of the participants in the research process (Denzin and Lincoln, 1998). In addition the participants were given the right to determine the limits of the study and the choice to stay in or opt out of the study. Lee (1993) notes that the researcher must give room to the respondents to define the boundaries of the research topic in their own way. This was achieved by being continuously aware of indicative signs. Wiles et al. (2004) point out that the author has to keep on being sensitive to recognising the participants' expressions of the desire to stay or exit.

In this regard, the author adhered to the guidelines of The British Educational Research Association which believes that all educational research should be conducted within an ethic of respect for persons, respect for knowledge, respect for democratic values, and respect for the quality of educational research (On line www.bera.ac.uk, 18th September, 2003).

However, there was a time when the code of conduct was bent and this is when the author withheld full disclosure of who she was. This happened when she was advised by the women ex-combatants not to introduce herself as someone studying in Britain. The women associated Britain with Rhodesia and the oppressive colonial activities that made them go to war in the first place. The women's perception was that they have never recovered from the traumas caused by the war in which the women participated to liberate themselves from the colonial rule. During colonial rule, the subsequent liberation struggle and after attaining the rule of independence, the women have always been oppressed and they partly blame Britain. Therefore, for as long as the author associated herself with Britain in whatever regard, access to the women was going to be difficult as she would be viewed as an outsider. The author responded to the advice and stated her position as a graduate student full stop.

Although the author was guided by research ethics in regards to full disclosure of information, the author took practical considerations and withheld some information about where she was studying in order to get the women to participate in the study. Punch (1986) argues that bending research ethics may be portrayed as a necessary or common aspect of fieldwork depending on the public benefit to be gained. Thus by paying attention to the women's concerns, the author had acquired the credentials of being an insider who could get information useful to the study that can be used to improve the position of women.

2.3 Qualitative approach

The study employed a triangulation qualitative methodology that comprised of phenomenological, feminist and grounded theory approaches because they were most appropriate for the study where little is known. Rossi and Freeman (1993) note that phenomenology is an approach used in studies where the author's interest is rather oriented toward the depth and detail that can be appreciated only through an exhaustive, systematic, and reflective study of experiences as they are lived. In this context, phenomenology is both temporal and historical; a position that made the author work around assumptions that the knowledge and understanding she sought to find were embedded in the lives and experiences of the women based on their war experiences. Denzin and Lincon (2000) who observe that a research starts with a basic set of beliefs that guide action support this view.

To this extent, the author relied on approaches derived from the philosophical work of Husserl on modes of awareness -epistemology and the hermeneutic tradition of Heidegger, which emphasises modes of being -ontology. Although these approaches differ from one another in the degree to which interpretation is acceptable, Morse (1994) points out that both generate a rich description that enlightens a reader as to the deeper essential structures underlying a particular human experience.

To get a bigger picture of the women's experiences, the author needed different methodological approaches; hence the adoption of a triangulation qualitative approach. Denzin and Lincoln (1994) point out that qualitative research is multimethod in focus where researchers attempt to make sense of, or interpret, phenomena in terms of the meanings people bring to them.

Schwandt (1997) notes, a good qualitative analysis often requires access to a full range of strategies. Reinharz (1992) concludes that as feminist research often draws multiple disciplines, so too it often draws on multiple rather than a single, method in a particular project.

Although there is considerable literature on the war experiences of women ex-combatants and civilian women, there has been little consideration given to health impacts. From this perspective the study about the physical and psychological injuries of war and the subsequent healing processes applied to heal the injuries is in its infancy, not much has been written about the population being studied. In this regard the author decided to learn from the experiences of the women through their words, actions and records, focusing on their subjective experiences and interpretations of the world and developing theories from these experiences through inductive reasoning. According to Cresswell (1994), a qualitative inquiry is a process of understanding a social or human problem, based on building a complex, holistic picture, formed with words.

Generally, inductive reasoning uses the data to generate ideas or hypothesis (Holloway, 1997). From this perspective, the author took the position that an interpretative understanding is only possible by way of uncovering or deconstructing the meanings of the phenomenon. Dey (1993) points out that the primary purpose of the inductive approach is to allow research findings to emerge from the themes inherent in raw data.

Thus the author adhered to the philosophy of phenomenology and belonged to the interpretative school of thought that can be traced to German sociologist Max Weber and German philosopher Wilhem Dilthey, where Dilthey argued that "there are two fundamentally different types of science. "One is based on abstract information and the other is rooted in an emphatic understanding of the everyday lived experience of people in specific historical settings" (Newman, 1997, p. 68). Weber argued that 'social science needed to study meaningful social action, or social action with a purpose' (Newman, 1997, p. 68).

To this end, the women's experiences are looked at from women's perceptions of the phenomena because one of the common features of the feminist methodology is an emphasis on the validity of personal experience. Reinharz (1992, p. 135) put it across "To address women's lives and experience in their own terms, to create theory grounded in the actual experience and language of women, is the central agenda for feminist social science and scholarship".

In this regard the health impact of war on the women is more represented by direct quotation than by secondary description. Further, where women's experiences and memories are varied, it is important to present several different testimonies on each point.

As human behaviour can not be measured, quantified or reduced in to statistics, the author sought an in-depth approach to understand the impact of war on women's health through their lived experiences. Truman et al., (2000) observe that from life experiences, one makes sense of data that are represented by words or pictures and not by numbers.

To this extent, the author explored the historical, political, economical and socio-cultural implications of war on the health of the Shona women, both ex-combatants and civilian as they shared the stories of their lived experiences.

The author, a Zimbabwean Shona female who could have joined the liberation struggle was a participant as well as an observer. Neuman (2000) points out that phenomenological approach requires the author to look at her own ontology and challenge herself to put aside or 'bracket' preconceptions so that she can work inductively with the data to generate entirely new descriptions and conceptualisation. The author's position meant that she had to try as much as possible to be objective by putting aside her own values, prejudices and preferences. Marshall (1989) notes that it is important for the author to try as much as possible to see things through the eyes of the women she is studying, as the author may not have the same focus, may not see the same things as important, or evaluate things in the same way.

The feminist approach was embedded in Marxism that refers to the emancipatory theory because the author believes that women in general, face some form of oppression or exploitation. The approach facilitated understanding among different classes and explored the meaning of events in the eyes of women. Crotty, (1998) notes that a feminist research method is always a struggle to reduce if not to eliminate the injustices and unfreedom that women experience however this injustice and unfreedom are perceived and whatever intensity and extent are ascribed to them. In this regard, the author wanted to uncover and understand what caused and perhaps sustains oppression, in all its forms. Dey (1993) notes that knowledge gained by illuminating the ways women interact to sustain or change social situations can be applied to improve the position of women.

However, Hammersely (1988) points out that the emphasis on personal experience leads to a rejection of structured research methods on the grounds that unstructured methods give access to women's experience in a way which other methods do not. Alasuutari (1995) is concerned that the feminist research has devoted much attention to interviews and other forms of data collection from the viewpoint of the research relationship. Hubers, (1991) supports feminist methodology in that it underlines the importance of learning from observation, from listening to or reading the accounts of others, and from examining one's own experience. This is the position that the author took in this study.

2.4 Literature survey

This study began by reading literature on women in war, the Zimbabwe liberation struggle, and liberation wars in general. Focusing on the key words, information was obtained by searching the library catalogue to identify the journals (print and electronic) and books with relevant information. In addition, internet sources, newspapers, published and unpublished works, added more insight to the topic.

The majority of studies on the health impact of war on women have been conducted in western contexts where the focus is more on the individual. There has been little work done on psychological effects of war on women in other cultural contexts. Other studies have shown that the general experience of women and war is a subject of debate by many authors. In this regard, the related literature ranging from the great wars that saw the involvement of Germany, Britain, France Ireland and others to African countries where liberation struggles have been fought cannot examine or reassess all the complex issues raised by wars. What the selected literature attempts to do is to give insights in to the experiences of women and war in different cultural contexts - European and African - then place these in the Zimbabwean liberation struggle context. The differences and similarities of the war experiences are then explored in an effort to determine how culture and attitudes influence the position of women when the war has ended. In this way, the literature illuminates both the ways in which wars are remembered and the ramifications of that memory in cultural, social and political terms by looking at the culture of commemoration, and the ways in which communities endeavoured to find collective solace and healing after the war.

2.5 Pilot study

Having grasped a fair knowledge of the topic under investigation, the author went to Zimbabwe to carry out a pilot study in October to November 2003 in order to test the proposed qualitative methodology. To this extent, the pilot study sought to test whether the semi-structured interviews were developed in a way that would adequately give a holistic view of women's war experiences and how these experiences impacted on their health. The issues that the interviews sought to address are;

- roles of women before, during and after the liberation struggle
- the physical and psychological traumas of the war
- women and education before and after the liberation struggle
- women and employment after the liberation struggle
- women and politics after the liberation struggle
- women's place in the Shona society after the liberation struggle
- the healing processes applied to heal the war traumas

Further, the pilot study was carried out to identify issues that may arise in researching a sensitive topic in a volatile political environment.

As pointed out by Polit at al. (2001) and Baker (1994), a pilot study is used as a feasibility study or a trial run done in preparation for the major study. In the words of De Vaus (1993, p. 54) "Do not take the risk. Pilot test first."

During this stage five interviews conducted with four women ex-combatants who were government employees and one who was self employed generated valuable insights for the major research. The insights that the pilot study gave the author included the need to:

- empathise with the women as they narrated their traumatic war experiences.
- paraphrase the guiding questions to make them clearer
- avoid interrupting the interviews to allow a smooth flow of the participant's thoughts

For example, during one interview, a participant was continuously brought back to answer questions that the author felt had been omitted as she kept on referring to the guiding questions that had been prepared. Sadly this appeared to have irritated the interviewee. When interrupted, the interviewee would look straight in to the author's eyes and say 'I told you that'. This experience informed the author to allow the narratives to take shape gradually and questions asked only when making connections between issues raised by the respondent. To this end Holloway (1997) notes that pilot study interviews are used to improve interview schedules and specific questions to allow smooth flow in subsequent interviews. Brannen (1988) suggests that the research topic should be allowed to emerge gradually during the course of the interview bearing in mind issues of informed consent.

The pilot study also provided the author with an opportunity to discuss the project with people from different backgrounds such as academicians, professionals, businessmen and women, clergy, rural people and teachers. The discussions centred on how to get access to the women and to be cautious and careful in asking them sensitive questions. The advice the author was given is that people in general were afraid to talk about the war and in particular women ex-combatants. To this extent the author needed to be introduced to the women by someone who was trusted by the women ex-combatants. The discussions gave the author an indication of the difficulties that may occur in recruiting participants because of the sensitivity of the topic. These were valuable insights of what to expect later during the major study and important reasons for undertaking the pilot study.

2.5.1 Access to documentation

In searching for material in Zimbabwe, the author visited Higher Institutes of learning such as the School of Social Work, the Institute of Development Studies, the National Archives and the University of Zimbabwe library. Little documented material on the research topic was found. However a few books and documented material from these institutes were archived. More useful literature about the liberation war was found as compared to the amount of literature written or published about the aftermath of the liberation war.

The documents and recollections (memoirs or oral histories) about the aftermath of the war were obtained from non-governmental organizations. These are The Women's Coalition, The Msasa project in conjunction with Womankind, Women in Politics Support Unit, Women's Action Group, Women in Law and Development. However, information about the liberation struggle and women's health was not available.

The other secondary data used came from books by historians. In addition the author collected photographs, memos, official reports, newspaper and magazine articles of the period, video films from Zimbabwe Television, dvd's from Zimbabwe Independent News Agency (ZIANA) and interviews recorded on tapes from Zimbabwe Radio One broadcasting Corporation.

2.5.2 People's reactions

The author had not realised the full extent of the danger associated with researching on the topic until conducting the pilot study. The danger was realised when most people often asked why the author chose the topic instead of other similar studies about which much has been written. Suggestions were made of researching a different topic where much has been written about. Topics such as black women under colonial rule were given and thought of as much safer by those who were pessimistic. The author was reminded that others who wanted to research on the topic gave up after realising how most powerful people would react. It was then that the author realised how sensitive the topic was. Sieber and Stanely (1988) define sensitive topics as studies in which there are potential consequences or implications either directly for the participants in the research or for a class of the individuals represented by the research.

In this regard, perhaps the concern was caused by what had happened to three black researchers from the University of Zimbabwe after the war. They had fallen foul of villagers who suspected them of having given information on guerrilla movements to the District Commissioner. The three were attacked: one escaped and the other two were killed (Reynolds, 1996). However, a sensitive research that Reynolds did later after this incident did not meet the same fate. Reynolds further acknowledged that threats of murder sometimes reached her ears, but she met no danger.

Although the scope and nature of the consequences of doing this research were not specified, the reactions appeared to be based on:

a)   not wanting to acknowledge any problems as these might interfere with different agendas. People would rather concentrate on what was being perceived as urgent and necessary. Some authors, Preston-Shoot et al. (2001), note how service providers are led by different stakeholders to pay less attention in other areas. They observe how the judiciary, human rights conventions and local government authorities are all different in their approaches. These authors comment, that in essence, the concern is that the policy rhetoric and social work values of respect for person, partnership and empowerment are undermined by reality of resource-driven and service-led provision. In the same light, it can be argued, the reactions of the people in the study suggest avoidance in dealing with controversial issues in preference to allocating scarce resources to less sensitive agendas.

b)   dilemmas involved in conducting sensitive research in terms of issues relating to cultural sensitivity and the potential dangers for those being researched, the researcher, or individuals represented by the research.

Thus it was unclear whether the concerns of the informants meant that people in general do not want to write or talk about issues that may be viewed as controversial or whether the informants were giving insights of what to expect during her investigations. However, Flame – a film produced by Sinclair (1996) caused controversy over rape allegations based on the accounts of women who joined the liberation struggle.

Although the author was concerned with safety issues based on the reactions of the informants, she weighed the benefits of abandoning the project in order to protect herself and the benefits of continuing cautiously with the project in order to gain knowledge that can be used by the society. After a careful consideration of the options she decided to fulfil her responsibilities to the wider society by continuing with the research. Denzin (1989) notes that it is better to learn to manage sensitive issues than to avoid them by pursuing only safe lines of research. In this respect others were supportive and felt that the research would spread knowledge that would be useful if not in the present but in the near future. Lee (1993) shares the same sentiments and notes that sensitive research is important because it illuminates the darker sides of society. Indeed, sensitive research addresses some of the society's pressing ethical issues and policy questions. Lee (1993) further notes that shying away from topics, simply because they are sensitive and controversial, is avoidance of responsibility.

To this extent, the author explained the purposes of the study and gave assurance that the aim of the study was academic and not to fulfil any political agenda. She then decided to carry on with the research despite the sensitive nature of the study. Steps deemed necessary to ensure safety for the women and the author were taken. These included maintaining awareness of all opinions circulating in the community in relation to the research and political climate.

2.6 The major study

The pilot study was followed by investigations of the major study conducted for a period of six weeks from February to March 2005. Thirteen interviews were conducted with one male healer of the African independent church, one male professional and leader of ZINATHA, one male medical doctor and ex-combatant, two female traditional healers, (one who lives in the city and the other in the rural area), one male traditional healer from the rural area, one Roman Catholic brother who lives in the city, two civilian women who live in the rural areas, a group interview consisting of one female ex-combatant and two male ex-combatants, one female ex-combatant now living in the UK.

The participants in the pilot study were made part of the main study sample because few women participated in the major study. Seidman (1998) supports the view that pilot study participants can be part of the major sample where it is felt that excluding them would result in too small a sample. To this extent eighteen participants in total were interviewed (five from the pilot study and thirteen from the major study) and all respondents ranged from thirty eight to seventy years of age at the time of the interviews.

The interviews were conducted face to face in Harare, Mt. Darwin, Marondera and Mrewa, recording everything the respondents said using a tape recorder. This gave the author time to concentrate on the interview and at the same time the author has a record of how the interview was conducted (Moser and Kalton, 1983).

The interviews lasted between 15 minutes and 120 minutes and were audio-taped and transcribed by the author. The pages of the transcribed interviews ranged from 2 to 14 pages.

In addition to interviews, the study used as its basis triangulation methods that consisted of narrations, literature, archives, field notes, personal diaries, DVDs and videos. Because the data collection and analysis processes tend to be concurrent, the author engaged in active and demanding analytical processes throughout all phases of the research. To this end, the author continued to collect data until she reached a point of data saturation. Data saturation occurred when the researcher was no longer hearing or seeing new information.

The data collected consisted of three concurrent flows of activity; data reduction, data display – for example, tables, narratives, all of which helps the analyst to see what is happening, and finally, conclusion drawing and verification which is the process of arriving at the decision on the meaning of data (Huberman and Mathew Miles, 1998).

The major research was undertaken at a time when preparations for elections in the following three weeks were taking place. To this extent, the author cancelled some scheduled interviews after she had been stopped and asked many questions about her political affiliations by members of a political party as she drove past the political gathering. It was a moment where the author had to be flexible and innovative in a volatile political climate. When, the following day, the author tried to contact the participants whose interviews had been cancelled, she was told *"Hatina nguva nevatengesi"* (We do not have time for sell outs). At a time such as this, 'personal safety' shifting alliances, and restrictions of movement were all concerns that had regulatory effects on the researcher. Liebling and Shah (2001) in their investigations of the 'Sexual Abuse of Women in Uganda and Girls in Tanzania' note that people's opinions include views about the researcher's motives. The participants whose interviews had been cancelled could have changed their opinions about the author and her research and decided not to have anything further to do with her.

2.6.1 Focus groups.

The author had not intended to use focus groups in the process of data collection. However focus groups were formed unintentionally, firstly during the pilot study when the informal gatekeeper, intervened to enable some respondents to continue with their participation even though the author could not meet their expectation of paying them 'something' first. As Seidman (1998) observes, an informal gate keeper has moral persuasion and the female ex-combatants managed to participate through her influence.

Secondly, a focus group was formed during the major study, as a female participant would not be interviewed without the permission of her bosses who were men. The men were reluctant to give permission initially, but as they discussed the purposes of the research with the author, they found the research topic interesting and gave their permission to the woman ex-combatant to participate if she wished. The men joined in the interview and the group gave very informative interviews.

2.6.2 Face to face interviews

Through face to face in-depth semi-structured interviews the author sought to understand, to listen to the experiences of the women ex-combatants and build a picture based on their ideas rather than explain or predict behaviour. May (1993) points out that in an interview process, one is able to make theoretical interpretations.

To this extent, the interviews enabled the author to directly access people's experiences and their interpretations. In this regard she did more listening than questioning. From the interviews the author was able to collect a broad range of views and explore certain issues 'in-depth' from the participants' perspective. In addition, the author was able to uncover new areas or ideas that were not anticipated at the start of the research

The interviewing process began at the recruitment stage by developing a relationship of trust and respect between the author and the women throughout the project. In this regard, the women were interviewed at a place of their choice and at their own convenience. Further, the topic was described in detail at the outset and the participants were given the opportunity to articulate the dimensions and boundaries of their war experiences.

At the same time the author tried to keep her word most of the times. However, this rule was broken when some interviews were cancelled due to the volatile political situation as described earlier. Weiss (1995) points out that it is important to establish a good relationship before the main body of questions is reached in order to create co-operation and trust between interviewer and respondent.

The first impressions were important as they enabled the women to open up and contribute to the study. To this end, Keats (2000) notes that time spent on establishing rapport at this opening phase is not wasted.

During the interviews, the author was able to take cues from the respondents and in the process avoided being judgmental. It was felt that being judgmental puts respondents on the offensive.

Therefore phrases such as 'you should have done this' were avoided. Further, the author condensed and interpreted the meaning of what the women described and "sent" the meaning back. This provided the women with an opportunity to reply, for example, "I did not mean that" or "That was precisely what I was trying to say" or "No, that was not quite what I felt. It was more like…" Lee (1993) suggests that the process of interpretation should continue till there is only one meaning left.

As the women spoke out what was in their mind the author remained neutral because she was aware that the women were observing and questioning her too. As such, the author was concerned about uncovering knowledge about how the women think and feel about the circumstances in which they find themselves than making judgements about whether those thoughts and feelings are valid. In this respect, the author continued to examine the context of thought, feeling and action and the interviews became a way of exploring relationships between the women and their war experiences. Kvale (1996) notes that during interviews, respondents tell what they experience, feel, do in relation to the topic and discover new relationships in what they experience.

Indeed Hutchinson et al. (1994) agree that in an interview, research participants can experience self-acknowledgement, a sense of purpose, empowerment, and healing (Hutchinson et al., 1994).

Although it is generally accepted that females are more comfortable when being interviewed by a female interviewer especially on sensitive issues, how conducive the author's presence was to the whole interview process, depended on the physical, emotional, and mental being of the respondents. Lee (1993) argues that the presence of an interviewer encourages the respondents to feel relaxed and therefore forthcoming. However, the presence of the author brought some sense of insecurity to both herself and the female ex-combatant being interviewed when she said,

> *"We are mad people. If you make me angry, I am a changed person. Even you, If you make me angry I am a changed person and I can hit you" (Female ex-combatant C).*

This interview was very emotionally involved and a very stressful experience for both the interviewer and the respondent. Brannen (1988) indicates that a number of issues that may threaten the interviewer arise when qualitative interviews are used to research topics which are highly personal, threatening or confidential.

When the respondent indicated that she could hit the author when she was a *changed person*, the author tried to empathise with the situation and showed sympathy by asking her, What do you think the government could put in place to help you? To which she replied

> *"I don't know, like therapy I think, because even my children do not understand me" (Female ex-combatant C).*

Shakespeare et al. (1993) testify to the importance of developing an awareness of the potentially exploitative nature of face to face research. They feel that other-awareness is a first step towards sensitive interviewing and an emphatic approach. This process was enhanced by the author's experiences of growing up and going to school under oppression and segregation during the colonial era, and the decision she had later taken to join the liberation struggle. Neuman (2000) notes that such issues are embedded within qualitative methodologies and epistemologies where the role of the researcher becomes part of the researched.

When the interviewer probed further and asked what her children do when they do not understand her? She replied

"Nothing. They say 'mamma watanga' (mum has started again). I can be unpredictable. I can change now as we are talking, I can change and you wont like me. And You wont like me for two seconds" (Female ex-combatant C).

By probing further, the semi structured interview guide yielded flexibility in that an answer influenced the next question the researcher wished to ask. Thus the qualitative interview provided empirical data to test expectations of the respondent. Gaskell (2000) notes that during an interview, hypotheses are developed out of a particular theoretical perspective.

More in-depth understanding offered by the qualitative interviews provided the author with valuable contextual information to help to explain particular findings. Arksey and Knight (1999) observe that interviewing is a powerful way of helping people to make things explicit and to articulate their perceptions, feelings and understandings. To this extent, when the respondent indicated that she could hit the author, she quickly realised that the situation was deteriorating, and she started to wind the interview down and asked the last question in preparation to terminate the interview.

Lee (1993) reminds us that a researcher has to exercise due care and diligence in the ways she approaches a sensitive topic, deal with the contradictions, complexities and emotions inherent in the interview situation and the conditions under which the interview takes place.

There were also times when there was total silence during the interview. The women appeared distressed demonstrated by increased disorganisation of their thoughts, unsteady voices, physically shaking, and becoming silent. Only the sound of a tape recorder would be heard. It seemed that both the author and the participant were each engrossed in their thoughts. Because the author did not know what interviewees were going to say, she accepted that interviewees would, at times, say things that she was not prepared for or things she would not understand. In this case the total silence was not expected, neither did the author expect to hear an interviewee threaten to hit her. That does not mean, however, that things unclear to the author have no validity. To the contrary the author was there to learn and in this respect, when the interview was done, she listened to the tape in order to understand what she had heard and experienced.

Marshall and Rossman (1989) mention that participants can raise topics, which the author might not have anticipated and which can be critical to the investigation and analysis of the interview.

By the difference in magnitude of responses the author was getting, she was made aware of her responsibilities to protect the confidences disclosed and the emotions which were aroused.

In this regard, it can be said that 'problems raised by sensitive topics have led to technical innovation and have contributed to methodological developments
(Liebling and Shah, 2001).

Although the qualitative interview - like other data-gathering techniques, has its strengths and weaknesses, it is argued that this method is a tool and that its utility depends on its pertinence to the research questions. The author supports the argument that the qualitative interview has power in the voices, expressions, emotions and the feelings that cannot be explored and illuminated any better than by qualitative interviews. Its strengths and weaknesses are functions of the expertise of the researcher who uses this tool to elicit information. Bell (1999) believes that a skilful interviewer can follow up ideas, probe responses and investigate motives and feelings, which other methods can never do.

2.6.3 Sociological and Historical Accounts

The study also employed qualitative strategies based on sociological and historical accounts. Denzin and Lincoln (1998) argue that social phenomena must be studied within the historical context. In this context, in Zimbabwe anyone one more than twenty five years old at the time of study lived through the processes of colonisation, direct or indirect participation of the war, independence and post independence. These different processes are important in trying to understand the significance of sociological and historical accounts as they relate to the women who participated in the liberation struggle. Similar sentiments have been shared by Cowans (1998). Referring to the inter war years between the first and second world wars, he noted that so much had happened to the French between 1914 and 1945 that there had been insufficient opportunity for people to digest the past, to argue over its meaning and to assign credit and blame

Until recently the focus of history was essentially political: a documentation of the struggle for power, in which the lives of ordinary people were given little attention except in times of crisis such as the English civil war or the French Revolution (Cowans, 1998). But today interviews can provide much more. They provided the author with means of discovering written documents and photographs, which would not have otherwise been traced. Indeed during the interviews for this research, a male western trained medical doctor and ex-combatant explained through photographs how women at times participated on equal terms with men. The photographs of the women ex-combatants stood as evidence in a way that a conversation could not. Ball and Smith (1992) feel that photographs can authenticate a research report in a way that words alone cannot; the visual is mediated verbally, images are translated in to words. Altheide (1996) feels that through photographs a researcher is able to explain that this is what the issue looked like.

To this end Thompson (1988) suggests that the historical approach allows evidence from a new direction as oral historians think now as if they themselves were publishers: imagine what evidence is needed, seek it out and capture it.

2.6.4 Narrative inquiry

The narrative inquiry approach was adopted for the understanding of the women's war experiences as lived, written and told as stories. Although narrative inquiry as a qualitative research method for the social sciences and applied fields is relatively new, it has a long tradition in the humanities because of its power to elicit 'voice' (Marshal and Rossman, 1999). During the interviews, women told the stories of their lives shaped by the liberation struggle. Some of their experiences were written and the analysis of written and oral stories characterised by signs, symbols, and expressions of feelings in language, validated how the women constructed meaning. To this extent, the narratives contributed to the understanding of knowledge situated in the women's talk and provided insight into the actual experience as described by the women. Marshall and Rossman (1999) note that narrations are particularly useful in developing feminist critical theory.

However, it was important for the author to remember that what was told is what the women wanted to tell. The narrations framed how they were perceived or indeed how they wanted to be perceived. Brown (1997) observes that the narrations allow the participants to share the details they think are important. To this extent, the stories themselves were not human experience but vehicles that constructed discourses about the past.

Thus the relevant reality as far as human experience is concerned is that which takes place in subjective experience, in social context and in historical time (Denzin and Lincoln, 1994). In this sense, the narratives offered insight into the identity of the Shona women by capturing political, economical, social and moral dimensions of life, and war experiences embedded in their stories. To this extent, creativity and imagination brought out the story teller's sense of identity in to light and the differences which existed between the narrated self and the narrating self. In a report about making sense of oral history, Roncaglia (2003) notes that conversation, reflection and analysis between the researcher and the researched are on the same continuum and as such creativity and imagination are considered important. For example, the reasons for going to war ranged from political to social. Some women went to war because they were disgruntled by racist laws such as going to schools only designated as 'black'. Some did not complete their education because of lack of financial resources. Others were running away from failed marriages as well as unsympathetic parents. Connelly and Clandinin (1990) point out that narrative enquiry is a way of characterising the phenomena of human experience; the importance of the inquiry lies in that humans lead storied lives and tell stories of those lives.

In this regard, narratives were a tool for recording the women's voices be they historical, political or creative compositions. Through the narrative inquiry, the author was able to discover the extent to which human experience is shaped, transformed, and understood through linguistic representation. To this extent, she observed that in the narratives, there were subtle explanations and meanings that revealed disappointment, hope, unfulfilled plans achievements and a sense of anticipation.

To this end, Sandelowski (1994) points out that the speech forms are not the experiences themselves, but a socially and culturally constructed device for creating shared understandings about them.

Charlie Mansfield wrote that "self-narration is a method of making a comprehensive history of the past. By using a theoretical language, available to us in the present, we can re-narrate events from our past in such a way as to come to a new self-understanding using those events which did not make sense at the time" (http//barthes.ens/Mansfield). To this end, most female ex-combatants said that they would never go to war again if the hands of the clock were to be turned. They did not know what the war involved before they joined the struggle, what the women ex-combatants now know is enough to make them not to want to go back to war, any war.

In this regard, the different interpretative approaches to historical materials show that a historian's account of the past is a social text that constructs and reconstructs realities of the past to come to a new meaning (Denzin and Lincoln, 1998).

Thus through analytic processes that help us detect the main narrative themes within the accounts people give about their lives, we discover how they understand and make sense of their lives (Reisman, 1993).

2.6.5 Recollection of events

The recollection of events by the ex-combatants and the civilian women may not have been as sharp more than twenty-three years after the events. Indeed Felice Lifshitz (1998) notes that struggles over memory inhibits and possibly prevents full understanding of both the modern and pre modern phenomena. Never the less, history is a story of lived experiences and as such the author transformed what was written or said to come to an understanding. Thompson (1988, p. 150) puts it "Every historical source derived from human perception is subjective, but only the oral source allows us to challenge that subjectivity: to unpick the layers of memory, dig back into its darkness, hoping to reach the hidden truth". To this end the author was aware of the fact that experiences of the women ex- combatants varied from person to person and the reasons for revealing or sharing the experiences were different. Brown (1997) argues that to better understand the experiences of the women, one has to be willing to accept the authenticity of their lives as they remember it.

While it was good to believe in what the women said, acceptance of everything the author heard would be inappropriate, but she believed that the women had something of worth to say.

2.6.6 Power relations in an interview

The author acted in ways that were none threatening by giving the respondents the choice to participate in the interview, to exit if they felt so and cultivated a relatively neutral role but compassionate towards the interviewee.

To this extent, transcribed interviews of the women ranged from two to fifteen pages, an indication that the women whose interviews were short did not wish to continue with the interview. This was particularly so when the women appeared reluctant to keep on talking about traumatic events in their lives.

Further, the author proved her motivation by interviewing respondents when it was best for them and not necessarily convenient for the author. To this end, the women were interviewed at places of their choice in order to make them feel comfortable and relaxed, a process designed to enable the women retain some power.

Further, by employing open-ended questions, it is hoped that the researcher avoided imposition of her ideas on the respondent. The open-ended questions therefore gave the respondent greater freedom in, and control of, the interview situation so that a fairer and fuller representation of their perspectives was produced. Brannen (1988) notes that interview topics are difficult to investigate with single questions or pre-coded categories. Thus respondents were put at the same level as the interviewer in order to balance levels of power. Newell (1994) observes that the interviewer can deliberately not intervene to allow the respondents to retain some power.

However, Cotterill (1992) notes that there are times when power shifts to the participant. This happened when, towards the end of the interview a female traditional healer asked the author to help her if she could.

> *"I would like to ask something. I hear in Britain they have doctors that can help one have a child. How can they help me?" (Female Traditional healer 1)*

The author was put in an awkward position. At the same time the author did not know how to let the respondent know that she couldn't help her in that area without making her feel used and thereby upsetting her. The author advised the respondent to seek help locally, as doctors who could do that were now available.

The author was relieved to leave Zimbabwe at the end of the research. As Melrose (1999) notes, leaving the scene is a detachment from the respondent, which is considered necessary.

However, the author wondered whether, during the interviews, there were situations when the author herself had put the respondent in an awkward position.

2.6.7 Purposive Sampling

It is often unfeasible to study all the people who have all the qualities we are interested in. The women ex combatants are widely dispersed both in Zimbabwe and in the UK and it is not possible financially and logistically to locate everyone concerned. Marshall (1997) notes that the larger the project, the more administration errors can occur in the co-ordinating and analysing of the data.

From what people said about the topic, the author chose purposive sampling because she knew it was going to be difficult to get women, ex-combatants and civilian, to participate in the study. In this respect the author used her common sense and judgement in choosing the women who were believed to posses rich in depth information central to the study.

Frankfort-Nachmias and Nachimias (1996) point out that the aim of purposive sampling is to explore the quality of the data not the quantity, because the real purpose of qualitative research is not counting opinions or people, but rather exploring the range of opinions and the different representations of the issue.

In this regard, the author acquired the services of two former female ex-combatants known to a member of the author's family. The female ex-combatants lived in different locations and were eager to participate in this study because they had a keen interest in a justice system as can be seen from the literature that has been written about women's experiences in the liberation war of Zimbabwe. One of the gatekeepers was self-employed and the other a government employee. Because the gatekeepers are highly respected by other women ex- combatants, the author sought access to participants through them. Seidman, (1998) writing about informal gatekeepers notes that in small groups, there is usually at least one person, who does not have formal authority, but holds moral persuasion. If that person participates in a project, then it must be OK; if she doesn't then the group feels that there must be a good reason for not doing so.

Snowballing could be regarded as a kind of strategic informant sampling. The author asked selected members of the population who else she ought to ask to obtain useful information and then repeated the process with each of those she was told about. Thus the number of informants snowballed. This technique worked quite well.

Truman et al.(2000 p. 68) notes that the danger in snowballing that the sample "is heavily skewed in favour of particular types of informants" can be minimised by using different starting points from which to contact the respondents.

2.6.8 Criteria for inclusion

Criteria for inclusion for the research was the age range between thirty five and seventy years of age, and Shona ZANLA female ex-combatants as well as Shona civilian women caught up in the conflict. Shona males, including professionals, who could facilitate access to female ex-combatants or who could give further insight in to the lives of the women were included. To this extent a male western trained doctor, a male university professor as well as male traditional and Christian healers were interviewed in order to get an understanding of the women's experiences that were presented to them. Male ex-combatants and a female ex-combatant were interviewed as a group because they worked together in the same office. Ndebele ZIPRA ex-combatants and Ndebele civilians were not interviewed because the author does not understand the language.

In order to obtain a purposive sample of respondents, who met the inclusion criteria, the author contacted two ex-combatants who fought in different areas and requested that they describe and explain the study to their colleagues/friends who fought alongside them during the pilot study. Those willing to take part in the study contacted the author and she arranged to meet the respondents at a time and place of their convenience. The combatants also referred the author to civilians in villages where they had fought and knew that women there had been affected and had their own stories to tell. This process was repeated during the major study when professionals contacted by the author referred her to other participants.[1]

2.6.9 Challenges

Women ex-combatants and civilians were faced with difficult situations during the liberation struggle. Specific problems such as sexual violence required the researcher to be careful in her conduct. The author's conduct demanded cultural sensitivity, that refers to the understanding and approach that enabled the researcher to gain access to women ex-combatants, to learn about their life styles and to communicate in ways that the ex-combatants, understand, believe, and regard as relevant to themselves.

The author demonstrated cultural sensitivity by listening to the women's concerns during the times that she was an insider as well as an outsider at the same time. She was an outsider when she had stated that she was studying in Britain a country that the women viewed as partly responsible for their position since it had colonised Zimbabwe. She was further an outsider when the prospective interviewees indicated that they would like to be paid 'something' if they were to take part in the study.

Political and cultural awareness of the relationship between Zimbabwe and Britain enabled the author to understand why the women would not be happy to be informed that she was studying in Britain. To this end she did not mention where she was studying so that she could be an insider.
After attaining the insider status, the author informed the participants that resources were not available to compensate them for their time. In the end interviews began after the informal gatekeeper intervened forming a focus group unintentionally in the process. *"Ladies, do not live to your reputation that female comrades do not understand"*. I was also an insider during the interview process as I shared

---

1   A professional was contacted through a friend and he referred the author to traditional healers. The Catholic Commission for Peace and Justice in Zimbabwe (CCPJZ) referred the author to a Brother who worked with traumatised civilians caught up in the conflict. An official of ZANU (PF) Zimbabwe African National Union (Patriotic Front) referred the author to ex-combatants (both male and female) who worked at the ZANU headquarters.

most of the cultural attributes with the participants. I speak the same language as them and share the same cultural background.

While face to face interviews generated useful data, the study faced challenges of a complex and contentious issue in a situation where much of the information that was needed for a full understanding was either not available or considered sensitive and therefore was withheld from the public. To this extent, some officials were reluctant to give information. This surprised the author who thought that since some officials were well known to her, they would give some information requested. The other challenge was that some would be participants were not willing to be interviewed despite having agreed to do so initially. There was a Pentecostal church healer, however, who agreed to be interviewed only if he was not tape-recorded. In these circumstances, the author recorded contents of the interviews in a notebook. Others refused outright stating that they did not trust anyone especially with elections that were just two weeks away. "Experience", they told me, "has taught us to keep quiet about sensitive issues such as the topic of the study under investigation".

2.6.10 Data analysis

The strategies used to collect or construct data and the understanding that the author has about what might count as relevant or important data in answering the research questions were important analytical tools. The process was very complex where her own biography constituted by her views of the social world, her recent reading, her background and training, her scripts and stories made the perspective from which the author approached the phenomenon.

The author's data base consisted of interview transcripts from semi structured, focused but exploratory interviews, narrations, recorded observations on videos and dvds, and photographs, field notes and personal diary. The tape-recorded interviews were typed and as typing was going on, the author began to note emerging patterns of the data. Many pages were typed, a process that assisted the author in the data analysis, for one of the advantages of thematic reflections data analysis was that the author was able to employ critical thinking skills as she read the typed scripts.

In this regard the author was able to define concepts inherent in the interviews in order to understand the internal structures. As trends were noted in the interviews, occasions for which they failed to hold true were searched for. This process allowed the author to categorise different types of attitudes, behaviours, and motivations and to find associations between experiences and attitudes; between attitudes and behaviours; and between circumstances and motivations. As the author sought for explanations - explicit or implicit – she was able to discover theories and new ideas.

The author did multiple readings of the transcripts for different levels of analytical complexity and reflexivity (www.coe.uga/html, 15 January, 2006). For example reading for the 'I'-participant's construction of self which is the ex-combatant's or the civilian woman's construction of self and reader centred which is how the author responded to the ex-combatant's account as well as how other readers responded to the accounts.

At the same time the analysis allowed the author to make connections between the women's voices and what has been written in texts (www.web.odu.edu/webroot/instr/AL/smoorti.nsf/pages/reflection, 15 January, 2006).

Themes that emerged from the personal experiences are; determination, resilience, survival, peace, patriarchy and pride in themselves for having achieved what they perceived as achievements. However, at the centre of the women stories were experiences of suffering, loss, betrayal, hopelessness and powerlessness.

2.6.11 Data reduction

Data reduction was achieved by selecting, focusing, simplifying, abstracting and transforming the raw data that appeared in written -up field notes and interview transcripts. Alasuutari (1995) writes that qualitative research should use techniques, which enable the reduction of the potential amount of observations into a more manageable number of chunks. In addition, one also has to limit the amount of data to be gathered.

To this end, the author tried to limit the material gathered from interviews by introducing the topic and issues that were assumed to have a connection with the theme being studied. For example, introducing the theme of health in the camps, questions were asked "How was your health affected by living in the camps?" The author sought to limit discussion of the different stages of the war that affected the health of respondents to discussion of heath in the camps as well as meaning from the World Health Organization's (WHO's) definition of health under the Human Rights perspective. Different questions were asked to gain an in- depth understanding of how health was affected by other different stages of the protracted war. Answers such as 'There were food shortages in the camps' or 'there was sexual harassment in the camps for example, guided the author to an in-depth analytical understanding of the relationships between nutrition and health or violence and health.

Despite attempts to limit data, qualitative research tends to lead to a large amount of information, but the text provided is rich in terms of possibilities for analysis.

2.6.12 The researcher experience

After data collection, the author thought through her research while for example, bathing, cooking, writing, discussing with others or reading the interview scripts. Although she felt as if she was talking and listening to the participants again, she was lonely. Moch and Gates (2000, p.79) put it "The researcher often feels quite alone and isolated during the research process; processing can provide connections with another and this connection can be useful for data analysis"

The opportunity to process the author's research experience, learn more about what participants might have experienced through the interview, and gain further insight for the data analysis and synthesis process, came through the supervision times that the author had with her supervisors

Sometimes she went to church where she got emotional support from the biblical teachings. Moch and Gates (2000) further suggest that researchers sometimes process the research through discussion with counsellor, psychotherapist, or spiritual healer and that all processes offer the researcher the opportunity to honestly deal with the reality of being affected by the research. Indeed the author felt that the emotional support she got from the church and through discussions with supervisors and colleagues helped her in coping with the research and in giving her the strength to carry on with the research. In addition writing helped the author cope with the difficult situations of the participants and also helped her experience the beauty in the courage that the participants had in sharing their personal lives.

2.6.13 Phenomenological interpretation

The author's story that she could have joined the liberation struggle influenced the way she listened to the women's stories, imagining what could have been her experience of the war had she succeeded in joining the struggle. Banister et al. (1999) point out that personal reflexivity is about acknowledging whom you are, your individuality as a researcher and how your personal interests and values influence the process of research from initial idea to outcome. It reveals, rather than conceals, the level of personal involvement and engagement.

Who the author is was not without problems as the author often encountered transcripts that reminded her that she could have been one of these women she met during the face to face interviews. To minimise the risk of being emotionally involved, the author kept on reminding herself that her role was that of an observer and not a judge

From a feminist research perspective, Reinharz (1992) suggests that many research projects begin with, or are part of, the researcher's life and, in fact, that the personal experience is a valuable asset to the project. Reinharz continues, saying that by working on a project that concerns the researcher, he or she is able to merge the public and the private.

Through the intense study of individual cases, the author attempted to uncover and describe the essential nature of the experience in such a manner that a person who had not experienced the phenomenon might begin to appreciate it. Hartman and Messer-Davidow (1991) observe that of particular interest is the applicability of concepts and understandings from feminist social construction to the observations.

To this extent, interpretation was not only involved at the final stages of a research study, it was also involved at the data collection and data analysis stages (Shakespeare et al., 1993).

The imagination of what the author could have experienced led to questions concerning modes of awareness or epistemology of who the author saw in the transcripts, what she was looking for in terms of "shape" of stories and what were the women's reasons for telling their stories and what did the author not see within the transcript that may give her more meaningful and insightful explanations.

Further, the talk between the author and participants involved analysis of the language of people in cultural context describing the social situation and cultural patterns within it. During the investigations, the author acknowledged and sought meaning in different forms of expressions such as cultural and linguistic codes, silences, repetitions, visual and oral cues. These nuances helped the author to explore how they contributed to what was shared by the participants. Spradley (1979) notes that an interview relates the social situation to cultural meaning.

To gain a deeper understanding of the women's war experiences, the talk required more than linguistic analysis. It further required the positioning of the interviewee in terms, of her education, ethnicity, gender, occupational position and marital status. This positioning enabled the researcher to understand the reasons why the interviewee was saying what she said or performed the various actions within the particular situation, which she found herself.

In this way, the study of personal experience indicated that it is simultaneously focused in four directions (Denzin and Lincoln, 1994). The directions are; inward referring to the internal conditions of feelings, hopes, aesthetic reactions, moral dispositions and so on; outward referring to existential conditions, that is the environment or what Bruner (1986) calls reality; backward and forward which refer to temporality, past, present and future (Denzin and Lincoln, 1994).

For example, female ex-combatant B shared experience of the inward direction.
"I am within the understanding that we will have a free Zimbabwe where nobody would call me a war vet or whatever in a derogatory sense. A free Zimbabwe where I can marry who ever I want without anybody telling me this and that".

A medical doctor and male ex-combatant shared the feelings of outward direction or the environment to be expected.

> *"When we said the Lancaster House Conference is over, we are now going home, we were all called by the commander, Rex Nhongo and he said, ma comrades the war is over but to you the war is not over, both male and female because you are going to face no longer the napalm bomb, no longer the bullets, you are going to face a disease. A sexually transmitted disease, I don't know its name but that will be your bomb that will kill you. And you will be given, they won't just come to you, because they have seen you , but the Rhodesian security forces will give you those girls to escort you where by the most beautiful girls, you will see them there. They are bomb."*

A male ex-combatant highlighted the experience pointing backward and forward.

> *What is painful is that people say who are comrades? Why should they be special? Today, we are surprised because some of the people in the cabinet never participated in the revolution.*

To experience an experience is to experience it simultaneously in these four ways and to ask questions pointing each way.

2.6.14 Constant comparative analysis

Methods such as constant comparative analysis are primarily used for the purposes of generating knowledge about common patterns and themes within the human experience (Hammersley, 1992). It is well suited to grounded theory, a design that the author used to study the women's behaviour and traumatic war experiences such as women going through stages of grieving for the loss of loved ones or assets, pain caused by the violent experiences, and the processes they go through towards healing. Bell (1999) notes that the aim of constant comparative analysis is to get answers to the same question from a large number of interviewees to enable the researcher not only to describe but also to compare, to relate one characteristic to another and to demonstrate that certain features exist in certain categories. Originally developed for use in the grounded theory methodology, Glaser and Strauss (1967) add that cross comparison strategy involves taking one piece of data (one interview, one statement, one theme) and comparing it with all others that may be similar or different in order to develop conceptualisations of the possible relations between various pieces of data.

2.6.15 Data validation

There are a number of ways that error can be introduced in an interview. "A respondent may answer in a socially desirable way, or may be ashamed to admit that he or she does not know the answer. Respondents may give accurate answers on questions dealing with recent events but make many errors in replying to questions about events that happened long ago" (Bailey, 1994, p.212). However an interviewer has the ability to ensure that the respondent answers every question adequately, answers in order, and answers with clarity. To achieve these, the author employed methodological strategies that demonstrated credibility, usefulness and trustworthiness (Gaser and Strause, 1967). To this extent, the author attempted to achieve credibility by ensuring that the theoretical framework generated is understood and is based on the data from the study. Further, the author has attempted to demonstrate that the study is worthwhile and that it has helped explain the experiences of the women. In addition, the author attempted to make the study worthy or showed the extent to which one can believe in the research findings (Glaser and Strause, 1967). In addition, the author improved the validity of the data by a process called phenomenological validation. Here the author declared all the influences in her biography, which may affect her interpretation of the data.

To achieve credibility, trustworthiness and a true impression of the phenomenon under study, due consideration to validity was borne in mind by looking at subject error, subject bias, observer error and observer bias.

- subject error – catching the respondent on a bad day (Robson, 1993).

For example, one of the respondents was coming from a funeral and had to go and see a doctor later. The respondent therefore told the researcher that he was not at his best considering the circumstances. The other respondent informed the author that these days some researchers come pretending to be scholars when in fact they were spies for the government. The interview was therefore shrouded in suspicion.

- subject bias – where the respondent gives the answers she thinks the researcher is looking for (Robson, 1993).

- observer error –where the researcher is having a bad day (Robson, 1993). For example the researcher was once denied entry to ZANU PF headquarters despite presenting the clearance letter she had got from the Director of Information. The author was informed that "You people from Britain, you are Tony Blair's informers".

Had it not been for the intervention of some government minister who was passing by and saw the commotion, the author does not know what could have happened. However the author was finally allowed in and did some interviews against the background of having been humiliated and frustrated.

- observer bias – where the researcher interprets the phenomenon wrongly (Robson, 1993).

However, some authors have pointed out that bias is an inevitable feature of any account (Hammersley and Gomm, 1997).

After the completion of the data analysis and interpretation the author would have been happy to give the interpretations back to the subjects. Guba and Lincoln (1985) note that in a continuation of a self-correcting interview, the respondents get an opportunity to comment on the interviewer's interpretations as well as to elaborate on their own original statements. However this was not possible due to technical problems of distance, postal efficiency and the reading capabilities of some respondents. The research was done in Zimbabwe and some of the respondents are not literate.

While recent years have seen a proliferation of texts within the area of qualitative research one area which continues to receive only limited attention concerns the detailed processes of data analysis (www.coe.uga/html, 15 th January, 2006).

2.6.16 Data analysis theory

The data themselves informed the theories that emerged from the women's experiences and what emerged were those of violence and powerlessness. The author viewed them under the Human Rights Framework tying them with conventions such as Declaration on the Elimination of Violence Against Women (1993), Declaration on the Protection of Women and Children in Emergencies and Armed Conflicts and Reproductive Health Rights.

In 1993, through the Declaration on the Elimination of Violence Against Women instrument, the Vienna World Conference on Human Rights devoted particular attention to the question of gender inequality in the full enjoyment of human rights. The Conference acknowledged that women's rights are human rights and that the human rights of women are an inalienable part of universal human rights and form an integral part of the human rights activities of the United Nations, including the promotion of all human rights instruments relating, directly or indirectly, to women' (http://www.unhchr.ch/women/, June 12, 2005).

During conflicts, women are often used as a weapon of war. The theory of Power Over another provides the common thread between war campaigns and violence against women. According to Arendt (1969) this theory says that it is allowable for a person, ethnic group or government to get what they want through power over another or over the powerless. Through the eyes of feminist theory, many of our conflicts in the world have their basis in the assumption that everyone wants power, and there's not enough of it to go around. Within that assumption power is something that can be possessed, like property. Patriarchy, as it manifests through these assumptions, is a dysfunctional system because it gives rise to behaviours that nearly always require violence. To this extent, Arendt (1969) saw violence as an indicator of powerlessness, not as a show of power. Violence is used to subdue people because those who have "power" perceive that their power is getting scarce. They are, in effect, declaring their powerlessness by using violence. Although the subjugated at this point have the upper hand according to Arendt (1969), they can, at the same time, experience feelings of helplesness and hopelessness.

In addition, the war experiences of women ex-combatants and civilian indicate that the women were depersonalised as they were violated against, leaving them with feelings of low self esteem, helplessness, hopelessness and powerlessness.

To this extent, Banister et al. (1999) argue that theoretical triangulation embraces multi-theories and breaks through the parameters and limitations that inevitably frame an explanation which relies on one theory. It recognises complexity and diversity and that multiple realities exist.

Grounded theory seemed ideally suited for the study of the war experiences of the women ex-combatants and civilians, given its focus on generation of theory from data collected in the field. The study under investigation is relatively new and the grounded theory approach, using data from a variety of sources including interviews, observations, field notes and personal diary, offered a qualitative strategy that employed interpretative procedures to generate theory grounded in the lives of the women as they reflected on their war experiences.

Chapter Three: ZANLA women in the liberation struggle and equality

3.1 Introduction

Political restlessness had been building up between the colonial government and the black majority in the mid-1960s and the 1970s when ZANLA young women found themselves leaving their communities. They were leaving for the promise of glory and success that lay beyond the village. Bhebe and Ranger (1996) note that in the excitement that came with the promise of patriotic adventure, as well as the threat of incarceration by the Rhodesian army, very few people had full awareness of what the war meant.

3.2 Reasons for joining the liberation struggle

The reasons for joining the war differed from woman to woman. However what was common to all women was the political climate prevailing in Rhodesia. Black people were oppressed.

> *"It came about as a result of the political situation in the country at the time. And partly as a result of the treatment that my father received as a teacher. Salaries of teachers were low. My father was successful, he was a teacher but he did not have the same salary with white teachers when you compare. My father was not even allowed to live with his own wife. So I could see racism, I could see oppression. I could see all that at a tender age of seventeen" (Female ex-combatants A).*

Other female combatants were politicised to join the liberation struggle.

> *"In fact, I did not have a decision to go to war. I was a kid by then and I didn't know anything. I was listening to the radio and it told us how suppressed we were. One day I went to fetch water from the river and the Smith soldiers asked me, 'Who is going to drink this water?' I Said my father, they said 'you lie, you know where the comrades are. Where are the comrades? I was doing Form One at Selous School then the combatants came to take us in 1975 to Zambia. I was scared" (Female ex-combatant C)*

> *"My decision to go to war was when I was at school. We were approached and told about how the white man came and took away our land and put us in reserves and why we were not allowed to go to town. Why we were segregated. I became very angry and decided to go" (Female ex-combatant D).*

"I was at school then, the comrades came to address us about the revolutionary war. They told us that yes you are being educated but do you know that there is oppression. They taught us about how this oppression led to the taking by force of our soil. We understood it and decided to leave this education business because it was not going to help us and go to fight the Boers who had stolen our soil together with the wealth it holds such as gold. So we left school as a group (ZIANA, 2000) [2].

2   Interview conducted in Shona by the Zimbabwe Inter-Africa News Agency and translated in to English by the author

Other female combatants joined because blacks had limited access to resources

> *"Those who lived in rural areas, had the most difficult life. In rural areas life was based on farming. They were given little land and the size of one's family was not taken in to account. My father was given two pieces of land despite the fact that we were eleven kids. They did not take in to account that some of the children were boys who when they get married would also need land to farm. It was often said the boys would look for their own land when the time comes. So this meant that the boys would move away from the parents to wherever they would get land. This is not what we were used to. Our culture is that a family will always be together"* (Female ex-combatant who has migrated to the UK).

> *"Yes, it was August 1976 when I was doing form three. And this is when I had been told you cannot come to school. What justice does God have to make me not go to school and yet there are other children who fail 3 times and still go to school in their father's cars. So I just wanted a way to find why it was like that. So it's like I had stayed for a term not at school. Then I was told to come back to school after I had lost a term because that school had no enough girls, heh, so they were looking for those who could fill in the gaps and I was going to get partial scholarship where you stay at school in holidays cleaning classrooms. Then part of the school fees was paid by the college and you also work. I did not like it because I did not accept it"* (Female ex-combatant B).

Others were collaborators (*vana chimbwido*) and wanted to experience freedom and riches.

> *"I didn't go to war really. I was a collaborator. It means an in between. Collecting information from Rhodesians and giving it to ZANLA. ZANLA told me the white man still owns the land, let's fight. I wanted to be free and prosperous"* (Female war collaborator E)

Another reason for joining the liberation struggle was the way villagers were treated in protected villages, called 'keeps' by soldiers and government officials. After witnessing the callousness of the Rhodesian security forces, the thought of living with the same soldiers in the protected village sickened Mildred Dengu, a *chimbwido* (war collaborator) who actually begged the guerrillas to take her with them to Mozambique (Nhongo, 2000).

One of the combatants, Marevasei Kachere, was forced to join the war because of the suffering she experienced in the 'keeps' (Zimbabwe women writers, 2000). Keeps were protected villages. The aim of forcing people in to keeps was to monitor movement and destroy the possibility of support for the guerrillas. Forced villagisation was a programme similar to that employed by the British in their colonial wars in Malaya and Kenya and by the Portuguese colonisers in Mozambique (McLaughlin, 1996). The Rhodesian security forces thought that by implementing harsh measures, the war was going to end.

However when they moved people in to keeps and closed schools, they actually facilitated the children to go and join the freedom fighters. Thus, by deciding to go to war as schools were closed the children exercised power which the author considers in terms of a scalar concept. Goverde et al. (2000) describe scalar concept as pure conflict on one end of the scalar and absolute consensus at the other. In this sense there existed pure conflict on one end where the children and colonial security forces had conflicts of interest and, at the other, absolute consensus - where the children out of their own will agreed to join the freedom fighters in an effort to defeat the colonial government.

However, not all women joined the liberation struggle for political reasons, as pointed out by Mahamba (1986) that some were running away because of circumstances they were in at the time such as failed marriages, husbands who were not understanding as well as parents who made life unbearable for their daughters who had got pregnant outside of marriage.

As news of the war spread, many young people including school children were caught up in the frenzy of the moment and joined the struggle, a decision that some have regretted later and attributed that decision to bad **spirits (Nhongo, 2000).**

3.3 The early women recruits – the peasants and roles they played

On arrival in the camps, the early women recruits found out that they were
^peeded for carrying supplies of ammunition, food and medicines. Training and fighting were reserved for men because there were no enough guns for both men and women as explained by a female participant.

> *" Initially there were more men in the battlefield because there were no enough guns. There were problems with guns. Women would carry logs just to get accustomed to weight" (Female ex-combatant B)*[3].

Thus in the early stages of the liberation struggle, men were given military training first and they were the ones who were given the few guns that were available. Women were given logs and allocated mothering duties of providing and protecting – domestic duties that have an affinity for nurturing, while men performed 'fierce' and war duties of fighting.

The late commander, comrade Tongogara put it, " the geographical barrier - the Zambezi - made it very impossible for us to have a continuous flow of supply...particularly weapons, food and other things. The people would go and get engaged for a week and then exhaust all the ammunition... they are carrying on their backs and...when the battle continues you run away because you have no weapons" (Nhongo, 2000, p. 41). By 1974, a Women's Detachment had been created specifically for the courier purposes (Nhongo, 2000).

To this extent, it has been pointed out that the actual role and status of women in any society is largely determined by the particular conventions, and prejudices existing about the nature and position of women (Marwick, 1977).
Thus the position of women is shaped by how they are perceived by both other women and men. In this regard Nhongo (2000) suggests that ZANLA men assigned women domestic duties because they could not face the reality that women too could fight. A male participant explained the initial roles that women played in the liberation struggle.

> *"When we opened the MMZ (camp) in Tete province in 1970 it was the women who were carrying makacha (boxes and boxes of ammunition). So the women initially were couriers of heavy ammunition, to a man he would collapse but to a woman she would just go on. . You see a woman with a big shinga rehuni (a big bundle of fire wood on her head). I don't think many men would stand that kind of thing. Its only a woman who would have that head and the neck to hold that shinga rehuni. That's what initially they started to do" (A male doctor and ex-combatant F)*

The President acknowledged that at the beginning of the war women were not regarded as real fighters. "At first we thought that the war had to be fought by boys alone, that's why at the beginning we sent

---

3   Interview with participant B was conducted in English in Marondera on 23 October 2003 and quoted verbatim

males for training in China. We thought the war was male business not women. We forgot that the first liberation was led by mbuya Nehanda (Female fighter who was killed by the whites in the late 1800s, whose spirit guided the fighters both men and female). The first women recruits were sent to places like Tanzania, United States and England to learn in various fields. We used to think that women do not fight. This ideology came about because of the ignorance of organizers that for any war to be successful, women and men had to be united and fight as one. This is what happened later. By 1974 we had quite a number of women in the war. I will just mention a few. Teurai, Sheba Tavarwisa, Dadirai, Garanevako, Serbia, Tracy, there are many. Some we still have, some we lost them" (The President comrade Robert Gabriel Mugabe at the 1984 Women's conference).

Fig. 2. Young girls pounding food substances in preparation for making a Meal in a camp

3.3.1 Burying the dead

Although women were initially expected to do domestic duties, war time necessities exhorted women to brave unfamiliar work such as burying the dead. A young peasant female combatant who was in company D for burying the dead tried some tricks in order to get changed from this company to where people fetched firewood or to other companies that had nothing to do with the dead. She was not successful (Zimbabwe women writers, 2000).

On one hand, by preferring to fetch wood or water, the woman was accepting patriarchal ways that see a woman as a domestic worker and men as performers of difficulty jobs such as burying the dead. Although the female combatant wanted to be a soldier, when the going got tough and the soldier had to bury the dead, she preferred to do the familiar jobs culturally designed for women, that of domestic chores. On the other, burying the dead might have been a job given to the less educated peasant women. To this extent class differences even in times of war, determined the allocation of jobs.

In Britain, although employment attracted women from all social backgrounds, class divisions existed as they had always been prior to the war. Blue-collar jobs were dominated by working-class women, white-collar jobs by middle and upper class women (Brayborn, 1981). Middle and upper class women who had been used to shop and dress elegantly volunteered to work in dressmaking and similar trades in an effort to fill their leisure time by doing something honourable (Brayborn, 1981). As the war progressed the upper and middle class women volunteers extended their work to welcoming refugees from Belgium (Summerfield, 1989). Some women - all of them unmarried - took the opportunity to go to universities where they earned professions in teaching and medicine.

3.4 The elite women's perception of the liberation struggle

From 1975 some fairly educated women who joined the liberation struggle thought it would be like the ones they see in the movies and then they would end up abroad where they would get professional courses of their choice.

> *"Well (laughter) like what we see in the movies, like the war in the movies. Eh, that you would be trained militarily then after training you would be sent to Russia, China for any course in nursing, teaching, any area that one would be interested in..... You can imagine I carried my beautiful clothes, bell bottoms, my platform shoes. Ah this was someone who was ignorant of what a war situation is like. So you can see from the type of dressing that I took with..." (Female ex-combatant A).[4]*

The professional training that female combatants hoped to get when they joined the war was noted by Raeburn (1978) who observed that the representatives of ZANU told people that they were going to have self-government in Rhodesia in a few months. They therefore needed more educated members to fill top jobs in administration. Jobs like clerks and District Commissioners. They were going to send people free to Canada or England to study.

Other female combatants were simply excited about the idea of going to war.

> *"Excited. I was very excited, extremely excited"(Female ex-combatant B)[5].*

3.5 The elite and roles they played

When they got to the camps, the educated female combatants were given jobs that were different from the ones given to the less educated.

3.5.1 Administration and caring

Some educated women combatants were given responsible jobs in administration as explained by a female ex-combatant

> *"The female comrades like in my case, I was responsible for the administration of ZANLA. I was responsible for the documentation. I was responsible for the finance, all the monies that was used by ZANLA; I was responsible for it. So whatever needed to be purchased, I was like the Finance Director of ZANLA..." (Female ex-combatant A)*

Others were given jobs in caring for the sick and injured.

---

4   Interview with participant A was conducted in English at the participant's house in Harare on 13 October, 2003 and quoted verbatim

5   Interview with participant B was conducted in English in Marondera on 23 October 2003 and quoted verbatim

Fig. 3. A young girl administering atropine to a patient

Fig. 4. A young woman caring for the sick

Fig.5. A young woman manning the underground pharmacy.

3.5.2 Keeping of security documents

There was a lot of information about the war that the combatants had to keep.
This required organisation, vigilance and security awareness as explained by an ex-combatant.

> *" So we would put the documents in trenches and cover them up with branches of a tree. After the war, we would then go and take them out…I was a member of the general staff. This was the policy making body of ZANLA. This was the body that would strategize on how we would want to carry out operations in the bush, carry out training programmes" (Female ex-combatant A)[6]*

However, when there was a shortage of manpower, even the elite female combatants did the jobs that were allocated to the peasant female combatants such as burying the dead. An ex-combatant describes this experience.

---

6   Interview with participant A was conducted in English at the participant's house in Harare on 13 October, 2003 and quoted verbatim

"So you will be surprised that a person like me, because I was a commander, when such a thing happened, even at 20, at 19, I would go to bury 20 people, you can imagine being a woman, you could not say ah, I am a woman, nor, you are a commander. So this is an area where you think there are differences and responsibilities that you could do – no. You could not cry" (Female ex-combatant A[7])

3.6 Anxiety of not being trained to fight

As the women were performing their different duties not knowing when they would be trained, they were increasingly becoming aware that war does not discriminate and so they were anxious about their safety.

"They had gone to the war to fight but only to be told , you can only fight when you have been trained. The anxiety, shall I go back home or shall I stay and fight? Ahh was really a toil seen to the mind of the young woman and men but more so on the young woman" (Male medical doctor and ex-combatant F)[8].

"It felt very bad. In fact I personally felt that I had made a mistake to go and join the war. I felt that what I had heard about it-what was going on- and the intention of this whole war was not really what was happening for me. I expected things just to happen systematically without any hiccups; so I felt it was not a very good decision that I had taken, but there was no way of going back home. In fact a lot of people tried to run away at that time because there was too much suffering and military training came much later….It was not until after four to five months that training started…. and military training was the same for men and women" (Female ex-combatant B)[9].

When a female combatant left home, she was in the company of *mukoma* (trained male combatant) under his protection. When she arrived in the camp she was no longer under that, she was on her own with her own colleagues. The sense of being not trained to defend one's self in a war zone, led to the symptoms that the male doctor and ex-combatant talks about.

"Can I defend myself? After all I came here to fight. And it took long, we are talking about a population of about 250 000 (two hundred and fifty thousand) young boys and girls, it's not a small thing. And we could just train a few initially. We couldn't train all of them at one time. And guerrilla training needs more training than conventional warfare. Guerrilla warfare requires a lot of training" (Male medical doctor and ex-combatant F).

3.7 Class differences and women's rebellion

Following the Chimoio battle in November 1977, women began to take a more active frontline role in the war. However, this outcome followed a slow-burning rebellion among the women in the army. Women decided to rebel against the practice of carrying war materials when they were not trained to defend themselves. The realisation for the need to be trained was reinforced by the arrival of new recruits who were fairly educated as compared to the earlier ones.

"…but when we joined, our situation was different because then we had students who had come in from all over the country. So the situation had changed slightly…One thing that you must appreciate is that when

---

7   Interview with participant A was conducted in English at the participant's house in Harare on 13 October, 2003 and quoted verbatim

8   Interview with participant was conducted in English at his home in Harare on 16 February 2005 and quoted verbatim.

9   Interview with participant B was conducted in English in Marondera on 23 October 2003 and quoted verbatim

we were in Zimbabwe, women were treated as women but in a war situation, the enemy didn't care. If it was an attack, it was attacking soldiers, and so you had to be a soldier. You forgot about sex. War knows no sex nor gender. War is war" (Female ex-combatant A)

Nhongo's (2000) analysis about women and education suggests that the low level of education in the early recruits determined women's inability to confront gender-based discrimination. Nhongo also suggests that women from wealthier and more educated backgrounds had a difficult time because their female commanders, from predominantly peasant backgrounds, saw them as 'soft'. The author would like to add that the findings of this thesis show that although women ex-combatants experienced unequal treatment with men, it does not mean that by doing nothing about gender discrimination meant that the early recruits with low education saw themselves less important as they were seen by men, the dominant class. Some of the early female combatants could have feared what they perceived as the risks involved and chosen not to speak or act against the unequal treatment.

However, these interviews provide new interpretation on Nhongo's (2000) argument that educated women were marginalised within ZANLA. Nhongo suggests that educated women had little impact on struggles for gender equality within the army. ZANU leadership warned women who challenged gender issues that they risked official ostracism and consequently their political demise. The author's interviews of women ex-combatants pointed out that the women's rebellion against carrying war ammunition whilst untrained took place after the more educated recruits joined the liberation struggle. Interviews show that more educated recruits were given leadership roles, which Nhongo's data did not reveal. For example, the daughter of school master, who had herself reached form four, reported:

"I was a member of the general staff. This was the policy making body of ZANLA. This was the body that would strategize on how we would want to carry out operations in the bush, carry out training pro-grammes." (Female ex-combatant A)

This informant was one of those who supported the move towards women bearing arms. She noted:

"When we joined, our situation was different because then we had students who had come in from all over the country… War knows neither sex nor gender. War is war" (Female ex-combatant A).

There was, then, a feminist alliance across the classes in support of greater gender equality. The threat by ZANU leadership against women who would challenge the status quo did not deter the women from rebelling against what they saw as unfair treatment between them and male combatants. In this regard, women knew that both men and women were fighting to liberate themselves from colonial oppression. In addition, women also knew that both men and women had to be trained equally to defend themselves against the enemy. The attitude of training men first suggests that male combatants were regarded as the real fighters, but with the arrival of educated female combatants, women argued that when the enemy fired, both men and women were attacked. The women who took action and rebelled were driven by their experiences and the general awareness that education brings. In this sense the author shares the views of Mullings' (1997) study on the oppression of the African American woman that greater oppression leads to greater consciousness and resistance. From this perspective, the suggestion that women viewed their oppression only in terms of racism they experienced in the colony under the white rule right to the end of the war can only be attributed to the interpretation and meaning of women's experiences at the time of Nhongo's (2000) study. At the beginning of the struggle it is true that oppression of the black race was the major factor that mobilised Africans - both male and female – to the war front. However, because educated women had not succumbed to the threats of their political demise, ZANU leadership appears to have temporarily placed fairly educated women to positions of authority in order to silence them and other disgruntled female combatants. To this extent, a female commander had to bury the dead when the need arose; her status did not count to ZANU leadership, it counted only to the other fellow female comrades.

Thus while the treatment of men and women in the camps was marked with the perception of gender differences, the allocation of duties among women was marked with the perception of class differences.

3.8 The Chimoio attack

The analysis of war – that it knows neither sex nor gender proved to be true when thousands of young women were killed at the Chimoio battle. The battle at Chimoio took place before most women were trained and so they died in thousands (ZIANA, 2000). A story is often told of how a woman ex-combatant spent four days in a pit latrine with the maggots crawling all over her during the November 1977 Chimoio attack (ZIANA, 2000).

Some vowed to keep fighting despite being injured by the enemy, those who had not been trained were becoming anxious about their safety. After the Chimoio battle women knew that they had to fight, if not to defeat the enemy, but to defend themselves. A male ex-combatant explained how and why the young women were caught up in the middle. On one hand they had gone to rebel, on the other they became the easy target of the enemy forces.

> *"Women actually took the biggest toll of deaths. I remember at mbuya Nehanda when the Chimoio attack came. At mbuya Nehanda, there were five thousand girls, they were all butchered by the enemy….And these were young girls who had run away from the refugee camps forcing themselves in to a military zone, military camp which was Chimoio headquarters and telling us that they had to be trained, they could not stay in the refugee camps for ever. They wanted to be trained….they were all butchered by the enemy. This is not a story I was told. I saw it with my own eyes. It was like a killing field where every woman was lined up as though they were going to march and it was a line of one by one being shot". (Male medical doctor and ex-combatant F)[10]*

> *"I was going to share an experience, where at Chimoio, when the fight was going on, we had a school for these children and the enemy went and killed five year olds, eight year olds and so forth. And I happened to have passed through the spot and saw children who had been injured. I do not know how they knew me, some cried out for help, you can imagine, the bombs are on and these kids are crying for help. I tried to ask the men, please help me these kids are injured. They said (voice raised) can't you see there is this war situation. I carried them on my back, I took my bandage, tore my clothes to stop bleeding and I managed to leave with five children who were injured… So I walked (voice raised) through, you know, at times you do not want to believe this but it happened. We walked straight, there were bombs, helicopters were there, I was never bothered. You know children are holy, there was no cover, I didn't fire because of these children. I could see people being killed, I just went with these children, and when I had come out of that environment, I saw some Mozambicans who were driving, I asked them to carry these kids to the hospital " (Female ex-combatant A)[11]*

---

10   Interview with participant F was conducted in English at his home in Harare on 16 February 2005 and quoted verbatim.

11   Interview with participant A was conducted in English at the participant's house in Harare on 13 October, 2003 and quoted verbatim

At the battle of Chimoio on 23 November 1977 thousands of people were killed. Refugees including children were 'slaughtered' along with their mothers. Some children were bundled together and set alive and they died while those still living were watching. Others had burns from napalm (Zimbabwe Radio 1 Broadcasting Corporation)[12].

The Chimoio attack marked the beginning of a struggle by women to liberate themselves from what they perceived as oppression and potential danger. By marching in to a military zone to rebel against staying in refugee camps untrained to fight while performing their domestic bound duties, women were risking their lives to achieve equal treatment in the military with their male counterparts. Gilligan (1982) notes that oppression in patriarchal societies can be regarded as a source of potential strength and power for women rather than merely a source of weakness. The deaths of so many women during the Chimoio battle became another source of strength to the women to go out and train as fighters.

> *"In 1978 in March, I remember after Chimoio attack, it was the women who actually swore by Mbuya Nehanda that it was better to die at home than here in Mozambique. And so they rushed to the training camps and they were trained" (Male ex-combatant and medical doctor F)[13].*

The battle at Chimoio was made possible by the army and air force who concentrated in causing confusion in the camps inside Mozambique. They did so by employing different tactics. One of them was the use of Selous Scouts and mercenaries as pointed out by one respondent,

> *"I remember being told, after the war, in 1987, by one who sat down with me . He used to introduce himself as sectarian commander from Gaza. He had painted himself black, he was white, he spoke perfect Shona (the local language spoken by the majority of the Zimbabwean population), and he sat down by my side and when he told me, did you know that it was me who sat down on that night at Chaminuka which was a security camp and you were briefing each other as what to do. So these agencies led the commanders to actually disarm the comrades the night before the Chimoio attack." The colonial government had successfully disarmed combatants in Zambia-Mukishi camp where ZIPRA forces were operating from and what happened at Chaminuka camp in Zambia was repeated at the Chimoio camp in Mozambique" (Male medical doctor and ex-combatant F)[14].*

The Chimoio attack was a repetition of tactics used by the Rhodesian forces at the1976 Nyadzonya attach where thousands of refugees and some combatants were slaughtered by the colonial security forces. The colonial government had successfully recruited Morris Nyathi who had risen to the position of commander in the ZANLA ranks to turn against his fellow comrades and become a traitor of his own people. On 9 August 1976 Nyathi led the Rhodesian forces to the Nyadzonya camp where he blew the 'emergency' whistle that was used as a command for all to assemble at the parade. In response everyone rushed to the Parade Square to await the instructions that they thought were to be delivered by those in command. Refugees and fellow comrades thinking that they were going to hear information about training were gunned down by the Rhodesian forces who had positioned themselves. Those who managed to escape using the only route available plunged in to the crocodile infested Nyadzonya river and perished there (Department of Information and Publicity – ZANU PF, 2005).

---

12   Radio One discusses an insight in to the battle of Chimoio. Recorded tape in English came from the Zimbabwe Broadcasting Corporation.

13   Interview with participant F was conducted in English at his home in Harare on 16 February 2005 and quoted verbatim.

14   Interview with participant was conducted in English in Harare at his home on 16 February 2005 and quoted verbatim.

A similar attach to those of Nyadzonya and Chimoio was recounted by a female ex-combatant who was operating from Zambia.

> *"Then you remember in 1975 we were bombed. We saw helicopters, jet fighters arriving. We thought they had come to attend the graduation of some comrades. We were happy so we did not group. Then they started dropping bombs. Some of us jumped in to the Mkushi river to hide. And there was one of our commanders called Bopoto, that girl was a brave soldier. She said 'I better be killed than run away from these oppressors. ' She said 'retrieve keep on retrieving' meaning run away'. If you are a commander, you command and not run away, so she died" (Female ex-combatant C)[15]*

Another combatant who was in the Mkushi camp narrated her experiences in little English and Ndebele, a language the author does not understand. However, her facial expressions on the video were those of one remembering the traumatic pain as she cried uncontrollably.

"We were defenceless. A lot of life was lost especially that of women and children. The combatant cries none stop for a very long time"(Female ex combatant, ZIANA, 2000).

3.8.1 Deaths at Chimoio

One of those who witnessed the horrendous events describes this battle.

> *"I was at Chimoio, that was my baptism, the first battle that I have ever encountered...... People died. They will try to minimize the figure but the figure came to somewhere around between 2 to 3 thousand people. The maximum figure agreed now is five thousand people. But it was all women and children. We had vatoto camp, va toto meaning children. It is a Kiswahili word meaning children. We had Vatoto camp which was holding around ten thousand, women as I said, fifty thousand that's where the massacre was. It was genocide if we could put it that way. One line after another, the women would go in front religiously to be shot. This I saw with my own eyes because I was perching at an anthill overlooking Vatoto base, Chaminuka, and mbuya Nehanda...... the young girls in mbuya Nehanda whom you see in mass graves did not even put a resistance, they ran in to the bar, they saw it was useless, they were told to come out , they came out, and they were told to line up, and they lined up, you know, in series. And then from 12 o'clock I remember, the guns didn't stop. It was gug gug gug gug and stop, another one gug gug gug gug and I would see them falling one by one. Look at the vatoto (the children) the same" (Male doctor and ex-combatant F)[16].*

Fig 6. Attending to the injured in the bush in Mozambique is a male doctor F and a colleague. ("This is me trying to take fragments from a patient while the battle is going on")

---

15   Interview with participant C was conducted in English in Marondera on 23 October 2003 and quoted verbatim

16   Interview with participant was conducted in English in Harare at his home on 16 February 2005 and quoted verbatim.

3.9 Training and deployment: equality with men on the battlefield

After the rebellion and the Chimoio attack, women like men were trained to fight and they went out to the war front as explained by a female ex-combatant.

".... So it was both men and women who trained militarily and they were sent to the front. The training took place in Chimoio and Tete-from there we were now deployed in to different areas. Some were sent to Gaza province, this is in Masvingo, some were sent to Manicaland and some were sent to Mashonaland' (Female ex-combatant A)[17].

Fig 7. The new roles that women took on after they rebelled against being confined to domestic duties. Here a young-trained woman carrying a rifle at her back is in the war front.

Others were determined to fight with the biggest weapons available usually used by men only.

"I will show you some pictures here, where a young woman would use even a bazooka. In her own right would say I want to use a bazooka, nothing else. Ak, yes I would use it but my biggest weapon is a bazooka. When we use a weapon called M90, virtually a bomb in itself, which would destroy a house like this. One woman would hold a barrel tube where she can slot this bomb, much to the destruction of the enemy. This was a big machine which would make the ground shiver. So to put a woman there, the power she would have to control the gun was great" (A male doctor and ex-combatant F)

Fig 8. A young woman holding a bazooka ready to fight

---

17   Interview with participant A was conducted in English at the participant's house in Harare on 13 October, 2003 and quoted verbatim

3.9.1 No excess baggage

Women were determined to fight for this is what a lot had come to do. Some of the women led battalions as explained by a male ex-combatant.

> "By 1978 in March, coinciding with the March Agreement, for the first time we had a woman's battalion sent in to the country to fight on it's own. This is the group you saw marching (A photo of the women) and it was a lethal battalion. No one would retreat. I remember they were sent through Mutare, Burma valley, Burma valley Gandayi. And there the Gandayi battle was bad news to the whites... I was talking about the women who said no excess baggage. They were led by a woman called Freedom Tichaona. She was under Perence Shiri who is now air force commander. She had her own team. No excess baggage. The only woman who became sectorial commander in her own right. The only woman who would say ngatichirarai pano apa vorara (this is where we will sleep and they would sleep there). Nothing about love affair, sex, Rara apa (just sleep there). I think, I think ahh, I don't know. Maybe (small laughter), it is in the mind of the female. But I tell you where ever we deployed women, they would say, no excess baggage. Don't bring a prisoner. Everyone must die, the enemy must die'" (A male doctor and ex-combatant F)[18].

Thus during the liberation struggle, women, just like men, learnt to take leadership, to give commands and to expect them to be followed (Sedman, 1984).

Fig.9. The women combatants whose policy was 'no excess baggage'

3.9.2 Women's determination

Through the orientation lessons they were given, women were inspired to keep fighting until the enemy was defeated. "Under a tree we were oriented about the war. The orientation had lessons about how our land was stolen and how our people were treated by the *Boers* (whites). We were also told that there were other people way before us who had fought the Boers in resistance to their occupation of our land. These early fighters were defeated by the enemy and they died declaring that their bones would rise and continue the fight. We were told that we were the bones that had risen. So this gave us a lot of determination to fight the Boers until the country was liberated. We saw ourselves as the risen bones of mbuya Nehanda and sekuru Chaminuka' (Radio One Broadcasting Corporation)[19]

Although some women knew then that liberating their country meant dying, they were not scared.

> "We were not scared because we were taught to accept the situation through songs, through orientation and some lectures. There were also some gallant women who had fought during the soviet war, the Chinese war, we wanted to be like them.....We were taught more about colonialism, We were taught about the situation, what the situation was in

---

18   Interview with participant F was conducted in English at his home in Harare on 16 February 2005 and quoted verbatim.
19   interviews done by Zimbabwe Broadcasting Corporation in Shona and translated in to English by the author. The tape came from Radio One archives.

China and Soviet Union who had gone through also revolution like ours. We were also taught about the experiences of Frelimo because they had fought a war of liberation against the Portuguese of Angola, the liberation of Angola. So we knew people had sacrificed their lives. They had lost comrades in order to liberate their country. A war situation meant that people would die" (Female ex-combatant A)[20]

A female comrade who had been shot during the Chimoio battle left a legacy for which she is remembered up to today.

"And a very good symbol when we were attacked at Chimoio for example, here is Muchazo, a very known female commander, who was shot and when she was shot, she began to sing, much to the ears of the comrades who were around 'Tinofa tichienda kuZimbabwe' (We will die marching to Zimbabwe). And she was actually coughing blood, and she was walking, dizzy, and she was singing 'Tinofa tichienda ku Zimbabwe). And the white guy who was shooting her came closer and closer and said to her 'Inofa ichienda kuZimbabwe (it will die going to Zimbabwe) and she died. That was the determination. Whether you are shot, whether you are hungry, that's irrelevant, war must continue. And that toughened the women. You couldn't say, I'm bearing the brunt of the war as a man when she was bearing the same as you" (A male medical doctor and ex-combatant F).[21]

Women combatants who were in the frontline have been described as "women of a new generation who wore trousers like men and could aim just as steady. They were women who killed and got killed. They were fit and strong, running through the bush and brandishing AK 47's and machine guns. These were women who crept into the village on their backs, they carried not runny-nosed babies but the hope of a new generation. They were as foreign to our traditional image of women as Eskimos" (Maraire, 1996, p. 168)

Thus when women needed to perform unfamiliar tasks, they did so. In this regard, Gilligan (1982) suggests that values and priorities stereotyped as feminine need to be integrated with masculine ones in order to provide an enlarged and more adequate conception of morality and a more adequate developmental ideal for both sexes.

Conclusion

The early women combatants were confined to domestic duties such as cooking and carrying weaponry when they arrived in the camps. Men were the only ones who were trained to fight as they were regarded as the real fighters. In addition to cooking and carrying war materials for use by male combatants, the less educated women combatants were given such jobs as burying the dead while the fairly educated women combatants looked after the sick administering medicines and did administration jobs. These interviews challenge Josephine Nhongo's findings, that educated and wealthier women were marginalised by the women commanders, who were predominantly of peasant origin. With the arrival of the fairly educated women came the realisation that war knows no sex nor gender and so the women rebelled against playing supportive roles to male fighters whilst untrained. However the rebellion took place a little late when more women untrained to defend themselves died in thousands at the Chimoio attack. After the attack many women vowed to fight and they too got trained and went in to the field. Some women combatants, including those of middle class origin, rose to the positions of commanders and led battalions.

---

20   Interview with participant A was conducted in English at the participant's house in Harare on 13 October, 2003 and quoted verbatim

21

    Interview with the participant was conducted in English at his home in Harare on 16 February 2005 and quoted verbatim.

Chapter Four: Traumas of the camps and health issues

4.1 Introduction

These are accounts of what happened during the liberation struggle of Zimbabwe, what life was really like for those who fought (Sinclair, 1996). Yet there are a few accounts of what happened to the women who fought beside the men. Sinclair (1996) notes that behind the women's stories lies a universal theme that women everywhere recognise the fight for independence, and then the isolation and disregard and suppression all accumulating to the trauma that follows.

The author shares the same argument with Sinclair (1996) that until women can talk about their war experiences and make a connection with their grief and anger, they will each still be unconsciously trying to get out of their own personal camps. The experiences are unique, but they are examples of the broader experience of cultural assumptions and attitudes towards women, how these permeate lives, and how the women, each attempt to survive them. Talking about war experiences is talking about trauma and suffering, it is about understanding the long-term health consequences but it is also about women's resilience and strength.

In this regard, the author reinforces previous studies on rape and pregnancies, shortage of food, killings, loss of limbs and adds detail on physical and psychological traumas looking at health issues such as hurricanes, migraines, matekenya and *madef* (stoppage of menstruation).

Talking about the war is talking about trauma and a female ex-combatant had this to say;

> *"It was traumatising. Some of the days we used to sing and dance, it was ok, but generally, it was bad. From my own experience, I wouldn't want my worst enemy to experience what I experienced" (female ex-combatant D)*[22]

4.2 Diseases and illnesses in the camps

Talking about the health issues experienced, the women looked like in pain brought out by remembering what they saw and what they endured in their passage through the bush and camps. The suffering endured is the extremity of misery that Des Pres (1976) describes as gross pain of flesh and of physically uprooted lives. This work reveals for the first time the range of unexplained and stress-related illnesses, including migraine, hiccups and cessation of menses, experienced by women in the camps. In particular, it reveals the prevalence of a mysterious phenomenon known as 'hurricanes'. This only affected females and overcame many women in the camps.

---

22   Interview with participant D was conducted in English in Marondera on 23 October 2003 and quoted verbatim

A male ex-combatant who used to attend to the health of the ex-combatants explained his observations.

> *"The worst impact on women I saw, was that the women had been terribly affected mentally by being displaced alone, not by war, by sheer displacement from home to a war zone even as a refugee. And the health problems which we faced with these women were 1) Some would go aaah, would feel as though they were sick when they were not sick – what we call psycho somatic diseases where a woman cannot walk and she cannot stand. She tells me she cannot stand, and sure enough she is falling but leave her alone to fall down aah you find that she doesn't need a hustle. You realize you are dealing with a woman who is psychologically traumatized. Some would go unconscious, You know you meet them, you laugh with them and all of a sudden, some would just collapse, go unconscious and after some time become round. They ask you, where was I? You tell them you are in the war zone as refugees not as combatants. All this was part of anxiety, where shall I stay, shall I go back? Some used to limp, (little laughter) as I say some big fish now in the politburo of ZANU PF" (Male doctor and ex-combatant F)*

4.2.1 Hurricanes

As the diseases began to take their toll in the camps, a disease, which had never been seen before, emerged. Even a medical doctor could not link this disease to anything he knew in medical terms and so the disease was difficult to treat.

> *"There were some who were limping without any injury at all. Literally limping you know and you say what is wrong? Eeh hence the over use of vitamin b complex. We used to call those women affected we used to call their conditions hurricanes coz they were limping. There was no pathological disease which we could pick up, just sheer limp. We used to call it hurricanes, abatwa ne ma hurricanes (She has been affected by hurricanes). The comrades would give the young woman limping an injection of vitamin b complex because the comrades who were medics were also not fully trained. There were very few fully trained medics. Aah, the worst, which I saw, besides the limping part, the fainting part and the collapsing part, the worst which I saw was a kind of hysteria. They would go hestirical. Aah a mass hysteria where one starts and then you get a chorus of the entire camp" (Male doctor and ex-combatant F).[23]*

> *'When we were in Mozambique, there was a disease called hurricanes. It used to attack only women and I do not know why. I myself suffered from it. Women barked like dogs and fell down. These hurricanes made women run and run until they fell down. It was not possible to stop running because the system is disturbed. So you would run and run until the knees gave way. Well these are some of the things that happened" (Female respondent in the group interview)*

> *"When one had hurricanes, say from 6 am, at around 2 pm you would be digging his/her grave" (Female ex-combatant in the UK)[24].*

The male doctor and ex-combatant F explained that the illnesses could not be identified pathologically, and anxiety caused by displacement and war environments could have contributed to the health conditions experienced by the women. There is still no clear medical explanation for this phenomenon, nor any study of potential long-term health impacts on the sufferers.

---

23   Interview with participant was conducted in English in Harare at his home on 16 February 2005 and quoted verbatim.

24   Interview was conducted in UK at the participant's house on 10 March 2006 in English and Shona and was translated in to English and quoted verbatim

4.2.2 Hiccups

" Munhikwe would go like this (she imitates) none stop. This killed children especially. You would have 5 to 15 children dead per day. There was a camp where some where assigned to stay at the grave because bodies kept on coming the whole day. There was nothing you would do to the munhikwe. Drinking water did not help. So sometimes people kept on running in the hope that munhikwe would go. They did not know how to cope, so they just ran. When they stopped, they were dead. The mental state of many people was disturbed, so that together with hurricanes made it worse" (Female ex-combatant in the UK)[25]

4.2.3 Migraine

Migraine was an illness that was common in the camps according to one participant.

"Most of the illnesses that I saw during the war in Mozambique, I have never seen such illnesses in Zimbabwe. When one illness had gone, a different type emerged, when that was over, another one surfaced and so forth. There is one that you call migraine. The one I saw was not migraine. That type of headache was not understood. When the headache started, in two minutes he was so hot that a wet cloth would start steaming as soon as you put it on his forehead. Then we knew that the person is gone. When the person died, you would see blood coming from the nose or mouth. We don't know what would have happened, whether it was the busting of blood veins or what, we never knew except that blood came out of the nose and mouth (Female ex-combatant in the UK)[26]

4.2.4 Matekenya

In addition to migraine, combatants got infected with matekenya (worms that ate the flesh)

"There was also Matekenya. If you look at my toes (showing the badly torn toes) this is matekenya. You got pimples here and there, very itchy pimples and then you would scratch and scratch. The itchiness would not go by scratching, the more you scratched, the more you wanted to scratch. You would not understand what was happening because you would enjoy the scratching but it would not end. What killed more people was that matekenya would go to the areas between the toes. Once the matekenta went to the toes, they would dig in to the flesh and that was the end of the person. Once a person had matekenya, he/she would survive for as long as they were outside the areas such as the toes, armpits or between the bottoms" (Female ex-combatant in the UK)[27]

Matekenya appears to have been a parasitic disease that affected combatants perhaps due to poor hygiene facilities in war zones. The
lack of personal hygiene could have also led to the breaking of skin among the combatants.

An ex-combatant explained the conditions in the camps that were conducive to the breeding of lice.

"And there was a lot of lice because we did not have soap to wash with. So lice was common. And the sad part was lice laid eggs and the eggs had some form of acid which breaks the skin. And because it is so hot, the lice come to eggs where the fresh air is coming from, so your hair is eaten. We did not have much of tsikidzi what do you call them those that eat blood? Yes bugs. We did not have much of these, but lice. I think it had something to do with dirtiness., dirty clothes, stench" (Female ex-combatant B)[28].

---

25   Interview was conducted in UK at the participant's house on 10 March 2006 in English and Shona and was translated in to English and quoted verbatim
26   Interview was conducted in UK at the participant's house on 10 March 2006 in English and Shona and was translated in to English and quoted verbatim
27   Interview was conducted in UK at the participant's house on 10 March 2006 in English and Shona and was translated in to English and quoted verbatim
28   Interview with participant B was conducted in English in Marondera on 23 October 2003 and quoted verbatim

While some people suffered beatings, others died from disease. The hair of combatants was full of head lice. Jigger fleas ate away the flesh between their toes (Zimbabwe Women Writers, 2000). Women in particular found life in the camps intolerable. Yet, tragically, as in death, one could not return to warn those at home to change their view of the war. Prudence Uriri's experiences at Tembwe, Mozambique, made her conclude that "I had made a mistake to go and join the war. I felt that what I had heard about it - what was going on - and the intention of this whole war was not really what was happening for me. So there were people who tried to run away and they were caught before they could go very far..." (Zimbabwe Women Writers, p. 76-68, 2000).These are not uncommon memories.

4.2.5 Madef (menses) and fertility during the struggle

Another problem that faced the women ex-combatants was about their menses nicknamed madef in the liberation struggle. While other comrades never stopped menstruating, others stopped and never menstruated again.

> *"Today, a lot of the comrades who had menstruating problems do not have children and this is an issue that the government should know and do something about. Maybe the poison that we drank in water, or eat in food was responsible, I do not know", (Female ex-combatant in the group interview)*[29].

> *Women suffered. I am one of those who suffered. We had no cotton wool to use for our menses. We started using leaves of trees (Silence). This is the period (Female ex-combatant in UK).*

> *"We never had any tampons, or cotton wool or things like that, so we had to make do with rugs. So we had to change that rug and it can be used by another person when they are menstruating. So it didn't matter whose rug it was. I do not know if aids was there, I think we would be all dead by now. I think we survived by God's will. We would use one thing" (Female ex-combatant B)*

> *" menstruation stopped. I think hormones (laughter) they just went haywire. You find most girls who participated, they are infertile. Some could not even have children. So that's one problem that we face" (Female ex-combatant A)*[30]

A male medical doctor and ex-combatant commented on the menses and explained that,

> *'' We did not understand why. They just went, what we call amenorrhea in medical terms. No bleeding at all. But the amenoria we found there was unique in that it affected a lot of young women. The women would confess that I am not pregnant, I haven't slept with any man. I know I am not pregnant"*

The significance of *madef* can be viewed from the importance attached to menstruation. The existence of menstruation, within the reproductive ideology, signifies the ability to bear children. The relationship between menstruation and fertility is also shared by Buckly and Gottlieb (1988) who observe that menstrual blood embodies a symbolic principle that makes possible human fertility in the form of babies. In most African cultures where the worth of a woman is measured against the children she bears, the absence or stoppage of menstruation could have caused a psychological problem to the affected women combatants because they knew that all other factors being equal, they would not be able to have children.

---

29   The group interview was conducted in Shona in Harare at ZANU-PF headquarters on 18 February, 2005 then translated in to English.

30   Interview with participant A was conducted in English at the participant's house in Harare on 13 October, 2003 and quoted verbatim

Other causes of secondary amenorrhea (stoppage of menstruation) in times of war include stress, depression, a sudden change in the environment, mal absorption, poor nutrition and starvation (APA, 1981).

4. 3 Factors that contributed to the women's health

The author suggests that in order to understand the women's health during the struggle, it is necessary to look at their experiences from the time they embarked on the journey to Mozambique to the time when the women started to face the conditions of the camps.

4.3.1 The journey to Mozambique

What started as a happy adventurous journey to end the oppression that blacks were enduring under the government of Ian Smith turned out to be a nightmare for some as described by one of the ex-combatants,

> "Crossing to Mozambique was not easy. Some never reached Mozambique. The journey to Mozambique was more difficult when crossing the rivers. Some girls I knew remain in these rivers up to day". (The interviewee starts crying and apologises for it saying she couldn't help it. These are painful memories.) The group encourages her to cry but to keep on talking because that way she will feel better. "When a comrade was hurt, we would carry each other, but sometimes we were confronted by the Rhodesian soldiers, then we would hide the hurt comrade. Sometimes we would leave the wounded comrade with the parents (any villager willing to do so). Then after the fight with the soldiers, some of us would go back to see how the wounded comrade we left in the village was. Sometimes we were told that she died and was buried by the villagers" (Female ex-combatant in a group interview)[31]

Other girls reported that they walked at night and in the day they hid in the bush. "Sometimes we were thirsty and hungry. I think we walked for three nights. So much has happened. I don't remember everything. Some things, of course, I will never forget. I was frightened when we met animals at night. Once we saw a wild pig and the comrades said they would have shot it but a shot might have been heard, so they left it. I was sad because I would have liked some meat. We only had berries and some water carried by comrades" (Weiss, 1986, p. 84).

Others said that on the way to Mozambique, they met some Rhodesian soldiers but these took no notice of them. Later they found out how lucky they had been. At night, they slept in the bush, and travelled by day to cross the border in to Mozambique where they were met by Frelimo. However, Frelimo was cross with them "because there were no comrades with us, just us girls. But later they were nice and took us to a camp, where we found others" (Weiss, 1986, p. 84).

Such male attitudes towards women fighters are not new. In El Savador, women were initially not accepted by male combatants in the civil war of the mid 1970s but later the male combatants realised the importance of having women fighting as well (Saywell, 1985).

4.3.2 Conditions in the camps

The girls had not been prepared of what they found in the camps.

---

31   The group interview was conducted in Shona in Harare at ZANU-PF headquarters on 18 February, 2005 then translated in to English.

"What we were told was that you are going to have your own gun. Imagine for a 13, 14 year old girl to have a gun. You have the power to kill a white man. But what we were going to find there, we were not told" (Female ex-combatant D)[32]

When the girls arrived in the camps they were terrified about the security checks they went through on arrival in the camps. They probably had not experienced such scrutiny before.

"When I arrived in Mozambique, I was scared because we were met with the security group, which would ask us why we had come" (Female ex-combatant in a group interview)[33].

As the ex-combatants reflected on their war experiences they appeared deep in thought as if they were travelling that same road again. The initial excitement of being able to do something about the oppression they were experiencing at home and the reality that awaited them in the bush were like two parallels. The conditions in the bush were like living in hell through man-made violence, they lamented.

"When I arrived…Ah well, life was tough. It was hot, very hot, it was empty, it was dry and we felt hungry, we were only given two portions. In the afternoon and in the evening, just to keep us going" (Female ex-combatant B)[34].

Indeed some female ex-combatants have described the conditions of the camps, that life was very tough there, there was never enough to eat, and that there were some comrades who refused to accept girls as freedom fighters (Weiss, 1986). The non-acceptance of women as fighters was similar to what women in Britain had faced during the First and Second World Wars (Saywell, 1985). Many of them operated as women alone or in a group of men where they combated not only fear of injury as do men, but also fear of the idea that was prevalent in men that women could not serve in any military capacity. Further it took courage to face being misunderstood, suspected of servicing men rather than serving a country or cause. As a result some girls got hysterical in the barracks rooms because they could not cope. Some of them had never been away from home before, and they didn't think they could stand it (Saywell, 1985).

Similarly, the women guerrillas who had been placed in Mozambican towns first and had experienced some home atmosphere were shocked with what awaited the women in the bush camps.

"Eh, when we were in town, in Frelimo camp, we used to sleep on beds, we had electricity but at Nyadzonya now, the situation changed, no soaps, no cotton wool…..no houses, no beds, we did not have blankets. Like I said that to us it was an adventure. We did not think that it was a place where people would suffer, where people would go for days without food…..In the camps, the position in the camp changed dramatically. No telephone, nothing (emphatically). So from that time we began to realise that we were in a war situation" (Female ex-combatant A)[35]

The Zimbabwe women writers (2000, p. 10) have summed up the difficult conditions that the ex-combatants found themselves in. "They lived in harsh circumstances without the backup of food,

---

32   Interview with participant D was conducted in English in Marondera on 23 October 2003 and quoted verbatim

33   The group interview was conducted in Shona in Harare at ZANU-PF headquarters on 18 February, 2005 then translated in to English.

34   Interview with participant B was conducted in English in Marondera on 23 October 2003 and quoted verbatim

35   Interview with participant A was conducted in English at the participant's house in Harare on 13 October, 2003 and quoted verbatim

arms supplies and medical provisions that are the prerequisites of a national army. The hardships required another form of resilience and as time went on, there was a grave shortage of food. Sometimes they would go without food for two to three days. They would drink water, and others would eat wild fruits".

4.3.3 Feelings of hopelessness

Women felt hopeless in the camps. People looked for ways to escape reality. There was a plant called mudzepete whose leaves could be rolled into a cigarette. If one smoked it, she would get drunk for a week and would forget her problems. Some would prefer to boil it and drink the water. It had the same effect as the cigarette. If one was caught trying to run away, she would be killed. It was so complex and everything and everybody was shrouded in fear. Women would never know who, amongst themselves would be taken in the middle of the night and never be seen again (Mahamba, 1986).

> *"I was very disillusioned. In Shona we say kusina mai hakuendwi. (literally means, do not go where there is no mum) because what I thought would happen is not what happened. The conditions were bad. There was hunger. There was everything bad that you can think of" (Female ex-combatant D)*[36].

Talking about *kusina mai hakuendwi,* (where there is no mother – do not go) is a reminder about the differences between civilian and combat life, it can be argued. In a civilian life, a mother is always there to advise and sometimes warn of possible dangers that come with the choices we make about life. In a combat life in the bush, a combatant had to live on commands from army commanders. Adjusting from civilian life where there was family to the bush life where there are strangers instead, must have been a difficult experience. In the bush camp, she had to live with the loss of family, friends and loved ones.

Thus the combatants had come face to face with the true meaning of war which they did not know before. They were to learn that war is confusion, discord, and strife. War brings conflict; it also represents a return to a primitive, savage state. In the face of savagery, civil life, in all its permutations, disintegrates. It is difficult and painful to admit that the stability of society is based on a fragile and easily disrupted foundation. War challenges the beliefs on which our lives are based. The sense of disbelief, of the inconceivability of war between people who lived together, was echoed again and again:

The women were introduced to a new way of identification from civil life and were required to share the scarce resources such as blankets, a system that some found very hard to get used to.

> *"Yah, this one is very hard. We were put in barracks, we had to stay within companies and the barracks had numbers. Section this of detachment this of battalion this in barrack number that. So we worked with numbers, a lot of them. The barracks were made of grass and poles. We shared one blanket. So you can imagine what happened when you have eaten a lot of beans and you had to share a blanket, you can imagine what you went through" (Female ex-combatant B).*

4.3.4 Displacement

A doctor participant believes that what he witnessed happening to the women was caused by displacement as he described.

---

36 Interview with participant D was conducted in English in Marondera on 23 October 2003 and quoted verbatim

"Way back in 1975, from 1975 a lot of young women from schools poured in to Mozambique. Initially in to refugee camps. They did not have any spare clothes. They went in to refugee camps. But the displacement of these young girls from the schools were there was food to refugee camps where there was no food, no medicines, virtually nothing. And some had to go roaming around trying to get some roots or leaves to eat, it made those young girls who had come from a very nice, cushy background lose a bit of sense of self control. Not in terms of sex or anything like that but in terms of sense of direction. Initially, they thought it was the best thing they could do but then only to realize that it was a world of very severe hardships. No food for weeks, water or muddy water here and there" (Male medical doctor and ex-combatant F)[37].

Thus the women found that life in the camps was very different from that at home when they were civilians. As civilians they experienced some form of freedom. They asked for permission from parents to go where they wanted to go and do what they wanted to do. They were people with rights in their communities (not in the country they sought to liberate). Within their rights people exercised civility, politeness and were cultured as well as refined. Here everything was different. There was an internal order such as attending lessons about colonialism, and that had to be followed by everyone. They had limited time and they had to follow the rules.

As the ex-combatants were going through the trauma of being displaced from a home environment to a bush environment, the civilian women were going through the trauma of being forcibly displaced from a home environment to keeps (concentration camps). The colonial Government designed keeps in an effort to cut the support those combatants were getting from civilians. Other civilian women were being displaced from their rural homes where the war was escalating to towns and cities where there was relative safety. A Roman Catholic brother who worked with the displaced civilians shared his experience.

"Well, there were a lot of people many of them women and children coming from the rural areas where the war was getting hot and settling in temporary shelters that they had constructed in what was later to be known as Chirambahuyo near the present Chitungwiza. People were fleeing the rural areas to where there was relative safety near the cities. Some had been forced to kill their husbands or to burn them or to beat them. Some have told me that they were even asked to cut their husbands' parts and cook them before they ate them in front of the perpetrators".[38]

These women suffered from multiple wounds. They were traumatised from what they had been asked to do, that is harming their own families and they were traumatised by being forced to eat the human flesh. These women experienced torture as they were asked to commit violence against their own families.

To this extent, Somnier and Genefke (1986) point out that torture and repressive violence are atrocious acts specifically targeted at individuals and groups with the specific intention of causing harm, forcing compliance and destroying political will, in a situation, of civil conflict.

As the Catholic brother began to visit the camps to do his pastoral work he found that what the women needed more was to talk about their experiences.

---

37   Interview with participant was conducted in English at his home in Harare on 16 February 2005 and quoted verbatim.

38   Interview with a Roman Catholic Brother was conducted in English and quoted verbatim at his Zambuko residence - Harare, on 20 February 2005

"Many times I'd just sit there and listened to the women talk. They wanted to share their pain with someone. I was one of those who decided to listen to their experiences. There was a lot of crying, and as they cried they relieved some of the pain, I would like to believe. It was very emotional"

What these women were going through forced the Catholic brother and some parish workers to do something.

> *"we found a big hall in St. Mary's township where we would invite the traumatized women to come and do anything they liked. We asked them to cry if they wanted, to share their future plans and so forth. Some rolled on the floor and just cried, some said they would want to go back to the rural areas but not where they had fled. They wanted to start afresh somewhere different. Some said they would never go back to the rural areas and some of the residents of Chitungwiza today are those who never wanted to go back to the rural areas. Some acted as if they were out of their minds. They would talk to themselves and laugh as if they were amused at something" (A Roman Catholic Brother)*

In this regard it seems that the trauma of displacement and experiencing horrors of the war parallels that experienced by female ex-combatants. What the civilian women went through has impacted on the Catholic brother's health significantly as did the war on women both civilian and ex-combatants.

> *"Today I am a very sick man, I have high blood pressure and am no longer very steady, I shake a lot and I have no doubt that what I experienced with the women as they narrated their ordeals, as they themselves mooed like animals, has contributed to my ill health. … Some of my colleagues were not eager to continue with this work but we had to help" (A Roman Catholic Brother).*

To this end, it has been found that where people have been subjected to extreme psychological abuse, it is not uncommon for people to suffer disability and chronic pain (Malloy et al., 1983). Malloy and colleagues further write that victims who have no detectable disability may suffer from chronic pain, a little as if the body carried a memory of the pain. It does not seem so difficult to accept that the body "remembers" pain, for the sceptics, ask women about childbirth pain: male doctors describe this as highly forgettable, but not so their female patients.

4.4 Food shortages

Lack of food led to illnesses and sometimes death. When it was available in the camps, it was of poor quality. However, combatants were still required to soldier on.

4.4.1 Food shortages and training

When training began, the women went through the routine whether they were fed or not. This was done to prepare and strengthen them in the event of an attack. A male ex-combatant explained the reasoning behind I

> *"Training still continued even though comrades were hungry. It was to strengthen their minds to say they shouldn't give in and say, I can't fight, I haven't had food, I was only given only one grain of food, therefore the war must be stopped, let's go somewhere and hide until we get food……I understood it, I understood it. Remember they had said there is a comrade who has just come from Britain who thinks the war must stop because of lack of food. Shall we stop the war or continue, who ever falls we bury, that's part of the war. If we don't continue, the enemy will just come and make minced meat out of us. And thumbs went up" (Male doctor*

and ex-combatant F)[39]

4.4.2 Food shortages and death

Lack of food leads to death. Des Pres (1976) argues that those who survive are trapped in a world of total domination, a world hostile to life and any sign of dignity or resistance – a world, finally, in which an anti human order is maintained by the bureaucratic application of death.

A male doctor and ex-combatant commented on the lack of food and death in the camps.

> *"That was the most devastating issue, aah, which made me even go in to Mozambique. Lack of food, shortage of food, led to 50 people dying per day in the five camps. And that's what made me go to the war zone and left even my Master's thesis unfinished, left even my part 2 fellowship exam which I was going to write the next month, I had to leave everything when I heard from a male combatant who was also a medical doctor saying this was a fact that 50 people in five camps per day were dying because of lack of food" (Male doctor and ex-combatant F)[40]*

A female ex-combatant believes that some children born in the camps were affected by lack of food.

"There was kwashiorkor. And if you see children who were older when they came back home, they were not normal children. They were a bit rough because they were born in rough conditions" (Female ex-combatant D)[41]

When the food was available, it was of poor quality.

> *"The food was horrible even a dog would refuse to eat it. The flies were so many, we couldn't remove all from the food. I don't know how we ate it but if we didn't eat, we would die" (Female ex-combatant C)[42]*

> *"For food, we would share, but it was bad and little" (Female ex-combatant B)*

A male doctor and ex-combatant explained the shortage of food

> *"One grain. And if you complain and say no we are starving, we cannot go on, we are starving, there would be a big cry, I remember I was working with patients, the malnourished ones, I had their own big camp and I said, comrades...and they were told, even though you are sick (unwell), you would be told to do exactly what another fed person does. In other words run from 3 am in the morning to 6am in morning. And I made a complaint to the commander to say, are you trying to make these people die anyway? And I remember all the comrades in various camps being called and they said, we have a doctor who thinks that lack of food should stop the war. Do you agree? And I got thumbs down. No it is better to die than stop the war. The war must continue. Ndo hondo yacho (that's the war)". ....They would have diarrhoea and diarrhoea and diarrhoea. Imagine you have been starving for two weeks being given one grain of maize per day. I went through that as well" (Male medical doctor and ex-combatant F)[43]*

---

39   Interview with participant was conducted in English at his home in Harare on 16 February 2005 and quoted verbatim.

40   Interview with participant was conducted in English in Harare at his home on 16 February 2005 and quoted verbatim.

41   Interview with participant D was conducted in English in Marondera on 23 October 2003 and quoted verbatim

42   Interview with participant C was conducted in English in Marondera on 23 October 2003 and quoted verbatim

43   Interview with participant was conducted in English in Harare at his home on 16 February 2005 and quot

In addition to the shortage and quality of food, it was discovered that it was not the food necessarily which was so short but that the system of camping was poor and the type of food was not appropriate. The male doctor and ex-combatant then came out with suggestions that included placing the ill combatants in to separate camps where they would be monitored closely.

> *"When I arrived there I had to sit down with the commanders because, this big bunch of people, especially at Doroi, that's where the people dying went beyond 50, I said to comrade Nhongo, let us sit down with the commanders, the best way to do it is to remove the sick people in to their own camp, the nutritional camp which we would feed with the food acceptable to them and that was also the start of the production unit within the ZANLA forces. Then they began to grow their own vegetables, grow their own onions, rear their own animals especially pigs and if you look at the pictures of Chimoio, you will find that the enemy was more interested in bombing not the comrades but in bombing food centres. The first bomb would land on the kitchen, and the second bomb would land where they thought you had stored your food, because they knew that food depletion was more lethal than their guns" (Male medical doctor and ex-combatant F)*

The colonial attitude of depriving the guerrillas of food was not only applied in the camps. After bombing food centres in Mozambique, the colonial soldiers realised that hungry guerrillas were not very active, and so they extended their policy to the rural communities inside the colony where the guerrillas were fighting them.

A desperate move to alienate the freedom fighters from civilians who were feeding the guerrillas was instituted. The government restricted the movement of civilians by imposing curfews and forcing people to move in to keeps.

In this regard it is often thought that where one might anticipate solidaristic organisation, time and space can be ordered and arranged to minimise the interaction and mutual awareness of subordinates, or even to render one group of subordinates invisible to another (Barnes, 1988). To this extent, the establishment of keeps was an attempt to stop the freedom fighters from interacting with the villagers as an ex-combatant recalls, "The strategy of the Rhodesian forces was to deprive us the fish from the people, the water" (ZIANA, 2002)[44]

To this extent the security officers locked civilians in the keeps. "One day our keep was attacked. We had spent seven days locked in the keep. No one was able to communicate with the comrades. So the comrades came in the evening at the keep and tore the fence. In the keep they started looking for those they knew and came to me and said 'Hey, we have come, we are hungry. We are here and we are many'. I think at that time I ran out of words, my jaws seemed stuck together. It was God who strengthened me and I said this is what war is all about. Inside the keep, the boys took whatever they could, mealie meal, chickens, etc. The DAs (District Assistants) ran away and assembled at the strong point where they hid in the holes they had prepared for such eventualities. When they hid in the holes, we started helping the boys transport whatever they wanted. These comrades could not be fed within the camp" (ZIANA, 2000).

Other methods of communicating with and feeding the comrades were introduced. One such method was the use of a Red Cross vehicle.

"We used to have a Red Cross car. No one stopped the Red Cross car. Even the Boers did not search it. So it is a car that also fought our war. The young man who used to drive it called Sheren (Shilling)

---

44   Interview with ex-combatant K conducted by ZIANA and quoted verbatim

helped the war effort a lot. When we were out of the mealie meal, we used to go to meet him at Howard. We used to meet with others there as well. We would load the Red Cross car with mealie meal. The Red Cross would bring medicines for malaria and other illnesses to give to the villagers and comrades as well. When the car came, it used to stop at that riverbank. Shereni then opens the bonnet in front and the doors at the back then pretended to fix something of the car. When he is 'fixing' the car, we would be taking bags of mealie meal out of the car as well as other provisions. We would hide these in the forest. The mealie meal would last quite some time. The comrades would be happy because food was there" (ZIANA, 2000)[45]

Thus, in spite of the hardship resulting from the deplorable conditions and the extreme situation of food and other provisions scarcity in the keeps, the civilians retained responsibility for the provision of the material needs of ZANLA fighters in those areas (Nhongo, 2000).

'' We kept on pounding maize for mealie meal for the freedom fighters and ourselves. We did everything within our power to support the comrades.

4.4.3 Sexual favours

Because there was so much food shortage, some women began to indulge in sex for food.

> " *If you were friendly, Nice… Very free with your favours then you would get a bit more*" (Female ex-combatant D)[46].

"…*Sometimes they would take advantage of the food shortage. Commanders used to have a bit extra, so a commander would call a woman to his poshto (private dwelling) to give her some food and then have sex with her…. When a woman was protesting, they would rape her*" (Female ex-combatant B)[47].

> ''*In addition one would get clothing and not going to the front. You know going to the front to fight was not easy for anyone but for women there was always an easy way out….You know when you sleep with someone for survival it's not by consent, its traumatic because when we were growing up we were told that you do not sleep with a mudhara (old man) for survival, you need his protection*" (Female ex-combatant D).

Others did not think that there were sexual favours.
"*I can't think of any sexual favours. But because it was a war situation, favouring anyone, because we talked about reproductive health issues during the war, there were people who were trained, so the consequences were very clear, so people made choices….. it varied from individual to individual*" (Female ex-combatant A)[48]

4.5 Bioethics and War

---

45   The interview was conducted in Shona by ZIANA and translated in to English by the author. The recorded tape came from ZIANA archives.

46   Interview with participant D was conducted in English in Marondera on 23 October 2003 and quoted verbatim

47   Interview with participant B was conducted in English in Marondera on 23 October 2003 and quoted verbatim

48   Interview with participant A was conducted in English at the participant's house in Harare on 13 October, 2003 and quoted verbatim

War poses hard ethical problems for the practice of medicine, making it difficult to identify medical ethics during times of armed conflict with medical ethics during times of peace (Online, http://journals.cambridge.org/., 18 April 2006). This sets up an enduring challenge for medicine, as doctors and other healthcare professionals weigh their responsibilities as caregivers against other responsibilities and obligations that citizens must shoulder during war (On line, http://journals.cambridge.org/., 18 April 2006)

When the male doctor and ex-combatant F joined the liberation struggle, he was thinking of survival but he found himself facing the challenges of bioethics in the liberation struggle. It is believed that the role of the "physician-soldier" is an inherent moral impossibility because the military physician, in an environment of military control, is faced with the difficult problems of mixed agency that include obligations to the "fighting strength" (Online, http://journals.cambridge.org/., 18 April, 2006) To this extent, the male doctor and ex-combatant described the dilemmas he faced and the trauma he experienced as a physician-soldier.

"My mind was set on survival of these people because I had said I will participate in the war but I will also help these people to survive so that they can continue to fight but they ignored all the ailments, all the lack of food, wounds, tattered clothes, they would say, you are lucky you are still talking, otherwise you would be dead. If the enemy comes now, would you say I'm sick?"

While the male ex-combatant doctor was facing a dilemma between choosing to withdraw the ill combatants from the tour of duty in order to treat them and letting the unwell combatants continue to fight, because of manpower shortage, civilian doctors in the colony were also facing a bioethics dilemma caused by the Government. As the war escalated, the Smith regime started to close mission hospitals. Women had to walk long distances in order to get treatment. The Medical Council of Rhodesia summed up the effects of closing health facilities (Reynolds, 1996). The medical council of Rhodesia under the presidency of Doctor Paul Fehrsen warned that dangerous infectious diseases and widespread epidemics could occur because of the war. The doctor spelt out that many small hospitals and clinics had closed, leaving millions of people without access to health facilities. Many monthly maternal and child health facilities had been closed in different parts of every district. Mothers, as a result, were not able to obtain advice about health matters: there were no accessible ante-natal or family planning facilities, and children could not be immunised against measles, diphtheria, whooping cough, tetanus, poliomyelitis and tuberculosis. A number of children susceptible to these dangerous infectious diseases were growing up having not been immunised (Reynolds, 1996). The report went on to say malnutrition, among adults and children, was increasing and was widespread in areas where stores had been closed and travel was dangerous. Malaria, bilharzia and other endemic disease control programmes were curtailed and much of the ground gained over the years was being lost. The report concluded by saying that as the tempo of the war increases, there is an atmosphere of hopelessness in many villages, there is more brutality and ever increasing misery and hardship. Dr Fehrsen said the Rhodesian Medical Association believed it was necessary to present these facts to all people of Rhodesia (Reynolds, 1996).

As Doctor Fehrsen was presenting facts about the deteriorating health services, some doctors were feeling that it was not a time to discriminate against any one who needed their help irrespective of what faction they belonged to (Reynolds, 1996). The medical superintendent felt that they were all humans suffering whether they were terrorists or not, the doctor's job was to patch them up (Reynolds, 1996).

4.6 Sleep depletion

Sleep saves energy. However in war times, it is difficult to sleep due to the unpredictability nature of the difficult times encountered in a war environment. A combatant explains how comrades were affected by lack of sleep.

"But there came another problem to the combatants now, I am now talking about the combatants, whether you were inside the country (Zimbabwe) or you were outside in the bases the other disease which affected more women than anyone else is what we call sleep depletion, you know, if you spend 3,4,5, days without sleep, definitely your mind doesn't really tune well. That's why the comrades who used to appear in various zones in the country, they would have spent about a week without sleep, and their eyes would be red shot, many people used to think that comrades smoke mbanje (intoxicating drug), very few smoked mbanje but sleep depletion was another tool of the enemy, even during the night, you would just hear the bomb thrown anywhere just to make sure that you do not sleep" (Male ex-combatant and medical doctor F)[49].

Fig 10. A comrade sleeps while others keep guard Fig 10. A comrade sleeps while others keep guard

4.7 rapes in the camps.

Some female ex-combatants narrated how they were treated. "There were many men. Imagine we had to sleep and have ten men, or okay seven men in a week. …..Your body becomes nothing. And you lose respect for your self as a woman. Ten men – okay, seven men – a week, different people it is something that normal women cannot do. So we grew up with all these experiences. I am sure they affect any one's later life. We were not allowed to say no" (Zimbabwe Women writers, 2000).

> *"Everywhere were there were men and women I think there was an average of 1 or 2 rapes every day per camp. It was very common and a very difficult crime to report because it was mainly done by seniors. And militarily, you do not report to a senior above your senior. So it has to start with your senior and it ended there. So nobody takes it up"* (Female ex-combatant B)

It would seem that commanders used their positions to abuse female combatants. The following account shows how a senior army personnel used his position to abuse the girl.

> *"I am one of those who was raped. I was raped by Mr. X. I used to carry his bag. One day he told me that only the two of us were going. So I asked him how we could go without someone with a gun accompanying us. He said, today there was no need for another person. Mr. X was coming from America. He was writing his book about the*

---

49   Interview with the participant was conducted in English at his home in Harare on 16 February 2005 and quoted verbatim.

war. I used to go with him and this time when we went the two of us only he raped me twice. It is difficult for me to explain what happened because (She starts sobbing uncontrollably)…

"It doesn't mean that I was a virgin. But to be forced by someone to sleep with him is painfu…. The only person I told when I could not bear it any more was Mai Sally Mugabe… He was so angry with me and he kept on saying it was me who raped him. It pains me even up to today" (Female ex-combatant now living in the UK)

One female recruit who joined the ZANLA army at the age of 15 had her first sexual experience with men who raped her in the camp - an all-too-common experience for many women recruits in the ZANLA forces during the liberation war (Zimbabwe solidarity newsletter 03. 02. 05).

These accounts show that during wars, women and girls are not just killed, they are raped, sexually attacked, mutilated and humiliated. The women paid prices for their sacrifices and when asked what it was like to be in the frontline, a female ex-combatant replied,

"Wonderful. In the front we got killed, At the back we got raped" (Female ex-combatant B)

The commanders who made combatants pregnant, did not want the responsibility associated with it, they left the girls behind while they went to further their careers.

"But what would happen is that the male comrades or commanders would be sent to a different base. Some were sent to schools in places such as Romania or China. While others were sent to school, some died during combat" (Female ex-combatant B)

In an attempt to protect women combatants against sexual attackers, the girls were taught about their sexual rights.

"….as they went in to the camps, the commissariat would teach them their rights to say you are a person just as good as me. I am a man, you are a woman, but you are a person, you can choose me to be your husband, I can choose you to be my wife or boyfriend. So you have every right. You can even sleep with me, no sex no nothing. Just talk and sleep because you and I have equal rights. And to those who were actually engaged in to a love affair, they were highly protective of their woman or men. You wouldn't touch somebody else's girlfriend or boyfriend. She belongs to so and so or he belongs to so and so. So they were protected by the commissariat led by men. And any pregnancies meant marriage and Mayor Urimbo who was the chief commissar would swear you as married couple" (Male doctor and ex-combatant F).

"…but we were also taught how to behave ourselves because we were away from parents and having so much freedom that could be abused. So we used to carry out, I do not know whether they would say gender training, so that women assert themselves, survival tactics, life skills, we started imparting them on the girls" (Female ex-combatant A)[50].

Despite the gender training programmes rapes in the camps were rampant because the success of the programmes depended on

- Whether male combatants followed or did or did not follow the sex code, which forbade rapes.

---

50   Interview with participant A was conducted in English at the participant's house in Harare on 13 October, 2003 and quoted verbatim

- On the reasons why some male combatants joined the liberation struggle - some rapists are reported to have been agents of the colonial government and they did not respect women as pointed out by one female ex-combatant.

> *"…We had people who were rapists at home. You know a war situation, criminals, rapists, murderers would come to Mozambique, some were running away from their own situation, some were reactionaries who were sent in by their agents to infiltrate us and destroy the revolution from the bases" (Female ex-combatant A).*[51]

In addition to gender training programmes, ancestral spirits through their mediums formulated the code of conduct towards sexual behaviour during the liberation struggle. An ex-combatant described how the code was enforced.

> *" Spirit mediums played very influential roles in checking and balancing behaviour of combatants. There is a song, nzira dzemasoja, (soldiers' ways); it tells you even about how a man in the battle, a woman in the battle should actually behave in terms of sex. Adultery was prohibited. And you would be told by a man or a woman that if you ever touched a woman in the battle, the next thing is we will bury you. But if you sleep with one and you love her, you want to marry her, no problem. But if you go from one poshto, we used to call them poshtos because we will sleep under tree. From one poshto to another, sleep with one, the battle starts, we will bury you here. Because you will have broken one of the laws of guerrilla warfare. No adultery in the battle field. And sure for your information, those who used to do it, died. Whether here, in the front or even at the back, they died. Uyu musikana uyu arikuramba achimhanya na so and so na so and so arikusara pano apa kana hondo ikauya (this girl is sleeping around with so and so and so and so, she will remain here if the battle starts) and she would die there" (A male medical doctor and ex-combatant F)*[52]

The code of conduct was in keeping with traditional ways where the ancestral spirits forbade sexual relations outside of marriage and exhorted married men to refrain from their wives before they went hunting or to war. Guided by the traditional moral code, unmarried girls were not permitted to attend ZANLA *pungwes* (night meetings) nor could they cook for guerrillas. According to Solomon Mujuru (Rex Nhongo), the ZANLA army commander during the liberation struggle, these regulations were strictly enforced in the early days and helped prevent rape and unwanted pregnancies (Mclaughlin, 1996).

However, rapes in the camps continued to take place despite the fact that there was a code of conduct in place that forbade such practices. A female ex-combatant felt that many male combatants through out the liberation struggle never adhered to the code of conduct.

> *"You know what, that is when they would turn a blind eye. There was a code of conduct but nobody followed it. You were lucky if someone said 'I'm living with this one as man and wife', but it was not always the case....There was rape, torture, threatening if you said you would want to go back home. If you didn't sleep with so and so, you were in trouble. So you were thinking of yourself and the people back home at the same time. And there were children who would accept anything to survive" (Female ex-combatant D)*[53]

The attitude of male combatants who sexually violate women in times of conflict brings us to the argument that gender relations in times of conflict are based on the subordination of women. "Women are reminded that whatever additional roles they are entrusted with, their original role as providers of sex comes first" (Turshen and Twagiramaria, 1998, p. 96).

---

51   Interview with participant A was conducted in English at the participant's house in Harare on 13 October, 2003 and quoted verbatim

52   Interview with participant was conducted in English in Harare at his home on 16 February 2005 and quoted verbatim.

53   Interview with participant D was conducted in English in Marondera on 23 October 2003 and quoted ver

To this extent it can be argued that the rapists used their power to force the girls to sleep with them against their will, because the men perceived sex to be the women's primary role in the war. Max Weber (1978) describes this type of power as the carrying out of one's will in a social relationship, something, which can also be accomplished through violence. 'Power' is the probability that one actor within a social relationship will be in a position to carry out his own will despite resistance, regardless of the basis on which this probability rests. Power as the exertion of influence over others, either in accordance with or, more significantly against their will, is in different variations and widespread throughout the social sciences. It also corresponds to our everyday understanding (Weber, 1978).

Women appear to have suffered more abuse at the hands of the guerrillas towards the end of the struggle when guerrillas were getting tired of fighting (Reynolds, 1996). A female ex-combatant confirmed this point.

> "Then there were women who were not exactly in the camps, those who were in neighbouring districts like Mutasa, those who would bring information. Those also had children from men in the camps. Up to now, nobody has tried to put an effort to try to match the children with their fathers; nor the fathers put an effort to look for their children nor the mothers put an effort to look for their children fathers nor the children put an effort to look for their fathers" (Female ex-combatant B)[54]

Thus, freedom fighters used guns that were perceived as tools for liberation by the villagers among whom they operated, to undermine the authority of community elders who normally regulated the sexual activities of young people. In this way, they seriously violated traditional African values, which were part of the cultural environment of the masses who hosted the war (Bhebe and Ranger, 1995).

However, not all rape cases reported were committed by male combatants. Government agents have been blamed by some who argue that infiltrators who raped women wanted to portray a bad image of male combatants and discredit ZANLA army.

> "The cases I knew myself, the cases I experienced, were perpetrated by I do not know whether you heard about Nyathi? The one who became a selous scout leader? He was sent by the Smith regime to cause chaos in the camp. And because people were not aware that he was an agent, he rose to the position of a camp commander and he used his position now to cause chaos to the girls.....raping girls at gun point. I told you it happened to me. He almost...was almost raped, and I refused to sleep with him. I said shoot me. You can kill me if you want. I would never allow anyone to violate my body" (Female ex-combatant A)[55].

> "In fact I was young. It was in 1978. It affected me school wise. Sexually, I was abused once, but I didn't notice it in those days. I thought it was natural. Mmm it hurts. I meet some of those people but they do not remember me. It's best to forget" (Female war collaborator).

In response to the rape cases, some male ex-combatants pointed out that rapes are not only committed by male combatants.

> "Let us understand that we are talking of a society. Church leaders are known to have raped people so rape can be committed anywhere by anyone. So rapes are not peculiar to wars only "(Male respondent in a group interview).

One female ex-combatant had a different view of what constitutes rape.

---

54   Interview with participant D was conducted in English in Marondera on 23 October 2003 and quoted verbatim

55   Interview with participant A was conducted in English at the participant's house in Harare on 13 October, 2003 and quoted verbatim

"People may say they were raped but it is not true. People were in love. Many knew that rape was forbidden. If done then the comrades would become weak and the enemy would defeat us. That's what I know" (Female ex-combatant in a group interview)[56]

The author argues that among some female ex-combatants the topic of rape is still a sensitive issue, and they are not enthusiastic to discuss or admit that rapes took place. Many others do not reveal that they are ex-combatants because they do not want to talk about the war at all. The reluctance to talk about rape leads to the question of rape representation. Whether in the courts or the media, whether in art or criticism, who gets to tell the story and whose story counts as 'truth' determine the definition of what rape is (Higgins and Silver, 1991). The personal experiences that the women ex-combatants revealed at the probe in to War Victims Compensation Fund, constituted counter discourse to official narratives about nationalist triumph, which had been popularised by male politicians and guerrillas (Chiwome and Mguni, 2003, http://www.gwsafrica.org/knowledge/zifikele, 17th July, 2005).

To this extent, the confession of the truth would have shocked society into reducing the moral and political stature of the fighters whom it had idolised in the first decade of independence. For those who materially benefited from the war, the revelation of the truth would have been considered as unpatriotic and subversive. Attempts were made to sweep the unpleasant truth under the carpet (Bhebe and Ranger, 1995).

This explains why after independence, men who participated in the war were never keen to allow women to spell out to society their side of the war. One female ex-combatant explained that male politicians try to make war experiences as 'nice' as possible so that they would remain the so-called trusted party cadres. They do not want the country to have the proper history of what actually transpired during the war (Bhebe and Ranger, 1995).

There is a feeling among ex-combatants that rapes that took place in the camps were the responsibility of the female ex-combatants because it is the woman who ought to protect herself. If sexual relationships took place, the women wanted them too because they had the right to say no. This argument was put across by a female ex-combatant.

"The truth is that women are the ones who look after themselves. Men cannot live without a sexual relationship for long. A man can not leave his wife for three to six months without indulging in ex marital sexual activities. Even when his wife dies, he is quick to enter in to a sexual relationship with someone. It was easier for young girls who went to war without having experienced sexual relationships to resist male advances than those who had left children behind or were bigger girls" (Female ex-combatant in the group interview)[57]
"What happens is that we are human beings and we have love for each other. Even female partners felt that they needed male love" (Female ex-combatant A)[58]

"Some women wanted to have sex anyway" (Female ex-combatant B)[59].

---

56   The group interview was conducted in Shona in Harare at ZANU-PF headquarters on 18 February, 2005 then translated in to English.

57   The group interview was conducted in Shona in Harare at ZANU-PF headquarters on 18 February, 2005

58   Interview with participant A was conducted in English at the participant's house in Harare on 13 October, 2003 and quoted verbatim

59   Interview with participant B was conducted in English in Marondera on 23 October 2003 and quoted verbatim

Thus female ex-combatants had different views about the attitudes of sexual behaviour in the camps. The differences appear to have been caused by the belief that people were governed by established codes of conduct. In addition girls were taught about their sexual rights and were expected to exercise them. But as some female ex-combatants testified, these training programmes do not always work and people do not always behave as expected.

A further analysis on the difference in opinion on what constituted rapes during the liberation struggle also appears to have been based on class differences among the women. The understanding that the peasant female ex-combatant in the group interview had about sexual relationships during the liberation struggle suggests that she believes that the traditional code of conduct was strictly followed and it guided combatants. In this respect rapes did not take place. Further, she believes that the onus of protecting a woman from sexual abuse rests on the woman herself because men are weaker when it comes to abstain from sexual activities than women are. Therefore, cases of rape are in fact cases of love affairs and sex by consent.

To this extent as Ziyambi (1997) notes, women are frequently the victims of 'traditional cultures', which deprive them of their human rights as specifically female individuals. 'Cultural rights' are often the rationale for masculine domination of domestic as well as national affairs. In this regard it would appear that traditional culture affects women's political, economic and social status. These factors are determinants of women's health. Although the educated elite women ex-combatants agreed that there were times that women wanted sex anyway, they feel that many times women were forced to have sex against their will and therefore they were raped leaving them traumatised.

Indeed after independence, there was controversy over rapes that took place during the liberation struggle and the difference in opinion about rape issues appears to have caused it.

The attitude of women ex-combatants who 'wanted sex anyway' draws parallel to women and sex during the First World War. "Thousands of women had seen their actual or potential mates swallowed up in that ever-increasing wave of death, which was the Great War. Life was less than cheap; it was thrown away. The religious teaching that the body was the temple of the Holy Ghost could mean little or nothing to those who saw it mutilated and destroyed in millions by Christian nations engaged in war. All moral standards had been submerged. Life and love were held for a short moment and irretrievably lost. Little wonder that the old ideals of chastity and self control in sex were, for many, also lost" (Woollacott, 1994, p.144).

4.7.1 Gender power

Raping women or forcing them to sleep with the men against their will could be explained by understanding the relationship of gender power. Men's power over women is seen to rest on the culturally developed ability of the male ego to have power over the female ego (Cosslett et al., 1996).

The politics of ego are based, not on any direct desire on the part of men to hurt women, but through men's need to derive their own strength and self esteem by over riding women's independent sense of self (Cosslett et al., 1996).

In this regard, rape experiences could have been a source of pride to perpetrators and a source of resentment to victims. In this sense reconciliation may be difficult to achieve, it can be argued and it is not difficult to see why the United Nations faces dilemmas on how to use conflict resolution tools to achieve healing where there are diametrically opposed views.

4.7.2 Physical and psychological injuries of rapes

There are many health consequences of gender violence. They can be non- fatal in the form of physical injuries, ranging from minor cuts and bruises to chronic disability or mental traumas. Doctors who have treated raped women have described the challenges they face. ''Initially they come with infections, vaginal infections, urinary tract problems – problems that are sexually transmitted. You cure the direct illness, but psychologically, they are not healed, they continue to be sick. And there are no services that specifically deal with the problems that these women have. There are some groups for widows and the like, but there are no groups to help women who have gone through rape'' (Turshen and Twagiramariya, 1998, p.96). Rape injuries may also be fatal, resulting from either intentional homicide or injuries sustained. In the case of mental trauma, women may commit suicide.

Thus the suffering and abuse endured by the female ex-combatants goes far beyond the actual rape. Mashall (2004) observes that rape has a devastating and ongoing impact on the health of women and girls and survivors face a lifetime of stigma and marginalisation from their own families and communities.

Women could also contract AIDS (Acquired immune deficiency syndrome) or other sexually transmitted diseases as described by respondents.

> *"Yes, if you were not an important person, you would die. Some of them were not so bad, they would feel for you. And some of us were virgins" (Female ex-combatant D)[60] .*

4.7.3 Rights to reproduction

Women ex-combatants feel that their right to reproduction and health was violated against when they were raped and when they were not allowed to use contraceptives. This resulted in unwanted pregnancies in some.

'' And as women we never got special treatment - we were the highly oppressed people. We were never even allowed to use contraceptives (Zimbabwe Women writers, 2000, p.125).

60   Interview with participant D was conducted in English in Marondera on 23 October 2003 and quoted verbatim

4.8 Torture of women

In some instances, in addition to being sexually abused, women were tortured too. A medical doctor and male ex-combatant explained that

"Way back in 1977 in June, I am talking about the diseases, I found together with anther male doctor that women were either tortured or being examined in their private parts by security security agents of our forces. Any pretty woman who entered the war zone, would be taken to the security camp and examined thoroughly. The more prettier she was, the more interrogation and examination she went through including putting the man's fingers in to her private parts looking for a disease.... So our security agents were oversensitive, to the extent that some women got burnt down there as if to say you will never have sex with any man" (Male medical doctor and ex-combatant F)[61].

4.9 Biological and chemical warfare

Agents of the colonial government used chemical weapons during the liberation struggle. They poisoned clothes, food and dropped napalm bombs.

"Those who got burnt by it (napalm) died instantly. We had only one whom we managed to rescue but even that girl didn't survive more than 24 hrs. She died. Phosphorous bomb, you just die because it will just penetrate and penetrate" (Male medical doctor and ex-combatant F).

In addition to using biological and chemical warfare against combatants and civilians, the colonial government was at the same time polluting the environment by poisoning wells and small rivers used by both human beings, domestic and wild animals (ZIANA, 2000).

A female ex-combatant explained how combatants suffered from wearing poisoned clothes and drinking poisoned water.

"Some people would bring chemical treated clothes from Rhodesia and when comrades wore them, they died and people would say 'afa ne aids' (he has died of aids) but that's not it. Sometimes comrades drank poisoned water. An enemy would come pretending to join the war, they brought chemicals, they were mercenaries." (Female ex-combatant D)[62]

Further, the Red Cross car that was used by civilians to transport food and medical supplies for combatants was infiltrated by the Rhodesian security forces as explained by a villager, "And the Red Cross was bringing us used clothes and the clothes had biological weapons in them. When we went in to the front line we started witnessing the problem of cattle death, human death and when the civilians and combatants were tested it was found that they were suffering from the effect of the biological weapons. It was mostly anthrax diseases, cholera etc. The same thing happened in Mozambique. Remember the Catholic bishop in Sofala who was running a clinic there, they found that most of

---

61   Interview with the participant was conducted in English at his home in Harare on 16 February 2005 and quoted verbatim.

62   Interview with participant D was conducted in English in Marondera on 24 October 2003 and quoted verbatim

the ZANLA combatants were actually infected by a certain hysteria and chronic illness which was causing the nerve degeneration" (Doctor Ngwenya, ZIANA, 2000)[63].

Doctor Timothy Stamps confirmed what he thought about the use of anthrax during the liberation struggle.

''The Rhodesian forces used anthrax, I am quite sure about that. In fact I didn't believe it myself at first but the evidence, though it is incomplete is there, that anthrax was used in the war" (Dr.Timothy Stamps, ZIANA, 2000).[64]

4.9.1 Food poisoning

One ex-combatant who survived the food poisoning shared the experience.

> *"Many people died, many. Some died of the poison, others died of fighting while the poison was cutting their intestines. One had to choose dying of the poison while fighting back or not to fight and wait to see the poison finish them. Some comrades sacrificed their lives by placing grenades on themselves and die than being taken as prisoners of war. So dying fighting was a better option. Other comrades who were a bit stronger, took with them guns that their dead friends had used. But the person who sold us did so because he had been given a tin of canned beef. Just a can of beef. This is why in the bible it is said that Jesus Christ was sold for a mere thirty pieces of silver" (Male ex-combatant 2 in a group interview).[65]*

4.9.2 Spirit mediums, poisoning and witchcraft accusations

As the Rhodesian administration was only too well aware of how much the mediums could offer to the guerrillas, an extraordinary "Shamanism Book" was compiled in 1970 to instruct administrators about the history, cosmology, and politics of spirit mediums (Ranger and Alexander, 1998). As the war progressed, the use of poisons was employed by the colonial Government in order to implicate and discredit the spirit mediums. To this extent, a "spirit index" was drawn up that aimed to include every priest and medium in Zimbabwe and to note which ones were supporting the "terrorists." Many mediums were arrested. Some were killed, either by Rhodesian soldiers or by guerrillas who believed them to be collaborating with the colonial government (Ranger and Alexander, 1998). When the guerrillas died from wearing poisoned clothes and eating poisoned food, both the spirit mediums (who guided the war) and the civilians who had supplied these were either killed or beaten badly by the surviving guerrillas as pointed out by Evelyn Taibo a *chimbwido* from the area, ''In 1976, then came comrades killing our people during our presence saying that they were witches and wizards. They killed our neighbours saying that they were sell outs. As a result life became hard for us. We had no one to depend on. We were afraid of both the whites and our children - the guerrillas" (McLaughlin,1996, p. 96).

Women accused of witchcraft were killed by guerrillas because they too feared that they would be bewitched and killed. Many of those identified to have poisoned the guerrillas and therefore witches were people believed to be politically untrustworthy or treacherous, those believed to be acting against the interests of the peasants as a whole (Lan, 1985).

---

63   Interview with Dr. Ngwenya was conducted in English by ZIANA and quoted verbatim.
64   Dr.T. Stamps is the former Minister of Health. Interview was conducted by ZIANA and quoted verbatim.
65   The group interview was conducted in Shona in Harare at ZANU-PF headquarters on 18 February, 2005 then translated in to English.

The persecution of women believed to be witches was also prevalent in England and Scotland during the seventeenth century (Rowbotham, 1973). In Scotland, the punishment was death, but in England, public humiliation was more common. In England, unlike on the continent, violence against the witches was spontaneous rather than organised by the church or state. It was believed that if you drew blood by 'witch pricking' you weakened the witch's magic and power for evil (Rowbotham, 1973).

Many of the women accused of witchcraft were old and poor. Thus the economic helplessness of old women meant they were common targets and when misfortune came people looked for someone to blame and disputes often arose between neighbours. Old women who argued back were obvious targets. Thus wise and cunning women became suspects (Rowbotham, 1973).

In some instances women admitted to being witches who made pacts with the devil. However one woman confessed not because she was a witch but because she was poor and tired of living from handouts. Confessing to being a witch would make people want to have nothing further to do with her, men would beat her and set dogs at her, no one would give her food and so she would starve to death (Rowbotham, 1973).

4.10 Personal care

Bathing was a rare commodity. The women ex-combatants described the hardships they faced.

> *"That is if there is any water. We are talking about the bush. So the same river supplied drinking as well as bathing water" (Female ex-combatant D)*

> *"Ah, you can't really say there was no bathing, Situation differed from one situation to another. Like in my case, it would be very difficult because there were all men, but in refugee camp and some other camps, there were camps for women so they could bath. But for cotton wool' they used rags. That's what they used, old clothes, they used rags, emm because there was nothing no birth control, no tablets, that's why…" (Female ex-combatant A).*

> *For soap, we used tree bark. You would crush it. I have not seen that tree here in Zimbabwe because it would make good detergent. So tree bark was for washing clothes and soap for washing the body not for washing (laundry). The soap was also used as lotion (Female ex-combatant B)[66].*

4.11 Pregnant women and Osibisa

When a female combatant became pregnant she would be sent to a special place called Osibisa camp. This is a place where pregnant women and those with babies lived. Some pregnancies came out of forced sexual relationships as pointed out by a female ex-combatant,

> *"There were big chefs who asked us to sleep with them and you couldn't say no. If you refused, you would be given a hard task that you won't forget in your life time. Silence. Pregnancies started coming up. Children were born. One was afraid to mention who the father was, so the children were born and the fathers were not known. This somebody had his own wife so the girls were scared to mention the responsible fathers. Sometimes the girls just mentioned the young men they had gone out with before as the fathers of their children…. And the girls who were old, they were forced to sleep with men. Some girls have kids and they do not know who the father is. Now you know in our culture a child will say 'Who is my father?' and the woman does not know because she slept with so many comrades. The child does not know its relatives" (Female ex-combatant C)*

66   Interview with participant B was conducted in English in Marondera on 23 October 2003 and quoted verbatim

Another ex-combatant reiterated what the pregnant young combatants went through in the camps as older combatants interrogated them.

"And then when the women were pregnant, the men were not there to see the women or children or to enjoy the child growing. So this child is growing in a home where the mother is thinking if the war starts I have just to pick this child and run. So the child becomes a burden instead of someone you are cherishing and loving, but you are so tied to them because its your blood. There is nothing you can do. You are sort of at risk. And at the same time you don't have guns except those anti air craft guns. And then the other aspect is that the woman who has come today, meets a woman who came two years ago, who was made pregnant by the same man. And this woman is the one taking roll call and she says What is your name? My name is Dotito (Fictitious name) Who made you pregnant? Comrade Hondo. Which comrade Hondo are you talking about? Oh the one in camp B. That's my husband. You are busy taking away people's husbands. Then they start fighting for a man who is not even there, right? And start pointing fingers at each other saying 'You are making my child sick because you want the man' but the man is not there and may never go there, so that's another thing in Osibisa camp. "It is a pity we do not have statistical data to support that almost a third of the babies born in the camps were a result of imposed sex" (Female ex-combatant B)[67]

There were also times when male combatants were afraid of female combatants in the Osibisa camp.

"I think there is something interesting that happened there. There used to be male guards. Like, its in the bush, so you had to put anti air craft stuff to protect mothers and children. Then women got so frustrated that they said they also wanted to be guards so that they would be with men to the extent that they women bribed male guards with food so that they (women) would have sex with them (male guards). So in the end the men refused to guard that camp. They couldn't cope with demand. And they had to be changed and the women started guarding themselves. This was just sexual needs…we also had clinics in the bush, in the camps and so we had nurses who would monitor the development of both the mother and the child. We had nurses, people who joined the struggle, some of them were nurses, some were doctors" (Female ex-combatant B)

4. 11.1 Children dying in the bush

Because life was not so easy in the camps, some mothers are known to have watched their young ones die. Many reasons are cited for this. The water was not so clean and the Rhodesian forces could have poisoned it. The children would not eat and eventually became very ill with dysentery (Urdang, 1989). Many other Zimbabwean women ex combatants went to celebrate independence in 1980 but left their dead children behind, somewhere in the bush. Today the women live with their loss and grief. Alexander et al. (2000) point out that for some ex-guerrillas, the pain of the past is just not history. It is a living present.

4.11.2 Recording of the babies

Children were recorded under the mothers' names only because most of the times the fathers' names were not known. The difficulties of recording the children under the mothers' names in the camps and later obtaining birth certificates for children in liberated Zimbabwe were spelt out

"Children were recorded under the mothers' names only'. Yes, not the father's, only the mothers. You were lucky to know who the father was. Some of my friends have children who they do not know who is the father because they would sleep with this one and this one…..I have got a friend who is very bitter. She has a daughter and she does not know who the father is because in one night she would sleep with about six men or more" (Female ex-combatant D).

---

67   Interview with participant B was conducted in English in Marondera on 23 October 2003 and quoted verbatim. The belief in witchcraft was prevalent among some combatants. This is why a baby's illness

If the father was known, he would not acknowledge the child as in most 'revolutions', the issue of gender equality was regarded as less pressing than other inequalities, by those men who fought for liberation which was settled at Lancaster House in 1979. In particular, no provision was made to regularise the social position of the children born to young women who had participated in the struggle (Zimbabwe Human Rights NGO Forum March 2001).

4.11.3 Experiences of children in the camps

Amidst all the hardships encountered in a war environment, women still have a 'heart' to save lives. Women looking after babies whose mothers had died in the war explained this role.

> *"There were other female comrades who were killed during raids or clashes and left babies behind. It was not uncommon for other mothers breastfeeding to feed an extra baby whose mother had been killed. I actually know of a child who after the war came to ZANU PF headquarters at 88 Manica road at the time and narrated her story that 'I was told that my mother died in Mozambique. One lady breastfed me and I am looking for her'. The one who had fed this child said ' The child I fed has a mark on such a place. May I see your mark?' When she was shown, she burst in to tears. The child also began to cry. So children were born during the war " (Female ex-combatant in a group interview)*[68]

Indeed wars are cruel: they kill, maim and wound anyone. Children are not spared either. They suffered anxiety, they got ill, and they suffered physically and psychologically. An ex-combatant explains,

> *"The children would learn wondering whether their parents are still alive. In the refugee camps there were no medicines and the flies that ate flesh were plenty. So the children suffered. The children were just there but their minds were not there. They just came to school because they were told to. They had psychological problems. Physically, they got ill because of lack of food or constantly hearing the planes hovering above them sometimes dropping bombs over them" (Male ex-combatant in a group interview)*[69]

4.12 Meaning of war

From the feminist perspective, the author of this study relied on the validity of personal war experiences and grounded theory to understand what the liberation struggle meant to women ex-combatants looking at violence, power and powerlessness. The three approaches - phenomenology, feminist, and grounded theory sought meaning of the women's lived war experiences. In listening to the voices of the women and reflecting on the meaning of their experience, what strikes is their innocence, their vulnerability, their complete lack of preparation or awareness of impending hardships brought by conflict: the unanticipated and incomprehensible event of war disrupting the fabric of life; the loss of home and the loss of innocence that was about to occur as they left their homes, naive, trusting and vulnerable. All participants shared these experiences.

---

68   Group interview with female respondent at ZANU-PF headquarters. She spoke in Shona and translation was done in Eglish.

69   Group interview with male respondent at ZANU-PF headquarters. He spoke in English and was quoted verbatim.

4.13 Trying times in the struggle

Apart from the direct effects of the war such as injuries and illnesses, there were other indirect psychological health effects on the female combatants due to gender differences. A female ex-combatant described how roles of combatants changed due to gender differences.

"Like I said, generally we had the same problems men and women. Then you had female problems due to gender differences. Eh women had children and a lot of women were on their own and they got isolated, those with kids. If you read my poem you will see that there was a camp called Osibisa. You will find that in the camp, you are no longer very functional, you are no longer very active on combat duties. Sometimes women would be sent home carrying materials" (Female ex-combatant B)[70]

Conclusion

The war women had in mind is different from the one they later experienced.
When the women got to Mozambique, what awaited them were conditions that some have described as conditions that can only be found in hell. Indeed some female ex-combatants have described the conditions of the camps, that life was very tough there, there was never enough to eat, and that there were some comrades who refused to accept girls as freedom fighters – they were only accepted as comforters of men (Weiss, 1986). The promise of glory that lay ahead turned out to be life full of difficulties, illnesses and diseases - including the mysterious and under-researched 'hurricanes' – all cumulating to traumas. Some thought that they had made a mistake by coming to the war but they could not run away, they could not go back. They started questioning themselves regarding the meaning of war. At home they lived under the guidance of their parents, in the camps they lived under authoritarian rule. At home they were not always forced to act in a certain way. In the camps they followed commands. In the hardships of these physical and psychological traumas, the women could not go back. They soldiered on.

---

70   Interview with participant B was conducted in English in Marondera on 23 October 2003 and quoted verbatim

Section 2

This section looks at the health issues of women ex-combatants post 1980.

Further, the author explores the elite and peasant ex-combatants' perceptions of how war affected their health looking at stress fertility and life chances.

The discourse of blame points to the issues of poisoning, children with downs syndromes, ectopic pregnancies and marriages as factors that have shaped their health and life chances.

Chapter Five: Health issues of women ex-combatants post 1980.

5.1 Introduction

"Zimbabwe needs to remember and to understand the war: to understand it at the level of high analysis and to understand it at the level of suffering and trauma. We need to understand it for reviewing policy, for making the record more complete, for healing memories" (Bhebe and Ranger 1995a, p1). To this extent, there is no question that the involvement of women in the liberation struggle as fighters, civilian supporters of the war effort, war collaborators, parents of the freedom fighters and forced camp residents were traumatic events. The Human Rights Forum (2000) indicates that 1 in 10 people over the age of 30 in Mount Darwin – one of the provinces in Zimbabwe where the soldiers, ZANLA combatants and civilians fought and participated in the conflict, were shown to have psychological disorder, physical or both.

5.2 Post traumatic stress disorders

The study of the women's war experiences of the liberation struggle revealed that post traumatic stress disorder is a phenomenon that can be buried but can break through the defences and memories after many years. Women ex-combatants had different perceptions of how the war affected their health. Although the cut off date for the study of traumas of the liberation struggle is 1990, female ex-combatants were still describing the long-term health consequences associated with the war that include psychological anguish of unexpected and disturbing flashback experiences twenty three years after the liberation struggle.

> "...in a war environment where I was, you slept with your gun on so that any time you could just wake up. As a result you know, it is not a normal situation. At times I do not sleep because all the time you're in a fighting mood. So any noise, I will wake up, even now. **We are not normal people** (giggles) **we are not normal people.** That's one thing the war does to people" (Female ex-combatant A).[71]

Kinzie et al., (1984) observed that many psychological disorders found in other groups exposed to war sleep disorders, and startle reactions were common. Sleeping with a gun indicates the unpredictability of when an attack could occur each night. Sapolsky (1994) claims that unpredictability makes stressors more stressful. Ex-combatants and civilians lived in unpredictable environments where they got threats to their well being but were never sure when the attacks would take place. The stressfulness of loss of control and unpredictability share a common element; they cause arousal and vigilance (Sapolsky, 1994). It would then appear that the effects of the sense of control on stress are highly dependent on context. Marks et al. (2000) note that there are stressors of living in a stressful

---

71   Interview with participant A was conducted in English at the participant's house in Harare on 13 October, 2003 and quoted verbatim

environment and both the psychological and physiological effects of each type of stressor are likely to differ.

The experiences of the survivors of the liberation struggle indicate that the symptoms most frequently described are increased fatigue, failing memory, an inability to concentrate, restlessness, irritability, emotional liability, disturbance of sleep, headaches, and various vegetative symptoms (Amani Trust, 2003).

5.2.1 Hurt and anger

When a human being is wounded, it is natural to feel hurt but when the hurt is so profound and ambiguous, people cannot express the pain, so they respond naturally with anger, as a protective response to the wounding (Cabrera, 2002).

Cabrera, (2002), further points out that when the pain is accumulated, the ability to communicate with others, to be flexible and tolerant is enormously reduced. This inability to function adequately was illustrated when the communication between the author and a respondent that appeared to have been going on smoothly took a sudden twist when she said,

> *"This is why they call us we are mad. If you make me angry, I am a changed person. I go back to square one. We are very unpredictable...my children at times do not understand me. They say 'mamma watanga' (mum has started again). I can be unpredictable. I can change now as we are talking, I can change and you won't like me. And you won't like me for two seconds. I can even hit you". (Female ex-combatant D)[72]*

The author observed that hurt and anger were some of the psychological disorders displayed by women ex-combatants studied. From this perspective, the liberation struggle has brought a lot of pain to women and children who are the most common targets of violence. Thus violence against women not only causes pain and trauma that impacts on women's health and lives significantly but the health of their families as well. In this regard, violence has a bearing on the population that was affected in Zimbabwe. When the violence becomes widespread and ongoing, the trauma and pain it causes affect entire communities and even the country as a whole. To this extent, Cabrera (2002) in her study about living and surviving in a multiply wounded country - Nicaragua, points out that the implications of trauma and pain are serious for people's health, the resilience of the country's social fabric, the success of development schemes, and the hope of future generations.

5.2.2 Witnessing

There is evidence, of enormous psychological effects not merely from those who suffered physical abuse, but also from those who witnessed traumatic events, such as murder, rape, or wartime torture (Amani Trust, 1997). Reynolds (1996) cites an incident where Mr Mudimba was killed in front of the whole village. As his wife bent down in grief, a soldier standing nearby shouted that she was the wife of a devil. With that, the commander ordered his boys to burn the granaries, which they did and all the year's food's supply was burnt to ashes. People were horrified and afraid. In a study done on the children's experiences of the liberation struggle, twenty four out of thirty five children interviewed in Musami, said that they had seen people being killed.

---

72   Interview with participant D was conducted in English in Marondera on 23 October 2003 and quoted ver-
      batim

They saw people burned to death, people drowned in rivers (their legs tied together), people buried alive, people shot, and people accused of being witches killed (Reynolds, 1996). Today, the interviewees in the study are no longer children. They are adults, some of them women who are living with the horrors of what they witnessed as children during the war.

It may be argued about what form this psychological disorder associated with witnessing traumatic events might take, but there is no doubt that there are some psychological effects on people who witnessed traumatic events as attested by some ex-combatants.

> *"All comrades, the civilians who participated, every ex-combatant, all these are affected. All the things seen are always in people's vision" (male1 in a group interview)[73].*

At times women witnessed horrendous acts such as seeing their children killed in front of them (CCJPZ, 1997). The women, in their grief, were asked to ululate while these processes were going on (CCJPZ, 1997).

An ex-combatant described the difficulties of living with images of the traumatic events witnessed.

> *"Many people saw dead bodies during the war. The soldiers of Smith used to take dead bodies of comrades, bodies that had been shot at several times, blood oozing and bodies that were generally in a bad state, hung them from the helicopter and showed villagers of all ages including young children and say 'look, this is what a terrorist looks like. Anybody who saw that means that her mental state will be affected at one stage in her life. The treatment that people got .....mmmmm.....Sometimes you hear people talking about ex combatants and say 'Oh these ones do not think and reason properly because the war affected them badly'. But a person who analyses correctly can see that an ex-combatant saw things that many have never seen and probably will never see...It is not easy to witness a person dying or to live with the memory of killing"[74].*

Fig.11. Rhodesian Propaganda Photograph of insurgent killed in action

---

73   The group interview was conducted in Shona in Harare at ZANU-PF headquarters on 18 February, 2005 then translated in to English.

74   The group interview was conducted in Shona in Harare at ZANU-PF headquarters on 18 February, 2005 then translated in to English.

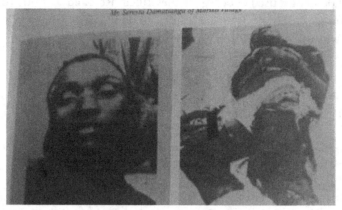

Fig. 12 Rhodesian Propaganda Photograph of insurgent killed. His body is partly undressed to reveal his identity

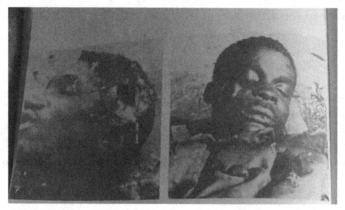

Fig.13 The villagers killed for supporting the insurgents

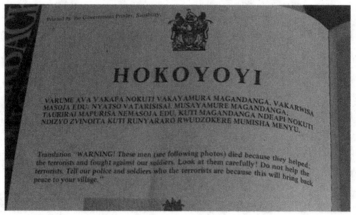

Fig 14 Photograph of a newspaper reading in both Shona and English.

The pictures of the dead bodies were distributed by the Rhodesian government in a newspaper that read in both the local language Shona and in English. Rewards were also offered for those who were going to give information about 'terrorists' in their area.

Photographs of Figs 11, 12, 13 and 14: Courtesy of The Catholic Commission for Justice and Peace in Rhodesia (1975).

5.2.3 Loss of loved ones

Losing loved ones is one legacy of any war. Many years after the Second World War, a Japanese woman described her state of mind "The 6th of August 1945 – which I do not forget – the things that happened this day are deeply carved in my heart. That cruel war that snatched so many precious human lives in one second – even now I shudder when I think of it. I am all alone after losing my father and mother and all my brothers and sisters. And no one can take their place" (Connelly et al., 1984, p. 94). The same may be said of the effects of the Zimbabwe liberation struggle on ex-combatants. After the liberation struggle, memories are still vivid as if it happened yesterday. The Government and the passage of time appear to have not been able to erase the horrific images of this war.

Ex-combatants left when they were very young and when they came back from the war, they found that their parents had disappeared. Ironically some parents disappeared at the hands of other comrades. The loss of parents was explained by another ex-combatant

> *"Some (ex-combatants) lost their parents. When they came back, they did not find any relatives. You can imagine. The fathers were either sold out by other villagers or killed by the regime or ex combatants. So you had those situations" (Female ex-combatant A)*[75]

Disappearances were abductions of individuals who were kept in secret detentions for long periods but were often executed in secret during the liberation struggle of Zimbabwe and after independence (CCJPZ, 1997). The disappeared person was perceived as an opponent of the government or powerful people. Mungazi (1996) noted how black employees disappeared after white employers had suspected that they were supporting guerrillas or might join the liberation struggle and reported them to the police.

In the Shona society, disappearance is not merely an event but an experience that has broad social effects in peoples' daily lives. In this regard women ex-combatants are living with the trauma of not knowing what happened to their family members. In a study of survivors of torture in Mount Darwin, the Amani Trust, (1997) realised that they were dealing with some people who were experiencing symptoms of continuous distress resulting from unresolved disappearances.

Payne et al. (2000) describe bereavement as the loss of someone or something significant, which typically triggers a reaction known as grief, which is manifest in a set of behaviours called mourning. Parkinson (1993) notes that bereavement is associated with more severe and chronic disturbance. The pain and grief that people go through indicate the bereavement. Parkinson (1993) further discusses that a common response to a crisis, such as the crisis of losing one's family members can manifest itself in one or two ways. One response is that things that were once very important become irrelevant. These may be things such as material possessions that were lost during the crisis or traumatic event and the person now finds them irrelevant for survival purposes, and therefore no longer important. However lack of information as to what happened to the loved ones appears to make life lost during the war relevant.

In the Shona culture, like in any society, burial rites signify the end of or closure to a person's life. When there is no closure, the pain and feeling of emptiness created by the loss of a loved one linger on

---

75   Interview with participant A was conducted in English at the participant's house in Harare on 13 October, 2003 and quoted verbatim

in greater depths as described by a civilian woman whose son did not come back from the liberation struggle.

> *"I have other children who died. I know that I buried them here. The one who died in the war, mmmm, I do not know where he lays. What I have are the last days I saw him walking and the last days I talked to him. The passage of time, that I last saw him, twenty-three years ago, is what makes me believe that he is dead. My heart has the last memory when he was alive. If he had been here and if he had been ill and I saw him, I would have known that he died because he was ill. Now I am in pain always. There is nothing that tells me he is dead except that he has not come back to me from the war"(Female rural villager MPC2).*

The new Government of Zimbabwe has neither official information about what happened to family members who did not return from the liberation struggle, nor those who disappeared during the struggle (Reeler and Mupinda, 1996). In this regard families are left to find out for themselves as to what really happened. Until they find out what happened, there is no closure to the person's life.

5.3 Women – ex-combatants' perception of their health post 1980

After any war, the manifestations of war traumas are many and may be described in a variety of ways but what is common is that these experiences are traumatic.

Post traumatic stress began to be significantly recognised in World Wars1 and 2. The names given to it were Da Costa Syndrome during World War 1 and it was coined Acute combat stress or combat fatigue during World War 2. Manifestations of the syndromes have been documented as abnormal postures, infectious diseases, exhaustion, brain damage and many others. During the Korean War, The Diagnostic and Statistical Manual of Mental Disorders (DMS-1) was developed. The following Vietnam experience was associated with post Vietnam syndrome, later to be known as post war syndrome and now known as post traumatic stress disorder (Barrow Neurological Institute, 2003).

The women ex-combatants have their own perceptions of war traumas and have described how these have manifested in them after the liberation struggle of Zimbabwe.

5.3.1 Stomach problems

The trauma that some ex-combatants described is associated with 'stomach problems. After the war, the stress disorders become long term health consequences. An ex-combatant describes the illnesses.

> *"They just complain about things which you say to yourself no that doesn't exist which we call psycho-traumatic symptoms, like mudumbu mangu munogarorwadza, handikwanise kudya zvakanaka (I am always having stomach upsets and I cannot eat well). When you say ok we have these chemicals, they will say no give me a disability percentage. They don't come to you with a disease to be treated. They come to you with a disease to be compensated because they are poor. They don't have anything. They want you to assess them and give a disability percentage" (Male medical doctor and ex-combatant F).*[76]

The illnesses that affect the 'stomach' are not unusual among war survivors. Braham's (1988) study on the holocaust survivors in Hungary, point out that among post conflict survivors diseases of the digestive tract are the most common, involving more than a third of the patients, with tendencies

---

[76] Interview with the participant was conducted in English at his home in Harare on 16 February 2005 and quoted verbatim.

toward diarrhoea and peptic ulcers being the most frequent. Braham (1988) further notes that peptic ulcers are most common in those who had shown signs of emotional disturbance after the war.

A traditional healer who has helped the ex-combatants after the liberation struggle explained the illness associated with the digestive tract in the following terms.

"I have been seeing a lot of patients. Most of my patients have been ex-combatants. Most of the problems I have seen are those to do with bombs. The patients told me they could no longer eat well because of the acids they swallowed from bombs dropped on them. So they needed medication to clean their stomachs. Civilians also came with war related problems. They cooked food and carried it to the comrades in the bush. In the bush, they were met in the crossfire and also swallowed acid from the bombs" (Female traditional healer 2)[77]

In this respect it can be argued that ex-combatants who have visited traditional healers and hospitals have health needs to be addressed. However, asking for ways to get compensation money indicates that in addition to health needs, ex-combatants have social needs to be addressed as well. If the ex-combatants are compensated with money, they can feed their families and perhaps get treatment from traditional doctors who are relatively cheaper and who understand the cultural interpretation of the specific illnesses. Traditional healing differs from the Western approaches in which individuals and their social context, the body and the mind are often perceived as separate, distinguishable entities (Honwana, 1997).

5.3.2 Trauma of rape and torture

After independence, the women ex-combatants were still experiencing the trauma of rape and torture. Later they refused to be silenced when they repeated claims which surfaced some time in 1995 that most of them were raped by their male comrades in arms (The Financial Gazette, Female guerrillas threaten to expose rapists, April 23, 1997). After being harassed by investigators over payments they received from the War Victims Compensation Fund, the women were threatening to release the names of the rapists, some of them were alleged to be senior government figures. The women claimed that 'Some girls of ten years were raped and we know the culprits. Some of them are very senior government officials, right at the top there' (The Financial Gazette, Female guerrillas threaten to expose rapists, April 23, 1997).

"Yes, some of our very high people. We had one old man. You would go there for protection and he would end up sleeping with you. If you had a boyfriend, a teenager also, he would say 'oh no do not do this kumwana (to the child) meanwhile he is the one doing it to the child instead" (Female ex-combatant D)[78].

"The big chefs (senior male commanders) used to ask for female companions from senior female leaders who used to look after the girls. The senior females would choose five to ten girls and ask them to go and keep comrade so and so company at his poshto (living dwelling made out of grass and wooden poles). The chef would then ask one or two girls to come back. No one questioned the move because we were under the law" (Female ex-combatant B)[79]

---

77   Interview with traditional healer 2 was conducted in Shona in Harare at ZINATHA headquarters on 11 February 2005 and translated in to English

78   Interview with participant D was conducted in English in Marondera on 23 October 2003 and quoted verbatim

79   Interview with participant B was conducted in English in Marondera on 23 October 2003 and quoted verbatim

Kriger (1992) goes further and suggests that there was need for redress for the trauma and injuries that civilians also experienced at the hands of the Rhodesian security forces, the guerrillas, and their fellow villagers. Trauma of rape and torture represents extreme forms of exposure to violence, in that the effects are premeditated, and designed. The processes usually involve attacks of both a physical and psychological nature, and, most importantly, rape and torture have an explicitly political purpose in a clear socio-political context (Amani Trust. 1997). Rape and torture represents extreme forms of exposure to violence, in that the effects are premeditated, and designed, the processes usually involve attacks of both a physical and psychological nature, and, most importantly, rape and torture have an explicitly political purpose in a clear socio-political context (Amani Trust. 1997).

Many civilian women and women ex-combatants were raped by soldiers and fellow guerrillas during the liberation struggle. One estimate sees 'government sanctioned rape and torture' as being present in 78 countries in the world (Jacobs and Vesti, 1992), whilst another estimate reckons that between 5% and 35% of the world's refugees, have suffered at least one torture experience (Baker, 1993).

Forced sex is a demonstration of power and control. Its negative consequences can be extensive, causing both physical and psychological damage and even death. Perhaps this is why it is generally agreed that the most evocative of all the female heroines is the defenseless victim raped or ravaged by war (Doyal, 1995). The women raped and tortured are not only those in direct combat but others as well. Dombrowski (1999) points out that female roles such as maid in waiting and helpless victim have existed simultaneously as complements to the vocation of the male soldier and as encouragement to his task. Therefore histories celebrating women's service in the armed forces of any country must be placed alongside those of women victimised by war's violence on all sides of a conflict (Dombrowski, 1999).

5.3.3 Difficulty in documentation

The pain is difficult to express because women cannot identify perpetrators for how can they conceptualise the government and government officials as perpetrators? How do the women conceptualise themselves as the victims of torture and sexual abuse?

An ex-combatant who experienced some form of torture could not or did not want to express herself.

> *"Mmmm, sometimes I do not want to talk about it. Sometimes the commander would say 'Move from here' and we would walk long distances during the night to a new camp" (Female ex-combatant C)[80].*

Further the trauma of rape and torture is extremely wounding as demonstrated by a *chimbwido*,

> *"Mmm, STDs, may be aids. May be I am a carrier, I don't know (almost crying)" (War collaborator)*

It can be argued that the female ex-combatant did not want to talk because she feared more harmful consequences, and so the buried anger is sometimes turned inward in order to cope. Bhebe and Ranger (1995) note that until recently it has not been safe to talk about rape cases that took place during the liberation struggle. As a result guerrilla experience has come to us through fiction rather than through history and autobiography.

---

80   Interview with participant C was conducted in English in Marondera on 23 October 2003 and quoted verbatim

To this extent, women ex-combatants are not only traumatised from the direct impact of the conflict, where fatal injuries resulted in death, loss of limbs, sexually transmitted disease or physical and psychological injuries, they are also traumatised from the indirect impact of the struggle ranging from the mental trauma they experienced as they were raped, tortured, and humiliated to the inability to talk about these experiences.

Lees (1997) argues that in general the type of questions inflicted on the minority of women who are brave enough to allow their cases of rape or sexual assault to be taken to court silence the women. Questions such as, 'What did you feel at each point as you were touched?' 'Could you describe loudly and clearly exactly what happened?' 'Why did you not fight back more strenuously?' are as humiliating to the victim as the rape itself. Lees (1997) further notes that the victims may feel that the questions are more deliberate and dishonest masquerading in the name of justice. In this sense, women would perhaps feel that silence is preferable, as reporting the cases does not help anyway. However talking to someone trusted may help. Living in silence may be likened to living with sudden fear the way others live with a chronic illness. It is helpful to note that speech is civilisation itself. The word preserves contact, it is silence which isolates. It is believed that expressing feelings allows us to resolve our emotions and get closure (Doyal, 1975). As a community some of this occurs with redress. As individuals, talking, acknowledging, listening with empathy can support the process of healing.

5.4 Fertility issues

Some women ex-combatants who had difficulties having children after the war have contributed the fertility problems to the effects of the war and described how society still makes them feel less human irrespective of what they went through in the war.

> *"Well of course. I did not have a child until I was 38. The first pregnancy I had was ectopic. I think it was the heavy things we used to carry. A lot of women have had problems with conception. There has been a lot of child bearing complications. And because that war was run by men, they would say oh, there are more serious things to worry about than that" (Female ex-combatant A)[81].*

Other female ex-combatants felt that the chemical weapons used by the Rhodesian soldiers were responsible for infertility problems and children born with defects.

> *"Chemicals affected women differently. Some women had babies who were down syndrome, some have one child and others are infertile. Skin diseases were many" (Female ex-combatant D)[82]*

Thus the reasons why some women ex-combatants have difficulties in having children may be attributed to extreme life situations over long periods of time, disease, lack of health services, and lack of proper nutrition (Enloe, 2000). The abdominal pain, cervical tearing, and infection which frequently occur in rape situations could have affected the ability to have children and contributed to difficulties and complications during childbearing (Enloe, 2000).

---

81   The group interview was conducted in Shona in Harare at ZANU-PF headquarters on 18 February, 2005 then translated in to English.

82   Interview with participant D was conducted in English in Marondera on 24 October 2003 and quoted verbatim

The fact that some women had problems with conception or could not have children because of what the war did to them is no solace. Mbiti (1989) observes that unhappy is the woman who fails to have children for, whatever qualities she might possess, her failure to bear children is worse than committing genocide; she has become the dead end of human life, not only for the genealogical line but also for herself. In this regard, failure to have children has a negative psychological impact on the women regardless of what caused it.

When she dies, there will be nobody of her own immediate blood to 'remember' her, to keep her in the state of personal immortality: she will simply be 'forgotten' (Mbiti, 1989). The fault may not be her own, but this does not excuse her in the eyes of society. Her husband may remedy the situation by raising children with another wife (Mbiti, 1989).

In a society where a woman's worth to a large degree is measured by her ability to raise a family, a barren woman ex-combatant is not a woman like any other woman in the eyes of most people (Enloe, 2000). The great importance of having children is not only a personal matter, but also a ticket to acceptance by society as a successful woman. Turner and Phan (1998) describe how Vietnamese women became barren as a result of their war activities and how their great contribution to the war can not compensate for what they have been reduced to today. Vietnamese women veterans lost their looks and their fertility after years of hard living and exposure to disease and chemical poisons (Turner and Phan 1998)

In this regard, male ex-combatants may prefer younger, healthier women as wives. In this perspective women ex-combatants of today rather serve as a symbol of the disenfranchised rather than as heroic women who helped win the war.

In the Shona society, a childless wife bears a scar, which can not be erased by anything. Schmidit (1992) notes that she suffers for this, her own relatives suffer for this; and it is an irreparable humiliation for which there is no source of comfort. In this regard Mbiti (1989) notes that when an individual suffers, she does not suffer alone but with the corporate group; when she rejoices, she does not rejoice alone but with his kinsmen, her neighbours and his relatives whether dead or living. Whatever happens to the individual, happens to the whole group, and whatever happens to the whole group happens to the individual: the individual can only say: I am because we are; and since we are, therefore, I am (Mbiti, 1989).

5.5 Life chances

The understanding of the existence of an individual in relation to others is what makes some female ex-combatants prefer to conceal their military past rather than risk social disapproval despite the great contributions that the women made in the liberation struggle of their country from colonial rule. As a result society at large and families too found it difficult to accept female ex-combatants who are generally a stigmatized group. This is because, the family, which is an institution that mediates between women and society, was fundamentally altered during the liberation struggle making the transition form war to a normal civilian life difficult as explained by a female ex-combatant.

> *"For instance my own family does not understand me. When I am around they talk as if I am a child or someone who is a sell out to the government. When the government gave the comrades a lump some of money, jokes were flown around about that money, some of the jokes where sickening and they made me*

very angry. Those around me said that 'You see comrades are no longer normal'. The only time a comrade is appreciated is when there are family disagreements. At such times they will say to each other 'Wait until the comrade comes. Each one of you will be sorted out" (Female ex-combatant in the group interview)[83]

It appears that accommodating stigmatised groups so that they become part of a society that understands them is a major challenge as these groups and their families often require more resources.

5.5.1 Women ex-combatants and marriage

The Human Rights Forum (March 2001) notes that female ex-combatants were widely perceived as rough and ready to fight at the slightest provocation. The Forum further notes that women ex-combatants were also perceived as 'culturally' unmanageable and unmarriageable, by their own families as well as potential spouses. As a small minority, women were subject to considerable social pressure after Independence to abandon their liberationist role and credentials, and to re-create their identities as demure, outwardly submissive, respectably married women.

"Our female comrades were shunned by the civilian men. They did not want to marry them, they said they were prostitutes. Apart from being isolated by men and then jumping from one bed to another, the man who goes out with her is not serious, you can tell and so they are being used again""(Male medical doctor and ex-combatant F).

> *"They are looked down upon. You see society labels them. For women, I know, you have to accept being rejected because the impression out there is, oh these are loose individuals, and you know a man would ehm…, you accept anything from a man, because you have no other choice, so he can harass you, abuse you and say you are a war veteran… When I look at war veterans, I really feel bad" (Female ex-combatant A)*[84].

Women who have participated in wars find themselves labelled prostitutes by many societies. In Britain the women were considered loose. The reluctance to accept equality with women who had participated in the Second World War led men to portray them as women who had lost their femininity as explained by a female Auxiliary. " Women were doing everything in England during the war. Churchill asked us to remember. But I don't think the army girls were ever very popular. I think most people thought we were loose women, just there to entertain the troops…. telling us how we were not really women at all, in our dreadful uniforms with our toughness. A real woman wore a picture hat and chiffon", Joan Cowey Anti-aircraft battery, Auxiliary Territorial Service (Saywell, 1985, p. 1).

After the Second World War, a popular Canadian magazine ran a cartoon that derived its humour from the feared possibility of a reversal of the sexual division of labour between male and female (French, 1992). The husband wearing an apron and standing with a mop in his hand and a bucket at his feet, frowns in annoyance at his wife in overalls coming home from the factory, heading straight for the refrigerator, tracking muddy footprints across his nice, clean floor (French, 1992).

---

83   The group interview was conducted in Shona in Harare at ZANU-PF headquarters on 18 February, 2005 then translated in to English.

84   Interview with participant A was conducted in English at the participant's house in Harare on 13 October, 2003 and quoted verbatim

Thus women's participation in war does not guarantee gender equality with men. Women are regarded as mothers and wives. The female ex-combatants who were not regarded as prostitutes after the liberation struggle and got married found out that they were not respected.

> *"Negative. Very negative. Because now I am married right? When I start saying things they say 'ibasa re ma war vets' (these are deeds of war vets, meaning they do not take war vets seriously). Because she went to war, that's why she is like this, being a strong character. But we have women needs. And most war vets are not married because of that…. Who wouldn't like to have rings like you have?" (Female ex-combatant D)*[85].

How the female ex-combatants thought and behaved was not acceptable. Until they were cleansed, they would continue to be unaccepted.

> *"…….. There is still a myth that after the fighting, people had to be cleansed, if not leave them alone. So there was this feeling among the civilians" (Female ex-combatant B).*

To this extent, most of the female ex-combatants who would have liked to get married are not married because they are shunned as noted by Nzenza (1988, p.54), "Who wants to bring in a bride who has been a freedom fighter, slept rough and lived a tough life? She is an absolute threat to her husband and is not fit to be a daughter in law". In Vietnam Vietcong women ex-combatants were left 'unmarriageable' and pushed to life on the margins of a society that values family above all else (Turner and Phan, 1998).

The female ex-combatants who got married do not want to admit who they are for fear of jeopardising their marriages. They do not even talk about sexual abuses they experienced to anyone because they fear rejection. They fear to be labelled loose.

> *"I remember that one comrade confessed that she never wanted people to know that she was an ex-combatant because this would jeopardise her marriage. Because the in laws and the husband would have never taken her as ex-combatants are supposed to be crazy people, arrogant and anti establishment. They were everything. But it was the freedom that they had acquired which perhaps was so much above everybody else. And people actually succeeded in making it a sin, to make them feel that they are wrong and she told me that it is just a year ago, the first time she was known to be an ex-combatant. I told her that I am proud to be an ex-combatant. So I asked her what did they say when you told them that you are an ex-combatant? She said they were just surprised. Because we have been married for so long, they couldn't do anything now" (Female Ex-combatant B)*[86].

In this respect, women who have been influenced by their experiences as soldiers have to repress the soldier part of their identity in order to be accepted because values of civil society and the values of the liberation army are often in opposition to each other (Zimbabwe women writers, 2000).

However, the marriages of some female ex-combatants who had been accepted as wives often did not last.

> *"Many marriages broke after independence. You see, no one except people like my husband. They do not want wives who are ex combatants. So many divorced" (Female ex-combatant C)*[87]

---

85   Interview with participant D was conducted in English in Marondera on 23 October 2003 and quoted verbatim.

86   Interview with participant B was conducted in English in Marondera on 23 October 2003 and quoted verbatim

87   Interview with participant C was conducted in English in Marondera on 23 October 2003 and quoted verbatim

It appears that men were not ready to accept that the war experiences that the women had gone through had changed them. Women's involvement as combatants in the liberation struggle represented a departure from the values and ways of life that their families had taught them. This is in contrast to the roles of males, which continue along the same lines as before. Men's gender roles are reinforced by activities associated with being soldiers. The war offered women a different perspective from that of growing up in a family that confined them to the domestic sphere. The perspective of the revolution was that women had to live and act similarly to men. In contrast to civil society, sameness instead of difference between men and women was encouraged during the war. To this extent, reverting to domestic values and normalcy proved difficult to women ex-combatants and marriages suffered in the process. The author argues that married women ex-combatants were caught in between the need to preserve their marriages by creating a new societal identity of themselves and the ability to suppress their war experiences. However, women ex-combatants found out that it is difficult to change the identities shaped by the war experiences because war traumas can neither be erased nor banished.

An ex-combatant describes the trauma that could have been responsible for breaking the marriages.

> *"But the trauma of having a child in the bush, and being forced to sleep with a man and later you are going to marry someone, is going to come back and it is going to disturb your relationship. People may not relate it to that and when it happened "(Female ex-combatant A)[88].*

The war had not only changed women ex-combatants but civilian women as well. Women and girls who had been left alone by their husbands and fathers who had either joined the liberation struggle or had disappeared in the hands of the colonial government, had learnt to managed their lives without the men's authority.

In the absence of the men who in the Shona culture, are custodians of women, the women were left behind to shoulder the responsibility of family as best as they could during this critical period. While men left their wives and children behind, women did not leave their children or husbands to join the liberation struggle (with few exceptions in cases of girls who got pregnant out of marriage and left the babies with their mothers). The female ex-combatants had learnt that they too could fight like men. All these new roles that the war brought changed the women. In this respect wars and armed conflicts produce a number of new social categories whose identity and status are not easily determined. The women could no longer continue to be demure and submissive as explained by a female ex-combatant.

> *"I had aspired a free Zimbabwe where nobody would call me a war vet or whatever in a derogatory sense. A free Zimbabwe where I can marry who ever I want without anybody telling me this and that" (Female ex-combatant B)[89]*

The failure of marriages involving ex-combatants can be looked at from the knowledge gathered about other countries that have experienced effects of secondary traumatisation. The United States and The Netherlands were cited as examples of post conflict countries where partners of veterans revealed

---

88   The group interview was conducted in Shona in Harare at ZANU-PF headquarters on 18 February, 2005 then translated in to English.

89   Interview with participant B was conducted in English in Marondera on 23 October 2003 and quoted verbatim

that close contact with a trauma victim over time can cause tremendous emotional upset, leading to marriage breakdowns (The European Society of Traumatic Stress Studies, 1998).

In the United States 38% of marriages of Vietnam veterans led to divorces within 6 months after their return from Vietnam. In the Netherlands, they learnt after the Dutch War in Indonesia during World War Two that material as well as physical and psycho-social support were paramount for the Veterans and their partners. They learnt that if the partner in the marriage is not given education and support, the family system fails. As a result, great care is taken to treat the Veteran and his or her family as a unit. In this regard, the failure of marriages involving ex-combatants may not only be attributed to the society's perception of women ex-combatants as 'rough and unmanageable' but also to secondary traumatisation, lack of education and support.

Because marriage is an institution that gives women an honourable identity in the Shona culture, it is taken very seriously and a young woman's social status is enhanced upon marriage. Schmidt (1992) notes that a Shona woman without a husband or children is 'held in open derision' because marriage creates a social bond between her kin group and that of her husband, extending the network of people who could be called upon in times of economic or military distress.

5.5.2 Parenting

The female ex-combatants believe that they did not only suffer from the direct physical and psychological 'wounds' of the war. The physical and psychological scars of the liberation struggle also indirectly affected their ability to good parenting. An ex -combatant described ways she thought would help her parent her children well, as the children do not understand her

> *"I don't know, like therapy I think, because even my children do not understand me...They say 'mamma watanga"(mum has started again) (Female ex-combatant C)*

Looking at the children born by combatants during the war, the author argues that these are children of trauma victims and may be directly or indirectly traumatised. Despite the silence, or perhaps because of it, the children whose parents are ex- combatants may attribute a number of negative consequences in their own lives to the unexpressed pain of their parents' war experiences. The multiple pathways of the trauma experienced by their parents create a variety of health consequences for their children as well.

Thus these children are reminders of what women ex-combatants went through, and the women ex-combatants burdened with the physical and psychological scars of the war may not fully devote their labour or creative ideas to good parenting. Richters (2001) feels that violence in all its forms and the associated traumas that follow drains women's energies, and may undermine all their efforts to further their own, and community's development. Development policies should therefore support women's health needs and help create the conditions of development and justice for all.

5.5.3 Integration of women ex-combatants in to civilian life

When female ex-combatants returned home, they were shocked to find out that while their male counterparts were accepted by the society, they were not. Women ex-combatants thought that with the considerable numbers of women joining the struggle in the late 1960s and 1970s, the image of the subservient and industrious mother or daughter would not prevail after independence (Gaidzanwa, 1992). Although there was discrimination in the guerrilla camps in that women were often headed into roles that involved cooking and caring for the sick and wounded, there was equality on the battlefield. Women proved to be just as able and dedicated to the cause for national liberation as their male counterparts. Therefore, there was little justification for continuing to regard women as inferior citizens who should revert to traditional roles if they were to be accepted (Gaidzanwa, 1992). However women ex-combatants found out that they were still ostracised and unaccepted leaving them psychologically traumatised. Gilligan's (1996) study on violence and its causes observes that the most frequent trigger of negative psychological well being is people feeling looked down upon, disrespected, humiliated, or ridiculed. Gilligan (1996) further notes that when people are not loved the resultant feelings can include bitterness and anger. Zimbabwe Women Writers (2000) have noted that women ex-combatants upon their return to civil society, were pulled between living up to the image of a 'liberated' woman while being looked down upon.

The position women found themselves in soon after independence appears to have been caused by the Government's failure to realise that one of the changes needed to successfully integrate ex-combatants -both men and women - into civilian life was social transformation through rehabilitation, education and counselling. Because this change was not given consideration soon after the war, most ex-combatants particularly women were not accepted by society. An ex-combatant believes that counselling programmes would have helped.

"And may be if the freedom fighters had created some method of rehabilitation, trying to counsel themselves becoming civilians. Just throwing the guns down is not enough. Doing something is not demobilisation. So doing something should have gone with demobilisation, which is not just giving someone a couple of a thousand dollars and tell them to go home. It is going through a process of what gonna happen. Because we were used to respond to slogans, to jump, how high? to run or things like that....So to rehabilitate, to demobilise so that they start functioning as individual units not as an army or group or numbers, we have to get out of those regiments and become functional as a greater family. It has taken a long time to realise that. And even now it has not been done. It looks like we are crazy, We are not, we are traumatised " (Female ex-combatants B)[90]

The demobilisation process was an attempt by the Government to provide for the ex-combatants, but as explained by the female ex-combatant above, it did not work. Although many ex-combatants were successfully re-integrated into urban or rural life after 1980, a substantial number slipped deeper into destitution and social ostracism. In 1980, there were approximately 65 000 ZANLA and ZIPRA guerrillas. About 20 000 of these became part of the new Zimbabwe National Army (ZNA). The rest, who were officially demobilised, were awarded a monthly pension of Z$185 until 1983 and encouraged to form self-help co-operatives and/or receive skills training (Musemwa 1996).

Beyond this, there was little national attempt to assist their socio-economic re-integration. Many ex-combatants also become victims of the twin scourges of poverty and AIDS. Many of the dead and dying were well-known in their local areas as genuine ex-fighters. After the war, however, they were ignored. Villagers were often resentful of party functionaries who eulogised heroes in death, yet ignored them while they lived (Musemwa, 1996). Some ex-combatants agreed that the Government ought to have put in place measures that would ensure a smooth transition from war to peace.

---

90   Interview with participant B was conducted in English in Marondera on 23 October 2003 and quoted verbatim

"The mistake we made was not to protect the comrades, we were concerned about political power. So the task was let's take over. So what do we do with the comrades? Unfortunately the comrades made a wrong decision. Tasunnguka, tatora nyika let me do what I want. And to try to tell them please wait, every one went to their homes before a decision had been made as what to do with them" (Male medical doctor and ex-combatant F).

> *"...... And I expected that they would receive some counselling. Instead what we saw was people enjoying themselves. They forgot about war veterans. They completely forgot that these people helped them during the struggle"* (Female ex-combatant A)

The failure by the Government to protect the ex-combatants has been observed in other post conflict countries where peace realities are that veterans especially women are not accepted. In the United States, there has been denial that post-traumatic stress disorder has and still exists among Vietnam veterans and, the road has been difficult to have PTSD accepted as a legitimate mental and public health concern (The European Society of Traumatic Stress Studies, 1998). Denial of the existence of PTSD also means that those who survived the war traumas suppressed the experience as soon as possible to the extent that it may have not been possible to detect (The European Society of Traumatic Stress Studies, 1998).

The unprocessed trauma in women ex-combatants is similar to that experienced by survivors of the holocaust. Even people who were able to have a new family, to pursue a career and in some cases even undertake active political work suffered nightmares – a German shepherd dog or a smoking chimney: these post-war symbols of reconstruction, took them back mentally to the concentration camps (Reiter, 2000).

If it has taken countries like the United States, with more financial resources and medical professionals a long period to understand war traumas, then it is more likely that the Government of Zimbabwe just coming out of the war may not have been in a position to understand the traumas of the liberation struggle. The issue of understanding war traumas after independence may be analysed from the President's speech at the 1984 Women's conference. In this speech the participation of women in the liberation struggle was acknowledged but how the war traumas have affected the health of women were not.

"Today is a big day in Zimbabwe. Never before have we had a gathering of this type. A gathering so important, a gathering for women liberated to talk about the liberation of the country. They have been chosen to be spearheads in the party, in the country, with which to make changes in the country. This is new. Those who will write the history of our country will note the importance of this day a lot. I thank you. Our history is a long history. We have come from far. The war that we have been waging meant death, suffering and a lot of sacrifice. This is the war that has brought us where we are today. It meant that the leadership had to be dedicated as well as the fighters. It meant that a lot of heroes died. We cannot name them all. Those we could write about war we wrote. Others died on the way to the liberation struggle and we had not registered them. These, we do not know how many. Others died while going to be trained in the camps. Up to today we do not know whether some are still alive or dead because we have not found them yet. We have been asked by the leader of the women's league to stand up in remembrance of those whom we lost during the war. I have written a few so that we can remember them all. Those we know and those we don't know. A lot others died in Nyadzonya, Chimoio, Tete and all other provinces. Where are those who were shot silently in the villages and those who disappeared? These are the ones who spilt their blood for our liberation, so that we can have a day such as this one today. Our independence did not just come like manner, that manner which is said to have dropped every Friday and people just go to pick it up. No, people had to fight for this independence. It meant that men and women united to fight the enemy. Today we must remember that women too died for the liberation of Zimbabwe. Women must be given the dignity and respect that they deserve.

A woman is an important creature. In her womb, that's where we were taken care of for nine months. If there is a man here, you did not fall down. Even Jesus Christ came from his mother's womb. If there is anyone who fell down from above can he come forward and present himself. The woman goes through different difficult faces until she delivers. Then she breast feeds the child. When the woman is doing this where is your breast you man? Yes because you men say the child is mine. Yours that fed the child where is it?

We hear that if a woman died during childbirth or soon after delivery or when the child is still very young, an aunt would be given medication through incisions cut in the breasts so that she is able to feed that child with milk. A man cannot do anything at that time. The hand that caresses the child, the hand that cooks for the child, the hand that cleans the child, the hand that sees to the growth of the child is that of a woman. A father finds it hard to make porridge for a child" (The President of Zimbabwe, comrade Gabriel Robert Mugabe).

In this respect, the effectiveness of a programme not well understood and developed is questionable although civilians and ex-combatants needed to be counseled and taught about readjustment to civilian life.

5.5.3 Women and the freedom of movement

When the women tried to exercise the freedom to move alone at night the society viewed the women as prostitutes.

> "And it explains if you trace the history of our independence. Immediately after our independence on the 18ᵗʰ the whole entire security of our ZANLA forces not ZIPRA asked the government to take all prostitutes anywhere and put them in the Zambezi valley because we were scared of this disease. And the operation, I remember in 1980, if you read something about operation Chinyavada, it was a mop up of all prostitutes within the urban areas and anywhere and put them in the Zambezi valley to isolate them from the rest of the population. It was a phase and it lasted until about 82, 83. …..Hotels, streets, were cleaned up" (Male medical doctor and ex-combatant F)⁹¹.

The societal perception that women ex-combatants were prostitutes was arrived at when after independence the women displayed freedom of movement by moving alone at night unaccompanied. The Human Rights forum (2001) notes that the women were rounded up by the police and put in police cells, they were harassed and humiliated.

The mopping up of those believed to be prostitutes was the implementation of a policy in fear of a disease from women that was discussed at the Lancaster House Conference of 1979.

> "When we said the Lancaster House Conference is over, we are now going home, we were all called by the commander, Rex Nhongo and he said, ma comrades the war is over but to you the war is not over, both male

91

and female because you are going to face no longer the napalm bomb, no longer the bullets, you are going to face a disease. A sexually transmitted disease, I don't know its name but that will be your bomb that will kill you. And you will be given, they won't just come to you, because they have seen you , but the Rhodesian security forces will give you those girls to escort you where by the most beautiful girls, you will see them there. They are a bomb." (Male medical doctor and ex-combatant F)

In this respect independence did not bring gender equality to all. The basic human right of movement was violated against. It is not surprising then that incidents such as this led to the formation of the Declaration on the Elimination of Violence against Women General Assembly Resolution 48/104 on 20 December 1993. The resolution in part stipulates that violence against women constitutes a violation of the rights and fundamental freedoms of women and impairs or nullifies their enjoyment of those rights and freedoms.

The idea that urban places were not for women was more prevalent for African women than for white women during the colonial rule. Jeater (2000) cites a Gweru African husband who stated categorically during a court case that the fact that his wife wanted to stay in town was proof that she must be a prostitute. He could not imagine a legitimate reason for a woman to be in town. In fact, she was staying in town to be near her mother, having left her husband's family following consistent verbal abuse from them.

In this regard, the colonial attitudes that encouraged black women to stay out of the urban areas had become integrated into the indigenous culture that believed that black women who stayed in the towns were prostitutes. To this extent, the exclusion of women from towns eventually becomes social and cultural norms even after the colonisers have left. This attitude of both black men and white men towards black women raises the central question of why urban spaces were not for them. In African perceptions, it was 'normal' for an African man to be in town, but African women were seen as very much 'out of place' (Jeater, 2000). In this regard it is argued that women who lived in towns, were not perceived or treated as full members of the society and, in this sense, they did not live in ways that gave them a proper, recognised cultural and social identity. The Government itself, which was expected to effect equality between men and women, found itself supporting patriarchal ideologies that oppressed women. African women could only walk publicly in the urban areas under the auspices of a recognised black male because a wife and women who could not produce a 'husband' were labelled prostitutes and socially stigmatised (McFadden, 2002). To this extent stigma has a negative impact on equality and social inclusion, and therefore has implications for health of the persons affected and of their families.

The rounding up of women in towns signified a division between westernised and non-westernised people, and has led politicians to search for a new African identity, something that combines African ways and modern European ways. Raeburn (1978) notes that in political terms, the search for new African identity manifests itself in the divisions between old-style of living before the arrival of the settlers and the new one after the settlers' arrival. In this regard the search for a new identity affected women significantly as people settled in urbanised areas after independence. The identity of a woman and her position in post war Zimbabwe continues to affect the women's health up to today.

To this extent, Nzenza (1988, p. 74) argues that "men want to preserve their culture from western influence but they only say that when they feel threatened by women. They drive posh cars, listen to western music, dress the western way, and eat western food but they advocate retention of tradition. They do not even see how much the women suffer and how they contribute to the suffering of the women".

While women ex-combatants continue to feel unaccepted by society at large, picture-poster images of women carrying guns portray the liberation of women (Cock, 1992). However, women's actual lives, experience in their own terms and language have illustrated that if women were optimistic about the potential for the transformation of gender relations through women's involvement in the national liberation struggle they were wrong.

Gender politics of the women's participation in the armed struggle tell a different story, that women are still not liberated. The very same pictures of women carrying AK rifles send other messages to society, that the women are not feminine. Thus propaganda reminded female ex-combatants that their roles during the liberation struggle did not make them natural. The roles made them behave temporarily like men. Hearn et al. (1996) note that these ideologies are ways of conducting social life and interpreting reality, which are inextricably linked to specific relations of domination.

5.5.4 Gender violence and development

The liberation struggle like any war, was a violation of human rights. Women and children, the most disadvantaged group, were violated by the events of the liberation struggle. Hayes et al. (1994) point out that international health and development projects that choose to listen to women for identification of their health needs are finding that gender violence is a major factor in women's strategies for survival and improvement of themselves.

5.5.5 Difficulties of obtaining birth certificates for children born during the liberation struggle

Difficulties of obtaining birth certificates where the fathers could not be mentioned or were not known raise other issues associated with women's development and the traumatic environment in which the affected parents conceived the children. These children feel the effects of the war in numerous ways. They may be sad and angry about their birth circumstances as described by one female ex-combatant.

> *"And the girls who were old, they were forced to sleep with men. Some girls have kids and they do not know who the father is. Now you know in our culture a child will say 'Who is my father?' and the woman does not know because she slept with so many comrades. The child does not know its relatives" (Female ex-combatant C).*

In this regard, on return to Zimbabwe, the children were often raised by their mothers' families. The children themselves often lacked birth certificates and, as a result, later experienced great difficulty in obtaining identity cards. Their civil rights were impaired by their problematic conception and childhood (Zimbabwe Human Rights NGO Forum March 2001).

Guerrilla names like Bazooka and Sub (sub-machine gun) could not help any woman get a newly-born child affiliated to its father's lineage as required by Shona or Ndebele customs, of which most women were part. Besides, the constant threats issued to women did not allow them to identify the biological fathers. As a result the war caused a moral dilemma in rural communities (Bhebe and Ranger, 1995).

However, after independence, some children born during the war managed to have some form of identity and were sent to school by the government as narrated by one female ex-combatant.

> *"Others had children but their male partners died in the war, then they were left alone looking after the child. But today these children who were born during the war have scholarships to go to school" (Female ex-*

combatant A).

5. 6 Response of health institutions to the needs of ex-combatants

After the war, the government embarked on a reconstruction programme that included the building and rebuilding of schools, clinics, roads, construction of dams, repairs of damaged bridges and factories. What was not immediately attended to was the rebuilding and reconstruction of the destroyed 'wounded minds and souls' of those whose lives have been changed forever as a result of their war experiences. The psycho-social support necessary to repair the psychological damage caused by the liberation struggle to many ought to have been given the attention it deserved in order to enable the sufferers to survive emotionally and socially. These observations were echoed by a male medical doctor and ex-combatant who felt that

> *"We also should have addressed some of these issues earlier but when we came back from war, what was on our minds was getting political power because we did not trust the Rhodesians. This means that some important issues that should have been given priority over others were not considered at the right time" (Male medical doctor and ex-combatant F).[92]*

It was not clear whether the issue of post-traumatic stress was well understood immediately after independence. In other post conflict countries, the understanding of war related traumas is fairly recent. Bracken (1995) notes that studies of post traumatic stress disorder are relatively new and arose in the 1980s as a result of trying to understand the experiences and problems faced by the American veterans of the Vietnam War. Reeler (1997) in his study about violence and torture in Zimbabwe points out that the psychological effects suffered by many people during and after the liberation struggle are perhaps not as well known, although there have been some discussions and explorations regarding war related trauma and violence. What appears to have been acknowledged and dealt with is that ex-combatants needed some form of treatment to deal with their psychological distresses. To this extent, some ex-combatants were sent to Harare hospital for western treatment and some were sent to Nharira for traditional treatment .

However, the ex-combatants were stigmatised by the hospitals that should cater for everyone. Ex-combatants found out that when hospitals attended to them, most of their health needs could not be addressed. A male ex-combatant narrated how hospitals failed to meet their health

> *"They always say suffer now and enjoy later. When we arrived in Zimbabwe, we were told that there would be free medication, free treatment. But when the free medication and treatment were announced, many of us went to get treatment. Because we were too many, the medication started dwindling. The countries that used to help us with medication were no longer able to do so. Even today, there are those with artificial limbs, and because there is no right material, they are now using sticks" (Male ex-combatant1 in a group interview)[93]*

In addition to the humiliation ex-combatants suffered when artificial limbs and medical help were not available for them, ex-combatants were sent to hospitals they did not trust.

> *"…..Yes they talk of a policy that stipulates that the families of ex combatants should be treated for free.*

---

92   Interview with the male medical doctor was conducted in English at his home in Harare on 16 February 2005 and quoted verbatim.

93   The group interview was conducted in Shona in Harare at ZANU-PF headquarters on 18 February, 2005 then translated in to English.

It is not easy for me to go with my family member(s) to Parirenyatwa hospital for example and say that I am an ex combatant, I need treatment, then show my card. By this I am exposing my self. I do not know how the person I have shown my card feels about ex-combatants. Maybe he will give me an injection to kill me. So it is better to go as an ordinary person and pay for treatment." (Male ex-combatant 2 in a group interview)[94]

" What is painful is that the doctors who we inherited are the Smith regime doctors. What interest does he have to treat me and make me feel better? Would he not give me medication to finish me off? How can I trust him?" (Female ex-combatant in a group interview).

While ex-combatants are not happy with the government's response to meeting their health needs, they are appreciative of some individuals who they feel cared for them.

"Yes, Dr. X was for bones, sculls, artificial eyes, and artificial hands. He was very helpful at Tsanga lodge in Nyanga where the ex-combatants used to go for physiotherapy".....The other person who helped was the late Mrs. Sally Mugabe. She was a mother who was full of love for others. When she met disabled ex combatants, she showed and gave her love to a child, a disabled child of the war.
She used to come to Ruwa technical college for the disabled ex combatants and spent a lot of time there talking to them. She would spend time which she otherwise would have spent with her husband the President. She donated wheelchairs etc. We say to her 'Rest in Peace'. In fact God should not have taken her before she finished doing what she wanted to do for the ex-combatants. If it was possible to know when death would come, we would have said 'Run mother" (Male ex-combatant 1 in a group interview)

From these views, it can be assumed that even though the Government may not have had enough resources to address the health needs of the ex-combatants, it could have reassured them that they have not been forgotten. Reassuring ex-combatants is important because the development of any nation largely depends on the well being of its people. To this extent Government institutions need to look at and address societal attitudes that disadvantage the promotion of women's health. This is particularly important when one considers that in Zimbabwe as in many other parts of Africa, health is traditionally defined as the harmonious relationships between human beings and their natural surroundings, between them and their ancestors, and amongst themselves. In this sense, Honwana (1997) observes that illness is thus considered primarily a social rather than a physical phenomenon. From this perspective, the women ex-combatants in Zimbabwe are living with a cumulative of liberation war traumas and societal inflicted traumas.

---

94   The group interview was conducted in Shona in Harare at ZANU-PF headquarters on 18 February, 2005 then translated in to English.

5.7 A table showing some traumas of the Zimbabwe liberation struggle

Causes	Health impact
Living and fighting in a war zone	anxiety - wanting to go back but not possible, fear of death, loss of body parts, diseases, all causing psychological and physical wounds
Bad/lack of food,	stomach upsets, malnutrition
Rape and torture	trauma, not wanting to continue talking about it
Displacement	wanting to talk and cry to someone, talking to themselves laughing and giggling as if they are amused at something
Disappearances	pain of not knowing what happened to loved ones and not being able to perform burial rituals until death is ascertained
Loss of life and assets	mental and emotional anguish, chronic pain of living without being officially informed of what happened to sons and daughters who did not come back home when the liberation struggle ended, grieving the loss of life and possessions
Witnessing	difficulties of living with the memory of killing and seeing a person being killed, difficulties of living with the memory of seeing paraded dead bodies and seeing a person being burnt to death
Reproduction	living with the pain of not being able to have children or having difficult pregnancies due to war injuries
Marriages	emotional pain of not being able to get married or being divorced because of social stigma attached to female ex-combatants
Sleep	^pot being able to sleep, startling reactions, waking up easily
Betrayal	words and signs of hurt and anger with the Government for failing to meet expectations, regretting joining the liberation struggle, mistrust of fellow comrades who raped women combatants.

5.8 Betrayal

After independence the women feel that their health needs have not been met despite the fact that the early years of independence saw the formation of a ministry specifically for women, the appointment of women to positions of permanent secretary, minister and deputy ministers and despite the call by women to change patriarchal attitudes towards them. Many people who had high aspirations for a free Zimbabwe were let down. The war traumas are exacerbated by lack of opportunities to improve the lives of ex-combatants and the development of their health consequently. Belle's (1982) study on women's lives and poverty reveals that poverty leads to depression. Belle (1982) further notes that the inequalities within societies are associated with reduced life expectancy and a variety of negative physical health outcomes. An ex-combatant spelt out the expectations of a free Zimbabwe that women had.

"We wanted people to be happy. Everyone to drive their own cars. But now we have changed from a white minority enjoying to a black minority. You know, what pains me most is that our party has good policies. If we followed these, this would be a very good country. But there are very few people who did not even go to war enjoying Zimbabwe. We are back to square one and what hurts me is that people who are benefiting are using the saying that 'oh takarwa hondo' (oh we fought the liberation war)…….Yes, and I went to liberate the people not myself. So when I see the very people I went to liberate being oppressed by a fellow black man, it hurts. It would be better if it was a white man…. the same system is still operating" (Femal ex-combatant D)[95].

"Today, we are surprised because some of the people in the cabinet never participated in the revolution. These are chancers who came because they are educated. During the war, not so many of us took scholarships to go for further education because we said we should win the war first" (Male 2 in a group interview)[96].

Those who benefited did not necessarily have to have gone to war. So what did they have to do to enable them to get more than others? Burke, (1992) feels that those who get more are the elite; the rest are the mass. He adds that the elite can exercise multiple overlapping and intersecting sociospatial networks of power. And the four sources of power that can be used by the elite are ideological, economic, military and political, all of which impact the health of the less privileged differently (Burke, 1992). An ex-combatant mourns the betrayal of the liberation struggle.

"You know during the war we used to have a slogan that said you and I have work to do. Today that slogan is - only me has work to do - that of suppressing another comrade. Only those at the top can correct the situation" (Male ex-combatant 2 in a group interview)[97].

The ex-combatants who expressed that they felt betrayed and let down by people they trusted appeared distressed. Mental health professionals have expanded the definition of trauma to include betrayal trauma which occurs when the people or institutions we depend on for survival violate us in some way (Betrayal Trauma, http://dynamic.uoregon.edu/~jjf/defineBT.html, 17th July 2007). To this extent, DePrince's (2001) study on post-traumatic responses, fear and betrayal discovered that trauma survivors reporting traumatic events and felt betrayed were distressed.

Contrary to what many thought, Independence did not bring advantages to women ex-combatants. They were relegated to the position of women –the position of subordination, which carries psychological traumas.

95   Interview with participant D was conducted in English in Marondera on 23 October 2003 and quoted verbatim

96   The group interview was conducted in Shona in Harare at ZANU-PF headquarters on 18 February, 2005 then translated in to English.

97

"I feel betrayed by my own people. I feel betrayed. Here again, I left at a tender age, there were opportunity costs. Some had to go for further education, I couldn't. And so, by virtue of that, so those who remained, they don't care, they don't appreciate, and that is painful". (Female ex-combatant A)

"No, they use us when they want. When things are tough, they use us. But it is unfortunate that some of us do not see that. There are no advantages because what I have, I have worked for it" (Female ex-combatant D)[98].

5.8.1 Land distribution

The betrayal views expressed by ex-combatants both male and female serve to explain why the Lancaster Agreement is viewed with suspicion.

"Even that Lancaster agreement, I do not believe in it. Many comrades do not. It was more a politician thing who were tired and wanted to come home. We who were dying and having wounds, we were almost through in achieving what we wanted. But somewhere on the way to Lancaster, something happened. ......I was actually telling people in 1986 that there were many crooks who have jumped on the train to Harare from Beira and this thing never had a face after that" (Female ex-combatant B).

McFadden (2002) notes that the Lancaster House Agreement of 1979 institutionalised the exclusion of women, from the possibilities that this moment of change provided.

To this extent, the opportunities that the Government provided for various groups within the society in the early years of independence, within the constraints of the Lancaster House Agreement of 1979 were both temporal and unsustainable. For the most part women are the ones who ended up losing as explained by some female ex-combatants,

"I still have memories as if it happened yesterday. But all the suffering was for nothing. I feel used...." (Female ex-combatant C)[99].

"You know like I said, we expected free education, free health services, we expected the land to go back to its original owners and that didn't happen. Look at it, When I joined the struggle, I was seventeen, I am now 46 and at 46 some of my colleagues are 50, some have died and what are they dying for? You will be shocked at the greediness that our people have. You find one family, each member of the family has a piece of land and these people did not even fight. I am not saying they are not entitled, but the greediness because they have had the opportunity either they have the relatives, the way they are abusing that trust the people had in them. They do not even consider those war veterans, whom are without jobs, its very painful" (Female ex-combatant A)[100].

Unequal land distribution between men and women is an example providing evidence that gender discrimination is largely cultural. In this regard women are frequently the victims

5.8.2 Betrayal as sources of strengths

98   Interview with participant D was conducted in English in Marondera on 23 October 2003 and quoted verbatim

99   Interview with participant C was conducted in English in Marondera on 23 October 2003 and quoted verbatim

100 Interview with participant A was conducted in English at the participant's house in Harare on 13 October, 2003 and quoted verbatim

Although the war was horrendous and betrayed many, it made some strong.

"It makes me a very strong person. I achieved what I wanted. But I was very lucky, because after the war, I decided I still wanted to pursue a career, so I went back to school. I realised that there was life after the war so I enrolled, sat for my 0 levels, and when I passed, I went to the States to pursue my two degrees" (Female ex-combatant A).

"Perseverance and the will to go on, and never to give up. Some people can have high blood pressure because of a little sickness. Well compare yourself with someone who is bed ridden. So it's the will to keep going. I don't think I would have had that if I did not go to war. Many people give up too easily ..... As a woman, I feel our society have men who will compare an outgoing woman combatant who goes to the pub with a cowboy. That does not bother me. Even my parents are starting to appreciate me because they thought I would have more problems settling down. I am a farmer, I write, I sing, I am a dancer, I am an artist. I do a lot of children's activities. I don't think I would have managed to do all these had I not gone to war. So going to war is an achievement " (Female ex-combatant B)[101].

Thus at regular intervals throughout the history of Zimbabwe, women have rediscovered themselves – their strengths, their capabilities and their political will although some are still very bitter.

"Impact of the war was an eye opener. It made me a stronger person, at the same time it made me a very bitter person because I had my beliefs when I went there. Even now, I have my beliefs. What happened is not what I thought. I am trying very hard not to be bitter" (Female ex-combatant D)[102].

5.9 Going back to war

If the hands of the clock were to be turned, would women ex-combatants go back to war?

*"**Never**, I would **never** go to war because of what I have experienced and what my other war vets are experiencing, that those who died have already been forgotten. The parents, no one has told them that your children died. They still have question marks. There has been no assistance. The assistance that people have received are those living war veterans. You can imagine how those who lost their children feel" (Female ex-combatant A)*

*"Mmmm no. War is everything brutal. You do things because you have to not because you want to. There must be another way of doing things without necessarily acquiring a gun. My thoughts are in my writings. Like you said 'would you go back to war?' **No**. I think there are many ways of getting the point home without fighting" (Female ex-combatant B)*

Another ex-combatant simply said ''**Never**'' (Female ex-combatant C).

And another ''**No** '' (Female Ex-combatant D).

There were no women who said they would go back to war if the hands of the clock would be turned back, an indication that although women do take up arms to fight they can also contribute to peace building initiatives given the support and recognition of what they are capable of doing.

101   Interview with participant B was conducted in English in Marondera on 23 October 2003 and quoted verbatim

102   Interview with participant D was conducted in English in Marondera on 23 October 2003 and quoted verbatim

The affinity to peace was further shown by a civilian woman who looks forward to a nation that has good relations with other nations because in that way no nation would want to fight another.

> *"I would like to see our country having good relations with many countries. I do not know whether we are going to live peacefully. All governments of the world should learn to govern well and not cause wars. They should consult each other and sort matters amongst themselves peacefully. This is what God wants, to love each other. To love one's neighbor. We want peace. Although this won't lessen my pain until I die because my son died for nothing, your children and those of tomorrow may live better. Many people die because governments of different countries have failed to agree. So what type of a world are we going to have if people are forever in disagreement and fighting each other?" (Rural villager MPC2)*

The realisation by women that the liberation struggle of Zimbabwe did not achieve freedom for all, and that the war they waged was, in many respects, in vain would have surprised an anticolonial revolutionary theorist Frantz Fanon (1967c) who provided a justification for people's wars, suggesting that they contributed to the reversal of oppression and the inferiority complex created by colonisation. Although Fanon was a psychiatry doctor, he appears to have missed the link between war traumas and their contribution to the state of mind. The study under investigation has shown that the perception of the women ex-combatants is that war traumas make them abnormal or be regarded as mad women.

Writing about the Algerian revolution, Fanon (1968) suggested that revolutionary violence held transformative potential for women as well as for men. He claimed that Algerian women's participation in the armed struggle altered their feminine colonised identities and family relationships in positive ways that challenged feudal, patriarchal traditions. Rather than remaining victims of historical conquest, he argued, the colonised became creators of history. In this regard it appears true that achieving dignity and equality were more important than life itself to the Zimbabwean men and women who risked their lives to achieve recognition of their humanity. Through violence the Zimbabwean men and women reclaimed their humanity. In this respect, according to Fanon (1968) violence frees the native, making him fearless and restores his self-respect.

Fanon's account of the potential benefits of revolutionary violence appears to have been influenced by Hegel's analysis of the constitutive features of consciousness in *The Phenomenology of Mind* (Hegel, 1966). Hegel insisted that man becomes conscious of himself only through recognition by the other. To explain the role of mutual recognition in the development of self-understanding, Hegel explored the complex dynamics of misperception: "false consciousness," mutual dependence, and "pure self recognition in absolute otherness" in the context of bondage or master-slave relations (Hegel, 1966). According to Hegel, the master becomes aware of his actual nature only when he recognises his dependence on the slave.

In this regard racism in the colonial context may be equated to the master-slave relationship where the white settlers became aware of their superiority nature by recognising the 'uncivilised nature' of the natives to whom they had come to spread 'civilisation'. However, Fanon (1967 a) challenged Hegel's analysis, suggesting that it failed to take seriously the effects of racism in colonial situations. Focusing on the dynamics of the master-slave relationship, Fanon argued that the superiority complex of the white coloniser produced more than an inferiority complex in the blacks colonised. The coloniser's conviction of superiority rendered the colonised invisible to the extent that the coloniser never recognised either dependence upon the colonised or the humanity of the colonised. Only violent confrontation could force the coloniser to see the colonised as agents capable of changing the status quo in which they were forcibly placed by the white settlers. For this reason, Fanon insisted, revolutionary violence was key to the restoration of the humanity of the colonised.

From this perspective Zimbabwean men and women fought in the liberation struggle to restore their humanity which had been eroded by colonisation. They achieved independence but faced other challenges in the post war era. Paying attention to the patriarchal legacies that the Zimbabwean women endure may help explain why participation in violence did not have the positive effects for women that Fanon predicted. Closer examination of patriarchal attitudes may also show why the active roles African women played during anticolonial struggles did not culminate in gender equality in newly independent nations.

The war experiences of women ex-combatants suggest that the events in the liberation struggle often undermined their sense of agency as a result of increased vulnerability to gender-specific human rights abuses perpetrated by the soldiers as well as by their own male combatants. These abuses include rape, torture, brutal abductions, forced pregnancies, forced sex work, and other forms of sexual harassment, molestation, and discrimination. To assess the merits of Fanon's theories regarding the beneficial role of revolutionary violence, then, it is important to consider the experiences of both men and women revolutionaries. Women's experiences of the Zimbabwe liberation struggle suggest that rather than serving as transformative as Fanon argues, the violence during the liberation struggle functioned as a degenerative force. The trauma and humiliation caused by the violent acts left many women ex-combatants and civilian women suffering from long term physical and psychological wounds. In this respect White (2003) challenges the degree to which Fanon believed that politically conscious and goal-directed violent confrontation by the colonised against their colonisers could have profoundly rehabilitative psychological effects, despite the risks of trauma. The author supports White's views because the long term psychological and physical wounds of the sufferers in any war make it difficult to weigh the benefits. If an ex-combatant ends up unable to sleep for example because of the reoccurring images of what was witnessed during the conflict, what benefit is the liberation struggle to her and her family?

However, Fanon died from leukemia less than a year before Algeria won its independence from France and did not witness the challenges that faced Algeria after the war (Bulhan, 1985). He did not have an opportunity to revise his theories concerning the transformative effects of revolutionary violence in the anticolonial struggles that have been fought in Africa over the decades.

Conclusion

This chapter has looked at the physical and psychological wounds of the liberation struggle. Women ex-combatants are living with the traumas of the war and they need healing to achieve the status of wellbeing that is necessary for the development of themselves and the nation.

Section 3

This section looks at the healing initiatives that were taken to address the health issues that affected the ex-combatants in particular women, after independence in 1980.

Chapter Six: Healing -Traditional, Christian and Biomedicine

6.1 Introduction

After attaining independence in 1980, the physical and psychological wounds in women ex-combatants appear fresh twenty three years after the liberation struggle. They are living with the trauma of killing and witnessing people being killed; suffering starvation; witchcraft accusations, being displaced, tortured and raped. There is a lot of pain, anger, bitterness and hurt because of what happened. The WHO report (2001) estimates that, in the situations of armed conflicts throughout the world, 10% of the people who experience traumatic events will have serious mental health problems and another 10% will develop behaviour that will hinder their ability to function effectively. The most common conditions are depression, anxiety and psychosomatic problems such as insomnia, or back and stomach aches. Investigations of this research suggest that the population studied suffers more from mental illnesses than other illnesses as explained by one of the traditional healers who attends to the patients.

> "Most of the ex-combatants came because they had lost their minds. It is because they had met with many different things during the war...... Some of their relatives were sold out by sell outs for nothing. They had not done anything wrong. The soldiers came and sometimes killed them....The person just talks nonsense, she has lost her mind, we call this mamhepo (spirit/s of the dead)" (Female traditional healer 2).

6.2 Healing approaches

In Zimbabwe women and their families might turn to three main different processes that can be applied to heal the illnesses and these are *traditional, Christian* or *Biomedicine* (Western)

Traditional medicine generally looks towards the 'spiritual' origin such as witchcraft and angered ancestors in order to cure an ailment (Chavunduka, 1998). The effectiveness of the healing approaches to meet the needs of the women depend on the cultural understanding of causes of illnesses and cultural responses and/or adaptability to given healing processes. Gelfand (1977) notes that in Zimbabwe and other parts of Africa, each medical system operates according to a cultural behaviour framework. He further notes that in these areas the general concept of disease causation is spiritual; therefore treatment is spiritual inclined employing methods of exorcism of spirits. Other agents of diseases are witches (usually women) who are believed to have the capacity to inflict illness at will.Countries in Africa, Asia and Latin America use traditional medicine (TM) to help meet some of their primary health care needs. In Africa, up to 80% of the population uses traditional medicine for primary health care. In industrialised countries, adaptations of traditional medicine are termed "Complementary" or "Alternative" (CAM) (WHO, 2002). Traditional medicine refers to health practices, approaches, knowledge and beliefs incorporating plant, animal and mineral based medicines, spiritual therapies, manual techniques and exercises, applied singularly or in combination to treat, diagnose and prevent illnesses or maintain well-being (WHO, 2002). In this study, traditional healing will be discussed under African Religion (ritual and ancestral healing). Chavunduka (1999) notes that it is difficult to separate traditional medicine from African religion because some traditional healers are also religious leaders and vice versa.

Biomedicine in contrast to traditional religion uses scientific knowledge to arrive at the diagnosis and cure of the illnesses. As pointed by Chavunduka (1998), germs, bacteria, bad food, accidents and poisons cause the illnesses. To this extent Western medicine or biomedicine looks at 'material causation' to understand and treat an illness.

Christian healing played an important role after the liberation struggle as people wanted to come to terms with their loss, physical and psychological injuries. The priest or *muporofita* (prophet) prays for the sick and plays a pivotal role in acquainting Christian doctrine on healing, pastoral practice and recruitment of members (Gundani, 2001). People believe that churches can heal or come out with answers or provide therapy to their own problems especially to issues concerning diseases, fertility problems in women, marital problems and traumatic experiences of the war. These churches meet the physical and spiritual needs of the people as Africans generally believe that there is no fixed demarcation between body and soul (Joyce,1989). Gundani (2001) notes that the rise of healing prophets who operate both within healing churches and as private entrepreneurs is a development in Zimbabwe, fuelled by the marginalisation of the poor from access to modern health care.

6.2.1 African religion

In order to understand the importance of traditional healing today, the historical background of the relationship between religion, land and the people, which has always been close prior to the arrival of the settlers needs to be considered. In the tradition, the land is intimately associated with the history of the chiefdom, with the ruling chief and with ancestral spirits (Shoko, 2006). Ancestor spirits known as spirits of dead relatives are considered the 'king- pin' of the Shona society (Shoko, 2006). They influence the activities and lives of their dependants, the living members of the community.

During the1896 and 1897 resistance called Chimurenga CheKutanga meaning the first War against European domination of the region, Mbuya Nehanda was the woman who inspired African forces to fight against the white settlers. Mbuya Nehanda and Kaguvi (*Kaguvi was a male resistor to European settlement*) were captured and after a trial were sentenced to death by hanging. They were hung on a hill near the capital city of Zimbabwe, Harare (Shoko, 2006).

Prior to her execution Mbuya Nehanda is famed for saying "My bones shall rise again" and this prophecy is one which has followed through generations causing mediums for Mbuya Nehanda's spirit to live on (Shoko, 2006).

6.2.2 African religion and the liberation struggle

Peasant religion formed an indispensable part of the composite ideology of the war. Spirit mediums (living human beings through which the spirits of the dead talk) were significant to peasant radical consciousness precisely because that consciousness was so focused on land and on the settlers' government interference with production. Above any other possible religious form the mediums symbolised peasant right to land and their right to work it as they chose (Ranger, 1967). Once the guerrillas had entered the locality, the mediums proved ideally fitted to play another and crucial role.

It was they who offered the most effective means of bringing together peasant elders with the young strangers who entered each rural district, armed with guns and ready to administer revolutionary law. Hence not only peasants but also most guerrillas themselves came to draw heavily on the religious elements within the composite ideology of the war.[103]

> *"There was no battle that would be started in any area without consulting the medium in any part of the country, no battle would be started, you can actually amass all the weapons and ditch them in mountains, whatever, but you wouldn't start any battle until you were given permission by the spirit medium of that area. And the spirit medium of that area was always a woman. So she had to decide whether you had to kill the enemy in her own area or stop" (Male doctor and ex-combatant F)[104].*

> *" I said earlier on that when we went to a fighting Zone, we first went to the head of the area and introduced ourselves and the purpose of our presence in the area. We would also tell them the weapons that we were going to use in the area. Our aim was to destroy the enemy and not the families in the area. And for sure, in some areas no lives were lost because the ancestors had been notified of our mission and the ancestors vowed that only the enemy would perish and this happened exactly like that" (Male ex-combatant in a group interview).[105]*

In keeping with the African religion, spirit mediums shared with guerrillas and civilians their intimate knowledge of the countryside during the liberation struggle. They led columns of weapon bearers in and out of the country and showed them the most secure places where these weapons could be concealed. But they did a great deal more than this. According to Lan (1985), their contribution to the guerrillas' success was their instruction in how to interpret certain signs displayed by animals in the bush. Protective techniques that the mediums had practised before the war were made available to the guerrillas. But the powers of protective medicine would fail and the guerrillas would lose their ability to interpret the signs unless they observed a complex set of restrictions, which the mediums imposed on them. If this account may appear dramatic to Bourdillon (1984) who contributes the power and legitimacy given to spirit mediums to Lan's persuasive represantations, the following account from the author's findings may add some insight into the relationship between spirit mediums and the guerrillas.[106]

> *"Some strange things happened during the war. Eagles would hit the enemy's fighting planes and the plane would fall down killing its occupants. People will not believe these stories….We relied on the spirits of mbuya Nehanda na Chaminuka na sekuru Kaguvi"* (Male ex-combatant in a group interview)[107]

Biourdillon (1984) challenges Lan (1983)'s account of the liberation struggle that gives power and legitimacy to a shared relationship between spirit mediums and guerrillas as instrumental to the success of the war. Bourdillon offers a different explanation, that the alliance between the spirit mediums and guerrillas could have been driven by fear of guerrilla violence and intimidation.

103   Ranger (1967), 188-189. See also pp.197-212. Like Lan he emphasises that 'some means was urgently required to give the guerrillas legitimacy in terms of Makoni's own past and to give to peasants some way of controlling the young men with guns. The spirit mediums provided just such a means'..

104   Interview conducted in English at the participant's house on the 1st of March, 2005 and quoted verbatim

105   The group interview was conducted in Shona in Harare at ZANU-PF headquarters on 18 February, 2005 then translated in to English.

106   Lan's (1983) thesis formed the basis of his book Guns and Rain, Guerrillas and Spirit Mediums (1985).

107   The group interview was conducted in Shona in Harare at ZANU-PF headquarters on 18 February, 2005 then translated in to English.

The argument given by Bourdillon (1984) that spirit mediums co-operated with guerrillas out of fear and/or intimidation because of the power and legitimacy that accrued from such an 'alliance' appears misleading, especially when one considers that during the1896 and 1897 resistance, Mbuya Nehanda and sekuru Kaguvi fought in the liberation struggle called *Chimurenga CheKutanga* meaning the first War against European domination of the region. Mbuya Nehanda and sekuru Kaguvi sentenced to death by hanging were to inspire African forces to fight against the white settlers through their prophecy – "My bones will rise again" To this extent, it was not fear but the belief in the prophecy and the inspiration from *Chimurenga Chekutanga* through mediums that strengthened the relationship between mediums and guerrillas. The ex-combatants regarded the liberation struggle as a continuation of *Chimurenga Chekutanga* fought by their forefathers.

Kriger (1992) appears to share the same views as Bourdillon and argues that the support that guerrillas got from peasants was a result of guerrillas coercing them to do so and not from the shared peasant guerrilla ideology as portrayed by Ranger (!985) and Lan (1985). According to Kriger, where peasants were not coerced by guerrillas, they were mobilised to support the war by other grievances such as gender and other inequalities. In this regard, Bourdillon finds it difficult to see guerrillas as sons and daughters of the peasants. The author of this study like Ranger (1985)'s study about peasant consciousness and guerrilla War in Zimbabwe supports Lan's findings. Ranger's findings and the author's are that whenever the guerrillas went to the front to fight, they started by consulting elders of their mission. The elders comprising of chiefs, headmen and parents in turn advised them to go and seek guidance from the spirit mediums. In this regard, the author argues that the relationship between the guerrillas and elders/spirit mediums can be likened to the relationship between sons or daughters and their parents. Children seek guidance from elders on what to do to achieve their goals. Parents in their wisdom give their children the best advice. The authority to run affairs of the family, community and society at large rested with the elders before the war. This explains why during the war guerrillas continued to consult them on how to carry on with their mission. This thesis supports the views of Lan (1985) who gives spirit mediums and guerrillas a pivotal role in spearheading the struggle and mobilising the peasants. However, a further analysis of the peasants' roles during the struggle by Alexander (1996) shows that Lan's and Ranger's accounts do not appear to give clarity of the position of chiefs in the liberation struggle. Both accounts appear not to recognise that some chiefs continued to support the liberation struggle despite the fact that they were also on the payroll of the colonial government. Lan's analysis of chiefs was that by accepting colonial payment, duties and their lowly position in the government hierarchy, the chiefs could not do anything else to support the guerrillas. Lan supports Ranger (1982) who wrote that while there was room for spirit mediums in independent Zimbabwe there was no room for chiefs because they had failed to support the liberation struggle. Alexander (1996) notes how in Chimanimani, headmen Gudyanga supported the freedom fighters during the struggle. At independence he was elected as branch chairman for ZANU PF. The Mutambara chiefs also supported the struggle and chief Samuel Mutambara was jailed from 1974 to 1979 for supporting the guerrillas, recruiting students to join the struggle and facilitating them to cross over to Mozambique. Never the less, as Alexander (1996) observes, there were other collaborationist chiefs who opposed the war and lost credibility as a result.

Credibility to the relationship between elders and guerrillas was also lost as the war progressed and some guerrillas started to demand food from *Chimbwidos* (girl war collaborators) for survival. The elders may have found it difficult to see their authority of controlling their daughters slip away. But such incidents can not deny that the relationship between the spirit mediums and the guerrillas contributed to the success of the liberation struggle as the author's findings have demonstrated. The complexities of the relationship between guerrillas and peasants have been summed up "Studies of the relationships between ZANLA guerrillas and civilians expound diverse and sometimes contradictory arguments, but they agree on one general point – that the guerrillas' entry in to rural communities demanded an adaptation to local agendas and ideas" (Alexander et al., 2000, p. 159).

The influence that spirit mediums had on the operations and well being of guerrillas was so powerful that some healers saw many new spirits begin to possess hosts during the war to protect their children (freedom fighters) from the enemies (Reynolds, 1996). In demonstrating the protective powers of the ancestors, ex-combatants shared how the religion shaped their journey to Mozambique. They were either rewarded or punished depending on whether they followed the advice or not.

> *"Crossing to Mozambique was not easy. We used to be looked after by the ancestors. In each group of comrades was a leader who would seek guidance of the ancestral spirits of the place we were staying or resting as we proceeded to Mozambique. At times we were advised not to eat certain foods or advised on what to say and do. If we followed the advice nothing happened to us. But as you know, in any group, some comrades would ignore some of the advice. At such times we would be bombed. Some never reached Mozambique"* (Female ex-combatant in the group interview)[108]

The spirit mediums who are living human beings through which the spirit of the dead are considered to talk, shaped and controlled social behaviour through designed codes. Operating outside the social codes was met with harsh punishments or other heavy consequences. An ex-combatant describes how social codes worked.

> *"…The other crime was never mess with the people because it was the people's war. Don't harass them, don't intimidate them. Let them take the war. That's why the spirit medium was the focus. If the spirit medium said to its own people, in this area, we are going to have a war the people will just automatically follow. A comrade didn't have to force anyone to say tipei sadza, tipei chakati (give us food, give us this and that), you know, support us in this or that. It was the spirit medium which would say give those who are fighting whether they are men or women anything you can afford. And hence the pungwes (night meetings), the food supplies"* (Male medical doctor and ex-combatant F).[109]

6.2.3 Honouring spirits and the work of the Mafela Trust

There is no more effective way of understanding the cost of war than remembering the individual who died fighting in the war. The unmarked graves of the liberation war dead, the plight of their dependants and the unresolved traumas of the war are a neglected aspect of the legacy of the liberation struggle. Hennessy, (1992, p. 2) in his book on the social history of post war Britain remembers Enoch Powell saying "what an important thing memory is, collective memory. It's really collective memory that makes a nation, its memory of what its past was, what it has done, what it has suffered, and what it has endured". In this sense, it is the memory of the ex-combatants who died during the liberation struggle that led to the establishment of the Mafela Trust. The Mafela Trust was initiated to honour the wishes of the late ZIPRA commander Lookout Masuku (Brickhill, 1995). His wishes were the publication of the war dead, commemoration of the deeds of the liberation struggle fighters, the propitiation of the war dead and the welfare of the ex-combatants and their dependants. The research team of the Trust with the help of *Sangomas* (a ndebele name for traditional healers) located

---

108   The group interview was conducted in Shona in Harare at ZANU-PF headquarters on 18 February, 2005 then translated in to English.

109   Interview was conducted in English at the participant's house on the 1st of March, 2005 and quoted verbatim

some unmarked graves and established how the ex-combatants died; these included ZIPRA, ZANLA and South African ANC fighters. The work of the Mafela Trust in regards to reburial rituals was to be followed by many survivors and n'angas in rural areas all over Zimbabwe in an effort to heal the psychological traumas of the war.

Igrejor et al. (1999) in their study of Mozambicans who died in the civil war observe that the dead or the disappeared are not accorded proper burial rituals because years of social, political and economic crises inhibit the people from fulfilling them. The same reasons apply to the dead combatants of Zimbabwe who were not given burial rites. As such, their spirits were not given respect. Writing about honouring ancestral spirits, Shoko (2006) states that failure to honour ancestral spirits invokes bad luck for both the individual and community. A traditional healer spelt out the burial honour accorded to departed chiefs and how the graveyards were kept clean as a gesture of respecting the ancestral spirits.

> *"We have places for chiefs, nobody in the whole of Zimbabwe is following our ways of honouring such places. These places called madzimbahwe (house of stones where chiefs were buried) used to be swept according to our ways and drums would be sounded by special people who were allowed and trained to do that. This rain is brought by God, together with ancestral spirits. Today, these places where chiefs were buried are in the open. Trees have been cut for firewood meaning that we have lost the African traditional way of life, paving ways for problems that we are currently experiencing..... If we follow God's teachings in the Bible and look at Abraham's life, we see that he was a prayerful person known all over by believers and non believers, but when he died, God did not want him buried in a place reserved for the holy ones, he said that he should be buried where his ancestors are laid to rest. This place is always swept to keep it holy" (Male traditional healer 3)*

Misfortunes like droughts, floods, crop failure, sickness and death are blamed on the presence of angered spirits because they have not been accorded honour with proper funeral rites. Moreover they would have been deprived of a very important ritual called *kurova guva* (ritual for bringing the spirits home) (Shoko, 2006)

However, after the war, some feel that the African religion that had played a pivotal role during the struggle was not given the same importance on a national level.

> *"When we went to war, we followed culture. As Africans, we would talk to God through the ancestral spirits. When we came back, that way of communicating to God was lost. I do not want to say we lost it but that those who were supposed to keep our traditional way of living by implementing the necessary policies and procedures did not do so" (Male ex-combatant in a group interview)[110].*

6.3 African Religion, Guerrillas and Christianity

Some Christians acknowledged the relationship between African religion and guerrillas. Realising the importance that traditional religion played in the liberation struggle, Christians began to support the liberation struggle. As noted by Nzenza (1988), the guerrillas had denounced Christianity on the grounds that the colonisation of Zimbabwe had been made possible by the spread of 'European civilisation' justified by the Christian religion. In this context, the author suggests that the fear of losing church members and influence as the population became more politicised by the guerrillas

---

110   The group interview was conducted in Shona in Harare at ZANU-PF headquarters on 18 February, 2005 then translated in to English. However this participant spoke in a mixture of Shona and English . The interview was translated in to English.

were the driving forces that made Christians realise that they had to understand the causes of the liberation struggle. To this extent, Christianity, especially from the Catholics became a religion that offered effective and practical support to ZANLA guerrillas (Maxwell, 1993; McLaughlin, 1996).

6.4 Healing needs

After the traumatic experiences of the liberation struggle, there was need for healing. Families, communities, ex-combatants and government officials realised the need after observing illnesses and the behaviour in other groups of people that could not be understood.

6.5 Illnesses

Traditional healers who may also be spirit mediums find that most of the times the avenging spirit possesses the host who may be either the ill person or the traditional healer herself and it spells out its demands.

"He just cries and cries. He wanted a proper burial......Sometimes the woman just talks nonsense, and nobody understands her, or sometimes she wants to rule the man, Sometimes she confronts her in laws and fights them. All these are caused by mhepo from her own home. These spirits are caused by the dead who have not been buried properly, or are asking why their persons were killed. When the woman comes here with her problem, we identify the ngozi. Then the family says 'Yes, we have a relation who perished in the war' Sometimes a woman comes and falls down, rolling all over the place, crying and talking about what she saw during the war. The woman is violent and talks like a man. Sometimes she tells me about the violent dreams she experiences from time to time. And at that time of the dreams, she is the man in the house" (Female traditional healer 1).

"Those who tell us their problems are still in their normal senses. Those who are not can not do so. So those accompanying the patient will just tell us to deal with the situation. The patient at the time is smashing items or attempting to hit healers. I was slapped once and my drink I had was snatched away from my mouth".... At times, when the husband can no longer handle the situation at home, he takes his ill wife to her parents and say 'may you please seek help for your daughter? I will come to collect her when she is well. At the moment, I can not cope with what is happening anymore' "* (Female traditional healer 1).

"Some of them are mental health and infertility problems. Some of them include being possessed by mhepo (the spirits that are not known). So families face difficulties in understanding the possessed mother or wife and many homes are broken... It was difficult for me to get married. I have never menstruated up to today. So I went to look for help in the apostolic churches. Then the spirit of my father possessed me and I would fall down crying.....In my healing time, I only attended to one man. All my patients are women.....They come being troubled by the spirit of their husbands or relations who disappeared during the war. ... ... What is worrying me is that my cousin sister whose father also went to the war can not have children like me. My sister menstruates. My barrenness comes from not being able to menstruate, but my cousin does but because of barrenness, she too was divorced..... My uncle, my cousin's father is not emotional stable. ....He came back from the war and did not go through cleansing ceremonies....He is always having problems at work" (Female traditional healer1)[111]

In the Western medical field, the different illnesses presented to the traditional healers are war related Post-traumatic stress disorders. Green et al. (2003) describe post traumatic stress disorder as the invisible injury to mental health.

---

111   Interview with traditional healer 1 was conducted in Shona in Harare at ZINATHA headquarters on 11 February 2005 and translated in to English

Chavunduka (1998) observed that people believe that such abnormal illnesses are sent by social agents such as ancestor spirits, angered spirits, alien spirits, witches or sorcerers.

Thus, the social world (comprising the spirits and the living) and the physical world are united within a larger cosmology. If this harmonious state breaks down, this is seen to result from the malevolent intervention of *varoyi* (witches and sorcerers) or a sanction by the ancestral spirits for incorrect social behaviour (Honwana, 1997).

6.6 African Religion and causes of illnesses

Participants explained causes of the illnesses suffered after the liberation struggle. The causes are explained in terms of the relationship between religion and the universe.

6.6.1 The ngozi phenomena

After the liberation struggle, it is believed that Ngozi caused the illnesses affecting people. *Ngozi* is the spirit of a fighter and civilian killed during the war who did not receive the proper burial rites to settle them appropriately in the after-world. Ngozi can also be a number of spirits of bitterness with the capacity to torment, provoke illness and even kill those who mistreated them when they were alive (Honwana, 1997).

An ex-combatant or civilian whose family committed wrongful acts during the liberation struggle may suffer from *ngozi*. *Ngozi* sufferers may also be affected by restless spirits of relatives killed in the struggle and did not receive proper burial rites.

There were other wrongful acts committed against families during the liberation struggle. Some civilians were sold out for crimes they had not committed. The avenging spirits later killed members of the family of the *mutengesi* (seller).

> *"Many members of that family that sold are just dying…. After the war nothing happened. Quite a number of years passed by before anything happened. When it started to happen, it was death after death. The family has also lost six children. Only three children are left together with the parents. -They say that the family that sold the other did wrong. Now it is being haunted by the ngozi spirit, that's why the six children also died" (Female rural villager MP1)[112]*

> *"The spirit of the dead then followed the person who gave that information. In our traditional way, the spirit of the dead will trouble the person who gave the information that caused his death. So the mutengesi (seller) comes here when he is mentally disturbed. So we sit down as healers and look for ways to help the patient. In addition the spirit can also trouble not only the person responsible for the death but other family members of the killer's family " (Male traditional healer 3)[113].*

At times those who are troubled may not have been in the war. However, if the people who committed these acts did not pay compensation and/or get cleansed through appropriate rituals, then they and future generations would continuously suffer misfortunes. In this sense revenge can even extend to people's families who have to pay for the behaviour of their relatives (Honwana, 1999).

112   Participant interviewed in Mrewa on 25 February 2005. Interview was conducted in Shona and translated in to English.

113   Interview with traditional healer 3 was conducted in Shona in Harare at ZINATHA headquarters on 11 February 2005 and translated in to English on the 1st of March 2005

In this case, the traditional healer who was troubled by the spirit of her father was born in 1970 and her father went to war in 1975 when she was five years old. She therefore did not go to war nor participate in the duties assigned to the *chimbwidos* (war collaborators).

> " *No I did not go to war but my father went. He went to war when I was five years old in 1975 when the war was at its peak. He also left a baby still breastfeeding. We have never seen him again. What we face are problems…Yes, and the avenging spirits are mainly those of males. They come to possess those who at times did not participate in the war because they were young, too young. However, it is like the sins committed by parents will haunt their children and grand children* "
> *(Female traditional healer 1)*[114].

In this sense the traditional healer was also a participant of the liberation struggle as she experienced what it was growing up in a war torn country without a father. Her perceptions to healing would be shaped by that experience.

As stated earlier, during the struggle, both guerrillas and civilians sought traditional healers, diviners and spirit mediums to direct offer guidance and protect them. In the post-war period, these links remain important because people fear the spirits of the dead will return to haunt and punish them. (Honwana, 1999).

Further in Post war Zimbabwe where burial rites are important, spirit mediums, traditional healers and diviners help by advising on the reburials of the dead in order to stop the avenging spirits from tormenting the living. In Tears of the Dead, Werbner (1991) observes how a family contributes its misfortunes to the failure of mourning their loved ones so that their spirits can join the other ancestral spirits. This family only returns to normalcy when the proper burial rituals are performed.

6.6.2 Witchcraft

The belief in witchcraft as sorcery exists around the world and varies from culture to culture. Historically people have associated witchcraft with evil and usually have regarded a witch as someone who uses magic to harm others, by causing accidents, illnesses, bad luck, and even death (Cohn, 1993).

However, some societies believe that witches also use magic for good, performing such actions as casting spells for love, health, and wealth. People around the world continue to practice witchcraft as sorcery, claiming to use magic for good or harm (Stephens, 2002)

Since the mid-1900's, witchcraft has also come to refer to a set of beliefs and practices that some people consider a religion. Its followers sometimes call it wicca, the craft, the wisecraft, or the old religion. However, many people, particularly conservative Christians, do not consider witchcraft a religion as they understand the term (religion and ethics, www.bbc.co.uk/religion/religions/paganism/subdivisions/wicca.shtml - 26k, 30th August, 2005)

In most African cultures witchcraft is evil and meant to harm others or get an unfair advantage over other people. In Zimbabwe there is a belief that witchcraft causes illnesses and harm to other people. However through the 2006 Witchcraft Amendment Act, Zimbabweans are now allowed to practise

---

114   Interview with traditional healer 1 was conducted in Shona in Harare at ZINATHA headquarters on 11 February 2005 and translated in to English

witchcraft as long as they do not use it to cause harm (The Herald, May 10, 2006). The new law recognises the existence of the supernatural and effectively legitimises many practices of traditional healers, but only if they are used for good. Until the amendment, The Witchcraft Suppression Act of 1899 made it a criminal offence to brand anyone a witch or wizard or to accuse someone of meddling in the supernatural, even where there was evidence (The Herald, May 10, 2006).

Traditionalists say the recent amendments show that the country was finally waking up to calls from the people who felt the Witchcraft Suppression Act was hindering the genuine development of African culture in the country (The Herald, May 10, 2006)

6. 7 Women and Witchcraft Accusations

In the Zimbabwean Shona society there has always been a distinction between which gender gets attached the label of witch (Hungwe, 2003). It seems that more women than men earn this title, old men living alone are not ostracised in this way (Hungwe, 2003). The woman accused of witchcraft is driven out of the family back to the family were she came from before she was married. This is because in the Shona culture, a married woman is an outsider and if convicted of witchcraft in the family courts, she is sent back to her parents who are expected to perform exorcism to remove the witchcraft spirit (Schmidt, 1992). The consequences of sending the 'witch' away were great. The children of the witch were isolated in case their mother, for bewitching purposes too, gave them some portion of the witchcraft. The family of the witch is bewildered and embarrassed.

During the liberation struggle, more women were killed because as Schmidt (1992) notes, there is a bias towards thinking that there are more female witches than male.

Hungwe (2003) notes that older women have always been accused of witchcraft, especially because of some features that they tend to have because of ageing. These include: red eyes; wrinkled faces; living alone; and the keeping of pets such as cats, which are said to be animals used by a witch for witchcraft purposes.

Although guerrillas killed women accused of witchcraft during the liberation struggle, there are other groups who did not believe in killing witches (Daneel, 1990). Zionists and Apostolics – African religious movements that grew from the early 1920's, out of the Christian churches' failure to adapt to traditional African culture and religion for example, believe in witchcraft but they do not believe in killing the witches (Daneel, 1990). Rather, they exorcise the spirits that cause the witchcraft (Hayes, 1995). As a result, the Zionists and Apostolics are much preferred by many families and by women in particular.

Because of their powers to predict, to heal and to render witches harmless guerrillas made great use of Zionist and Apostolic prophets. Although the Zionists and Apostolics regarded African religion as diabolical; forbade the worship of ancestors; and claimed that the voice of God was truly expressed by their prophets but corrupted and distorted by the belief and practice of ancestral worship, guerrillas who believed in African Religion still made use of them (Ranger, 1999). Since guerrillas also made great use of spirit mediums, these two forms of religion were brought together during the war (Ranger, 1999).

6.8 Seeking help

Zimbabwean people have always had strategies that were employed to help them know what to do when faced with important decisions and to cope with traumatic situations. With the coming of settlers, Western biomedicine was brought to Zimbabwe. After the liberation struggle, western, church and traditional therapies were sought by individual families in an effort to find solutions to the stressful events and misfortunes that were being experienced. The stressful events resulted in a person suffering 'abnormal' illnesses. *Madzitete ne madzimbuya* (aunts and grand mothers) get together as families begin to discuss what they could do to help.

As pointed by Summerfield (1995), most people exposed to the effects of war and trauma in the non-Western world do not go through these events as a private or individual experience; the events are generally faced as collective experiences in which the traumatic content of the experience is not attached to the event itself but to the pain and negative consequence associated with it. Honwana (1999) points out that by focussing exclusively on the individual, western therapy undermines family and community efforts to provide support and care.

6.9 Healing approaches

As a collective body, family meetings recommend the best possible healing therapies. The healing processes that can be applied were pointed out;

> "We have illnesses that can be treated at hospitals, others at churches and others at traditional healers. There is no difference at the effectiveness of the healing processes as long as the problem should go to where it should. Some problems are for hospitals. But if you take a problem to a hospital and the problem should have been taken to a traditional healer, then the problem won't go and vice versa. I can say a problem should be directed to its rightful placer for healing" (Female traditional healer 2)

> "Yes, they (church people) couldn't help me. The spirit was so violent that I beat them up and they chased me away. My mother gave up on the church" (Female traditional healer 1)[115].

> "As a family, one looks at ways that will help. You could go to the prophets, n'anga or svikiro ('witchdoctor' or spirit medium) because you alone are facing the difficulties and challenges of life caused by what happened during the war. This way you can get help. You could also tell other comrades where you got help" (Male ex-combatant in a group interview)[116]

The responses given about where patients go for healing could be an indication of different beliefs patients have in the effectiveness of the healing processes. The author argues that colonisation and missionary work brought healing methods which were not known to the indigenous people of Zimbabwe. In the process, people got confused as to what methods work. Western medicine was introduced by missionaries in Zimbabwe, like in many other colonised countries in Africa (Waite, 2000). The missionaries who had brought medicines for their own use discovered that they could work more effectively if the natives were introduced to Western medicines rather than leaving them exposed to their traditional medicines which the missionaries called 'witchcraft'. The missionaries believed that traditional medicine with its 'magic' threatened the spread of Christianity. The Salvation Army

---

115   Interview with traditional healer 1 was conducted in Shona in Harare at ZINATHA headquarters on 11 February 2005 and translated in to English

116   The group interview was conducted in Shona in Harare at ZANU-PF headquarters on 18 February, 2005 then translated in to English.

officers and teachers were always on the alert to prevent their African converts from being treated by the 'heathen'. In Botswana, where the Africans were using Western medicine, Christian work had advanced (Waite, 2000).

Prior to the arrival of settlers, the Shona culture had always taken a holistic approach to illness because the culture believes that illness does not occur in a vacuum, it occurs in a society where there are other factors such as *mhepo* (spirits moving about) that cause the abnormal illnesses. In a discussion about *mhepo*, Pfofessor Mararike explained that *mhepo* may make it impossible for the biomedicine to come up with the right diagnosis. Sometimes the doctor may not see anything wrong with the person. The temperature is normal; all other indicators show that there is nothing wrong with the person. When the family takes their patient home from the Western doctor they are not able to sleep as the patient displays abnormal illness[117]. Gelfand (1977) notes that in Zimbabwe and other parts of Africa, each medical system operates according to a cultural behaviour framework. He further notes that in these areas the general concept of disease causation is spiritual; therefore treatment is spiritual inclined employing methods of exorcism of spirits. Other agents of diseases are witches (usually women) who are believed to have the capacity to inflict illness at will.

In this regard, Western therapies may not effectively address traumas in people with a different culture. Boyden and Gibbs (1997) have shown, in a study on the psychoanalysis of war traumas on children in Cambodia, that individual therapy conducted by western psychotherapists can be ineffective because it does not account for the place that ancestral spirits and other spiritual forces have in the causation and healing processes. They further observe that Western biomedicine and Western psychoanalysis become too narrow and restricted for the understanding of post-traumatic experiences and the healing of the traumatised from a cross-cultural dimension. This is because western concepts of trauma do not seem to embody a socialised view of mental health (Boyden and Gibbs, 1997).
To this extent, when the patients go to the traditional healer, they would have agreed that the illnesses are abnormal and most modern doctors are unable to attack the ultimate cause of abnormal illnesses, namely *varoyi* (witches or sorcerers) and the various types of spirits (Chavunduka, 1998). The family then focuses on applying alternative treatment that includes traditional and spiritual treatment.

Irrespective of which therapy is adopted as humans, we do have several universally shared values which cross boundaries of ethnicity, class, gender, culture, nationality and religious belief. These universal values stem from universal human constants which characterise human life everywhere (Shah, 2002). In this regard the existence of pain and suffering is a constant in the human experience, but the way in which they are interpreted, understood and thereby given meaning changes over time and varies by culture (Summerfield, 2000). During conflicts, the universal values pertaining to mental, physical and social well being of humans, are violated against and healing everywhere depends on the social and cultural context.

---

117   Discussion with Professor C. Mararike about 'mhepo' at the University of Zimbabwe

6.10 Challenges women face in seeking healing

When misfortunes come in to the family, it is the woman who suffers in many ways. A female respondent gave some insights in to how women bear the brunt of the misfortunes.

> *"First and foremost, the women are the ones who suffer because of the problems brought by ngozi (avenging spirits). It is the woman who carries a child for nine months, it is a woman who gives a painful birth, it is a woman who grieves seeing her child being tormented by spirits, so it is the woman who comes to seek for help" (Female traditional healer 2)*[118]

6.10.1 Power versus powerlessness

When a woman wants to seek help to end misfortunes tormenting her family, she may suffer from power relationships often found in the Shona culture. In this culture a woman is a minor and needs a man to represent her affairs including health issues (The Zimbabwe Human Rights NGO Forum, 2001). In addition to the Shona Culture the other way, in which African women were kept under the authority of men was through the use of Christian religion. Christian African women's groups called *Ruwadzano* (Fellowships) were encouraged to teach African women about God and how to maintain a home that measured up to Christian standards of cleanliness (Schmidt, 1992). The Victorian ideal of virtuous wife, selfless mother, and tidy, industrious housekeeper was the goal for which all African women had to be taught to strive.

Thus women ex-combatants have suffered disabilities, being subordinated by 'African customary law'. Under Customary Law, an African woman remained a legal minor all her life under the custodianship of her father, husband or eldest son as her life progressed from childhood, to marriage and widowhood or old age. (Zimbabwe Human Rights NGO Forum Special Report 2 March 2001). These patriarchal ideals lead to oppression that causes trauma in many women especially when the male members of the family refuse to take up the responsibilities agreed at the family board meeting. The women are traumatised further as they cannot get help in their own right. The interaction of patriarchy and war traumas can have devastating consequences, especially in a post conflict society where women ex-combatants are affected by their traumatic war experiences. In a study on War and mental health in Africa, Musisi (2005) observes the long-term outcome of those traumatised by wars and notes that women are more affected than men because of patriarchal attitudes towards women. The author argues that

the existence of norms, values and behaviour which are defined for each gender by the Shona society determine what it means to be men and women. To this extent women's status socially constructed provide an infrastructure conducive for psychological distress.

The restrictive measures in the Shona culture have led women to come out with alternative ways to meet their health needs. This means that they have to break the rule; the rule of being represented by males.

> *"When I wanted my uncle and others to help me sort out the problems I was facing, they actually beat me up. I had to seek help for myself because my uncles, my father's brothers are not bothered about it. I am not their child suffering. So they do not care. My brothers and a friend accompanied me to the traditional healers. When my father finished possessing me and stated what he wanted done, he stopped troubling me.*

---

118   Interview with traditional healer 1 was conducted in Shona in Harare at ZINATHA headquarters on 11 February 2005 and translated in to English

Now there is another spirit that possesses me. I do not know how these spirits call each other…Some times, I want to kill myself. The problems that women face in families come from the fact that the men who should assist do not want to know" (Female traditional healer 1)[119].

Although it is difficult to monitor those who refuse to take up their responsibilities and operate according to the laid down procedures, a professional male participant felt that people are monitored by their own spirits through a self monitoring process and punished for their offences. In this sense male representatives and traditional healers are monitored by their own spirits.

"It is very difficult to monitor them, however their own spirits monitors them. So there is a self-monitoring process. If the healers operate outside the boundaries as laid down by the spirits, then the spirits punishes the offenders not ourselves. This is the beauty of the system" (Professor Gordon Chavunduka).[120]

Similarly, the male members who refused to seek help for the afflicted female appear to have been punished for that.

"So the problems he faces today, we do not know where they are coming from. Perhaps they are family spirits punishing him for refusing to do the duties as he should as a father to the family. Now his own daughter has the same problems I have. That must be paining him" (Female traditional healer 1)[121].

Female traditional healers are aware that male representatives may not be there for the women who need healing, and so they came out with ways of by passing this requirement. The following case study shows how women are taking control of their own health by departing from the traditional norms where males are custodians of women's health.

"The woman tells us that the husband does not even want to discuss the problems. He pretends not to see them. He does not intend to do anything about the problems and he does not care what happens next. We will then talk to the spirits of mbuya Nehanda, sekuru Kaguvi na Chaminuka and pray according to our traditional ways and explain that the husband is not bothered. We cannot let the family perish because of that. Can you intervene? The ancestral spirits will then discuss this with other spirits and the woman can be helped with or without her husband" (Female traditional healer 2)[122]

Thus one of the few times when women are in control is when they are spirit mediums. The author argues that the experience of being spirit mediums gives women unassailable authority cutting across the hierarchy of male structures of authority, and keeps them outside of those structures. The female traditional healer used this authority to help women who came for treatment on their own without male representatives as required by the traditional culture. Unquestioned authority of spirit mediums over men is why the liberation struggle was powerfully driven by the spirit of Mbuya Nehanda through female spirit mediums.

---

119   Interview with traditional healer 1 was conducted in Shona in Harare at ZINATHA headquarters on 11 February 2005 and translated in to English

120   Interview was conducted in English at the participant's house on the 13th of February, 2005 and quoted verbatim

121   Interview with traditional healer 1 was conducted in Shona in Harare at ZINATHA headquarters on 11 February 2005 and translated in to English

122   Interview with traditional healer 3 was conducted in Shona in Harare at ZINATHA headquarters on 11 February 2005 and translated in to English.

Some women though exercise authority over other women in ways that both serve their own interests and that of the patriarchy system as a whole. For instance when a man takes more than one wife, the first wife has authority over those who follow. As Schmidt (1992) notes, junior wives work under the supervision of the senior wife and are often labourers working for room and board only – a situation that is stressful. In the liberation struggle, senior women actually helped male commanders in selecting women who would be raped.

Whatever form the oppression of women comes in, women need to liberate themselves as did the female traditional healer who treated women who came without male representation. Zimbabwean women's lives can no longer remain shaped by traditional religion because their mentality has changed due to their experiences of the liberation struggle and their position in the post war era.

In this regard, the women can take stock of the experiences of the liberation struggle and continuously work towards improving their position socially, economically and politically in order to achieve the state of well being paramount to the human developmental needs. However, as Coote and Campbell (1982) note, women have never yet secured the means of communicating their endeavours truthfully beyond the boundaries of their own movements. To this end, women of Zimbabwe are finding that although the setting is new, the battle they are fighting is essentially the battle that Mbuya Nehanda fought; the battle of freedom from oppression.

6.10.2 Economic hardships

When the mother goes to get help regarding the misfortunes in her family, she may be faced by yet another constraint, this time - economic.

> *"Most of the times the woman has no money. We vanambuya nanasekuru (female spirit mediums and male spirit mediums) can not let her go without getting the help. If there are other organizations that can help us with funding to keep us going because we do not do any other jobs except healing, we would be grateful. The western doctors will charge. When you have no money, the hospital doctor will not attend to you so you may die. We will still attend to you but we have no other means of earning a living" (Female traditional healer 2)[123].*

Thus some challenges that women face in meeting their health needs are not necessarily brought by the avenging spirits but by cultural practices.

6.11 Healing processes

After the liberation struggle, The concept of treating mental disorders, the total person and the spiritual part of it in terms of medication and therapy, needs an understanding and explanation of roles played by spirit mediums during the liberation struggle. In the traditional and spiritual treatment, the *vadzimu*, (ancestral spirits) are consulted and via a medium, would tell the family what is causing the misfortunes and advise on what to do so that the misfortunes end.

The role of ancestral spirits in describing the cause of mental illnesses and other disorders is common in many other cultures and religions for example in Cambodia as noted by Boyden and Gibbs (1997).

---

123   Interview with traditional healer 2 was conducted in Shona in Harare at ZINATHA headquarters on 11 February 2005 and translated in to English

Some misfortunes can only end when compensation has been paid and others when certain rituals have been performed as explained by traditional healers.

"Whatever experiences they are, they have to be dealt with and not to be ignored. The way to deal with ngozi is kuripa (paying compensation) to the aggrieved family " (Female traditional healer1)[124].

6.11.1 Compensation

Compensation takes different formats. Herds of cattle, goats, sheep, and even human beings are given as compensation. Human beings are usually young girls, virgins that would bear children, many children so that there is no loss in the form of family continuity suffered by the killed member's family. The girl given in compensation grows in the strangers' family and when she eventually gives birth to a child who has the same sex as the killed member, then her duty is fulfilled. Reynolds (1996) points out that after giving birth, the girl was free to marry in this family if she wished with full roora paid (bride wealth) to her family or she could return home.

The consequences of a girl given as compensation are great. The young girl has had her right to dignity, choice and self-respect violated. If the girl refuses to go as compensation she and other girls in the family may not get married at all because of the misfortune brought by *ngozi*. As noted by Reynolds (1996) not being married is frowned upon in the Zimbabwean society. In addition, her family would further suffer other misfortunes caused by the avenging spirit of the dead person.

Realising the adverse effects of giving girls in compensation, the government has abolished the practice of paying compensation in human form as explained by one healer.

".....goats, cows and money. No human beings anymore. When the spirit of a dead person asks for a girl as compensation, so that she can go and bear more children, we the healers will tell the spirit that it is no longer allowed. We say that because we have been told by the government to stop practising compensation in human beings. This practice used to grieve the girls because they were forced to live with men they did not love or knew. A long time ago, human beings could be paid in compensation. When a spirit demands a girl in compensation and it is refused, then usually it will ask for so many cows. Again, we will intervene and ask the spirit to be reasonable because the family has accepted responsibility and would like to live in harmony with the aggrieved family" (Female traditional healer 2)[125].

6.11.2 Acceptance of compensation

To end misfortunes, compensation must be accepted. Refusal of compensation has consequences on the family that has refused to accept it.

"The family members of the murdered person accept the compensation because they now know how their member of the family was killed. Some times the spirit of the dead person will posses members of its living family and tells them that 'I am so and so. You will see people bringing cows or whatever. You must accept because they have paid for murdering me at such a place'. The compensation will then be accepted. If they refuse the compensation for whatever reason, then the spirit of the dead person will trouble its own living

---

124 Interview with traditional healer 1 was conducted in Shona in Harare at ZINATHA headquarters on 11 February 2005 and translated in to English

125 Interview with traditional healer 2 was conducted in Shona in Harare at ZINATHA headquarters on 11 February 2005 and translated in to English

family but this is rare. After the compensation is paid and accepted, then another big ceremony uniting the two families is done. Beer is brewed, even a cow slaughtered mbira dzorohwa (traditional music played). The two families can now talk to each other. There are no hard feelings harbored by each one" (Female traditional healer 2).

Thus the compensation process, is in keeping with the Shona culture where the healing, just like the traumatic experience, is not an individual affair because the individual is conceived as part of an extended living and a dead family, special group, or community. In this regard compensation is a process that is expected to heal not only an individual but all members of the family too.

6.11.3 Distancing from the perpetrator

For others there is no compensation that is asked for. The families can not reconcile and so they move away from each other. A villager gave an example of families that do not see eye to eye because of the traumatic events of the war.

"The two families are no longer staying in the same village. The family that sold the other moved kuminda mirefu (the long fields. These are resettled lands formerly owned by whites) The two families do not see eye to eye" (Female rural villager MP1)[126]

In this regard reconciliation as a healing process becomes debatable; for how does one reconcile the psychological and mental being of 'broken hearts', of people who as a result of the historical and war experiences, have hatred for each other. Do people forgive and forget? The only way that other traumatised people have dealt with their traumas is moving away from the perpetrator.

6.11.4 Rituals on a family level

When a family member is murdered, there are two ceremonies or rituals that are performed. The victim's family, to make the dead person's spirit rest in peace, performs one and the perpetrator's family, to cleanse the murderer, performs the other. If these are not done, it is feared that the dead person's spirit will be restless and cause misfortune. However, these rituals alone do not effect total healing. They have to be accompanied by reparation or compensation as discussed earlier.

The significance of the ceremonies differs. The ceremonies performed by the victim's family asks the spirit to go to its killers and demand an explanation of why the person was killed in order that compensation may be paid. By paying compensation to the victim's family the perpetrator's family is accepting responsibility.

Honwana, (1997) notes that in the post-war period cleansing and purification rituals purify and protect relatives from the atrocities they experienced during the war. Ritual cleansing is tied to the notion of 'social pollution', which must be eliminated before the links to the past can be cut. The healing process consists of several symbolically charged rituals aimed at restoring the identity of the individual and reintegrating him or her back into the community.

The aims of the ritual ceremonies mirror those advised by The United Nations High Commission for Human Rights (2004). The commission points out that reparation should cover all injuries suffered by victims, and embrace three kinds of action. These are restitution (seeking to restore victims to their

---

126   Interview conducted in Shona at the participant's house in Mrewa village on the 18th of February 2005 and translated in to English

previous state); compensation (for physical or mental injury, including lost opportunities, physical damage, defamation and legal aid costs); and rehabilitation (medical care, including psychological and psychiatric treatment).

Traditional healers describe the rituals performed as part of the healing process.

> *"So we perform the cleansing ceremonies and prepare a dancing ceremony where there is a lot of brewed beer and mbira (traditional music). When the dancing is at its climax, the spirit of the dead person will come out and introduces itself and say 'I am so and so. Mhuri yenyu (your family) killed me at such and such a place. I want this in compensation, then I will go away from your family'. When the spirit of the dead person wishes not to speak then the troubled family pays compensation as directed by masvikiro (spirit mediums)"* (Female traditional healer 2).

> *"Sometimes we cannot trace where mweya wengozi (the avenging spirit) is coming from because people killed during the war were from as far as Mozambique, Zambia, Mutare, Bulawayo and so on. In such cases the family that has a member who killed must accept the avenging spirit which comes from where ever, through proper rituals and live with it in their family. This avenging spirit then becomes a new member of the family whose member committed the murder"* (Female traditional healer1).

Similar rituals were also performed by ZINATHA (Zimbabwe National Traditional Healers' Association) which was formed with the help of the government. ZINATHA uses the knowledge it has about healing those tormented by *ngozi*.[127]

> *" There were rituals held every night for these patients to give them an opportunity to talk about their war experiences. The patients would scream at times and when asked what they were seeing they would say 'I killed him and he is chasing me, look, look. He wants to kill me. When the screaming stopped he or she would be asked if they killed anybody during the war and they would say yes. So I think the environment was conducive, out there in the bush where local people who liked ex- combatants would come and join in the ritual ceremonies"* (Male professional G)[128]

The screaming patients are mediums through whom the spirits of those who died during the liberation struggle enter and afflict the individual and the community. In this sense, individuals who have been in a war, who killed or saw people being killed, are polluted by the 'wrong doings' of the war. Honwana (1997) feels that pollution comes from being in contact with death and bloodshed and in this regard social pollution constitutes an important factor in the context of post war healing.

Because, the people who suffer war traumas do not go through these events as a private or individual experience, the spirits of the dead that haunt them disrupt life in their families and villages. From this view, the spirits afflict not only the individual who committed the offences but also the entire family or group. In this respect, Honwana (1997) suggests that the cleansing process is seen as a fundamental condition for collective protection against pollution and for the social reintegration of war affected people into society. Howana (1997) further notes that the cleansing rituals are thus aimed at dealing with what happened during the war and are a subsequent break from the past.

---

127   Zinatha is an organisation that represents traditional indigenous religions. The head of that organisation is a retired university Professor.

128   Interview was conducted in English at the participant's house on the 13th of February, 2005 and quoted verbatim

6.11.5 Rituals on a national level

Mupfudza (2004) suggests that 'individual' cleansing ceremonies in themselves are not enough because war pollutes not only 'individuals' but the earth as well. In this respect, pollution is a sin against the creator and the nation, and people need to be pardoned from this sin[129].

To this extent, there are some spirits mediums who would not support guerrillas during the struggle because they did not like the shedding of blood. Reynolds (1996) cites Mande, a spirit medium, who was in contact with the freedom fighters frequently through the years of the liberation struggle. He did not help them because his spirit hated bloodshed. His spirit did not allow killing and so he could give comrades neither courage nor power to killing. The comrades were annoyed. However, Mande used his powers to cleanse the soldiers returning form the war as the killing they had committed had polluted them.

Thus, shedding bloodshed is sinning against *Mwari* (the creator of life). Mupfudza (2004) explained that human beings, who are children of mother Earth and *Mwari*'s breath, have sinned against both by killing one another. The shedding of blood defiles divine nature in them and it pollutes the earth. In this light, it is apparent that Zimbabwe has sinned against mother Earth and *Mwari* on many occasions but has held no cleansing ceremonies, or rituals of *kugadzira*, which would make the nation clean in the sight of *Mwari*, and bring the nation back to the Creator's presence' (Mupfudza, The Daily Mirror, 17 Nov. 2004)

The idea of pollution and cleansing may be tied to the Christian Biblical notion of land defiled by bloodshed. ''So you shall not pollute the land where you are; for blood defiles the land, and no atonement can be made for the land, for the blood that is shed on it, except by the blood of him who shed it. Therefore do not defile the land which you inhabit, in the midst of which I dwell; for I the lord dwell among the children of Israel" (Numbers 35:34-35)

Indeed one ex-combatant shared the views on the need to cleanse the earth that was polluted by the blood spilt when people killed and were killed during the liberation struggle.

"The country needs brewed beer called chitovapasi (beer for cleansing the earth as well as appeasing the ancestral spirits). This beer should be brewed at each of the holy places such as Great Zimbabwe, Mutiusina-zita, Matojeni, Chinhoyi caves, Chirorodziva. Flags of the liberation struggle - were hoisted on these places at the start of the liberation struggle. Therefore it is quite befitting to raise flags at the same places to signify the end of the liberation struggle. Even the wealth that we want, why is it that the British people still cry for the same wealth from our country? It is because they know what wealth Zimbabwe has. So when we ask from our ancestors, when the country has been exorcised, when our children have been exorcised at their homes, then we will get what we are asking for " (Male ex-combatant 1 in a group interview)[130].

"Today the government goes to Mozambique to do what they call bash. They go with the educated comrades with musical bands to perform rituals. This is not how cleansing or bringing the spirits of the dead home is done. The ministry of information just arranges these things without consulting our parents or us. I think those who participate in these bashes do so to have a nice weekend. This is what is causing people to fight each other even though they fought for a common goal during the

129 'Individual' means family, group or community ceremonies, because traumatic experiences affect not only the individual but others as well. However, here they are termed 'individual' because the ceremonies do not represent cleansing the earth which belongs to God and the nation.

130 The group interview was conducted in Shona in Harare at ZANU-PF headquarters on 18 February, 2005 then translated in to English.

liberation struggle. It is causing opposition parties to engage in violence and spill even more blood at a time when we should concentrate on building our nation. It is causing road disasters killing more people. N'angas (traditional healers using the knowledge of herbs) are called to perform their ceremonies but what are n'angas compared to national stability?" (Male ex-combatant 1 in a group interview)[131].

The views expressed by the male ex-combatant suggest that ritual cleansing performed using modern ways – through festivities called 'bash' or bands playing live music cannot bring peace to Zimbabwe. In this sense the educated ones who have allowed cleansing through modern ways are perceived as the westernised ones who are ill advised by n'angas . He prefers religious healing that comes from ancestral spirits through spirit mediums.

"N'angas are worms. We even believe that those who were witches during the struggle died because it was something forbidden. We are here today not because we were the clever ones who could escape bullets from the enemy. It is because the ancestors looked after us" (Male ex-combatant 1 in a group interview).

In this sense the ex-combatant recommends that people should follow the traditional way of life guided by the ancestral spirits.

"If we could live our lives as was directed by mbuya Nehanda and sekuru Kaguvi following our culture and respecting holy places, then we could have few problems in life. If we follow the western culture, we will forever have problems, Even this aids can be a health problem of the past if we follow the traditional way of living" (Male ex-combatant 1 in a group interview)[132]

A traditional healer supports the view that most illnesses could be treated if the Shona culture of respecting and asking guidance from the ancestral spirits was followed.

" Even this illness called aids can be eradicated as was the case with influenza years ago". Older people used to ask ancestors to stop the illness because people had perished and the illness would go. So why is this aids killing people without end? We have been told at different traditional forums that it is our way of life that is causing aids to devastate people because no one wants to ask the ancestors what to do......Even us traditional healers, if I heal according to ways prescribed by our culture, following mbuya Nehanda's teachings and sekuru Kaguvi, that patient will be healed. Today I am so happy that I wish many healers were here to share in these discussions so that we could draft a code for traditional ways of healing. I am sure the ancestral spirits would have been pleased and our healing could be more meaningful" (Male traditional healer 3).

Because spirit mediums played important roles during the liberation struggle, it is not surprise that most ex-combatants still regard them as pillars in overcoming their health problems as they did in protecting them during the struggle (Shoko, 2006)

---

131   N'angas as opposed to ancestral spirits, cause havoc. They treat normal ailments from learned remedies but they can be manipulative. Reynolds (1996) notes that n'angas are dedicated to the development of backwardness in Zimbabwe because their knowledge is claimed. N'angas have caused a lot of misery to families they accuse of witchcraft. It is then not surprising that N'angas have been referred to as worms by an ex-combatant.. However it is important to note that both n'angas and spirit mediums operate under the umbrella of traditional hears and are registered under ZINATHA. Many people prefer religious healing through medium spirits,

132   The group interview was conducted in Shona in Harare at ZANU-PF headquarters on 18 February, 2005 then translated in to English.

6.11.6 The burial rituals

Reburial rituals are meant to effect healing in the post war trauma society of Zimbabwe. Realising the significance of reburials to healing, the government embarked on a programme of exhumation and burying the remains of the deceased in an effort to help the nation recover from the devastation of several years of violent conflict and war (Shoko, 2006).

When the avenging spirit asks for a proper burial rite normally through *ngozi*, certain rituals are performed.

> *"So we slaughtered a goat and took its head which we placed in a coffin and started the morning process as if the head was the body of my father. Many people came for the funeral and the burial ceremonies were performed.....she (mother of the traditional healer/wife of the deceased) was in mourning for a year wearing black as is with the tradition" (Female traditional healer 1)[133]*

The slaughtering of a goat symbolises the relationship that the living people establish with their dead loved ones and this relationship was disrupted during the war, as they could not bury them with proper rites. Igrejor et al. (1999) note that the years of social, political and economic crises inhibited the people from fulfilling these vital obligations. After the war, the living perform the burial rites because they believe that their well being depends on honouring and performing established ceremonies and rituals surrounding death.

Indeed, after the burial ritual was performed, the traditional healer experienced some changes in her life.

> *"The following year, I was properly married but the marriage did not last because I could not conceive. The husband said he could not live with a barren wife. I tried every traditional means that I know of but without success. I have now lost hope. If I am barren and I cannot live with a husband because of that, so be it" (Female traditional healer 1).*

However, there are others who do not believe in the traditional rituals. A civilian mother who lost her son during the struggle believes in a church ritual.
Referring to a traditional ritual where the head of a goat is mourned as if it was the body of the deceased, she said that

> *"I can't do that because I believe in everlasting rest that comes through our lord Jesus Christ. So I would like to call the church to pray for his soul and the rest of the family so that we can accept what we cannot change. I don't see how burying a goat's head will be a substitute for burying the body of my son. My belief in God makes me feel better praying for his soul wherever his remains are. A long time ago, before Christianity came, people followed the traditional way . However, there are some who still choose the traditional way of burying a goat's head in the absence of the body. I choose to pray" (female rural villager MPC2)[134]*

6.11.7 ZINATHA (Zimbabwe National Traditional Healers Association)

---

133   Interview with traditional healer 1 was conducted in Shona in Harare at ZINATHA headquarters on 11 February 2005 and translated in to English

134   Interview conducted in Shona at the participant's house in Mrewa village on the 18th of February 2005 and translated in to English

After independence in 1980, the new government sought to officially recognise the role-played by traditional healers and spirit mediums during the liberation struggle. The importance attached to the roles of spirit mediums during the liberation struggle contributed to the formation of a body- ZINATHA- that would encompass them under the ZINATHA Act of 1981

> *"Many of us including some traditional healers saw the need of forming a body of certified, registered healers to help with the needs of the public This would give the public the assurance that the healers were not bogus and at the same time one would know where to go to get the help.....The nature of most of the illnesses required the patients to stay at the center for long periods. Therefore it was a good decision in my opinion, that the association was established in a rural area where rent, food and other costs are much cheaper. So the centre was established at Nharira in Chivhu" (Professor Gordon Chavunduka).*

Through referrals by ZANU PF many patients affected attended ZINATHA as explained,

> *"There were rituals held every night for these patients to give them an opportunity to talk about their war experiences. The patients would scream at times and when asked what they were seeing they would say 'I killed him and he is chasing me, look , look. He wants to kill me. When the screaming stopped he or she would be asked if they killed anybody during the war and they would say yes. So I think the environment was conducive, out there in the bush where local people who liked ex combatants would come and join in the ritual ceremonies.... The nature of most of the illnesses required the patients to stay at the center for long periods. Therefore it was a good decision in my opinion, that the association was established in a rural area where rent, food and other costs are much cheaper" (Professor Godrdon Chavunduka).*

Brickhill (1995) reveals that the traumas of the war are still very much alive for both the perpetrator and the victim. The work of the Mafela Trust was an
attempt through field research, to list the names, next-of-kin and places of burial and the ZIPRA dead'.

Although traditional healing has played an important role in meeting the needs of the ex-combatants, Professor Gordon Chavunduka, head of ZINATHA observes that Christianity has been disrespectful toward, traditional healing. Indeed the Dean of the Mutare Cathedral once protested over the appointment of Professor Chavunduka to the Board of Governors of St Augustine's School calling him 'the Head of the Witch-doctors' Association'. He wrote that Scripture clearly points out that God's people can have nothing to do with supporting things clearly shown to be contrary to the Word of God (Ngwabi and Ranger, 1995).

6.12 Christianity

The patients who believe in the Christian perception that traditional healing is heathen, go for Christian treatment which also encourages Western/biomedicine treatment. In general when there are no answers some people turn to God. Maxwell (1993) notes that during the struggle, Christians met regularly to reflect on their daily trials and sufferings. Their theology was of hope, action and endurance. Its content expressed in the idioms of song and testimony and in the concept of sacrifice and martyrdom continues to help rural Christians make sense of the many struggles they face in the post independent Zimbabwe.

Although Christianity (European and African) helped the communities make sense of the suffering brought by the war, European missionaries often accused Zionists and Apostolics of being disguised pagans but in fact their relationship to African religion was quite different. Zionists and Apostolics opposed ancestral worshipping (Ranger, 1999).

It would appear that the European missionaries who branded Zionists and Apostolics as 'pagans' did so because they believed them to be anti-European settlers. Indeed Ranger (1999) observes that Zionists and Apostolics refused the authority of the colonial state and they were persecuted and repressed.

Nevertheless, civilians still consult both Christian movements for healing especially those who do not charge. If churches encourage tithing of 10% of earnings and the individual's earnings are zero then she pays zero. Therefore churches provide a coping strategy as well as comfort zone especially for the poor who have nothing. Further, people believe in divine powers of faith.

> *"We choose the church because there we are told about verses in the bible where God comforts those who are troubled. ..... I like Job's story because Job had many children but when he was tried, all his children died. All his livestock died. He was given sores. Later God saw that Job was courageous and he comforted and rewarded him" (Female rural villager MPC1)*[135]

In addition to acting as a forum where women get healing and share experiences, the church advises them on self help projects

> *"...The church also advises women to grow vegetables for sale so that we can help ourselves. I wish we could get a bit more money then we could start chicken rearing... When we meet at church we tell each other that Zimbabwe is better than what we see happening in other countries. We see piles and piles of dead bodies covered in tents. Let us concentrate on our grandchildren. They are our children now. War is a terrible thing but let us not dwell on it" (Female rural villager MPC1)*[136]

A faith healer agreed that he sees a lot of women more than men. He believed that many women suffered in the liberation struggle and they come to hear God's healing words through him. He does not use the Bible because he does not know who wrote it and in addition teachings from the Bible forbid polygamy. He has two wives, one of them lost her family during the war; when she went to him for healing, she ended up being his second wife. He feels he has done God's work by being kind to the woman who later became his wife. They had ten children together, unfortunately two have died.[137] In this context the belief in healing through divine faith was and is open to abuse of women and girls. This has profound consequences such as the spread of sexually transmitted diseases including aids or marital problems emanating from such practices. The World Council of Churches (1998) points out that there are many stories of rape, domestic beatings, sexual trafficking and abusive employment practices by church institutions.

However, healing that comes from worshipping appears to be temporal as explained by a villager,

---

135   Interview conducted in Shona at the participant's house in Mrewa village on the 18th of February 2005 and translated in to English.

136

137   Discussion with a faith healer in Mount Darwin on the 15th of February 2005. Discussion was in Shona and he did not want to be tape recorded because he feared for his life. With his permission, notes of the discussion were noted in the author's diary, then translated in to English.

"Singing makes me forget my worries for a day. Some words also make me forget for a while but as soon as I come back home I am immediately confronted with the same problems. . I don't know what happens to other women when they go back home because I find myself still thinking about my loss" (Female rural villager MPC1)

6.12.1 Christian healing questioned

One ex-combatant asks why church ceremonies should be performed for healing the wounds today, when at the beginning of the war, and during the war, such ceremonies were not used.

"When we came back from the war, we were supposed to be exorcised but this did not happen. Today, when you talk about the need of exorcism, you are asked to which church you belong. Are you a Catholic, Anglican, Seventh Day Adventist and so on? If you talk about being a comrade they say you are heathen. Those who are ruling today, they do church ceremonies but where were the churches while we did our worship through the ancestors? If you look at it there are two clashing religions. The religion of the settlers and that of the traditionalists. Because that means that there is the question of who is the greater one? Who controls the material resources? This means that there is now a problem ... When I was born, I was given my traditional name. When I started going to church my name was not accepted, so I was given a Christian name from the bible. So who am, I? The schools where we go to today, teach that to go to God, you go through Jesus Christ. But during the war, we did so through our parents, our ancestors, sekuru Kaguvi, Sekuru Chaminuka and mbuya Nehanda. So when we came back, our ancestors were not informed that we are back, the mission was accomplished" (Male ex-combatant 2 in a group interview)[138].

This accounts shows that some ex-combatants believe that Christianity was a tool that was used by the colonialists for imperialistic purposes and as such it is not to be trusted.

6.13 Biomedicine

Western models consider the person as a self-contained unity, an individual completely independent of others (Brackken et al., 1995). In this way, many challenges are raised when research on trauma and post-traumatic experiences is done with traumatised people from societies where the individual is part of an extended family.

Post-traumatic stress disorders as described by western scientific education appear to have no links to fear associated with the belief in supernatural danger caused by committing evil actions. The author sees 'the fear of supernatural danger' as the fear of *ngozi* that has led many to seek healing. In this regard, the significance of cultural variations in concepts of sickness and health should not be underestimated, especially when there are differences between manifestation of disease and the experience of illness in the minds and bodies of individuals (Eisenberg, 1977).

Although many families chose traditional healing soon after the war, some ex-combatants sought Western psychiatric healing and were displaying symptoms as described by an ex-combatant,

"Soon after the war in 1980 to 1981 there were many comrades who were at the psychiatric centre at Harare hospital. They were shouting that look the aeroplanes have come to bomb us" (Female ex-combatant in a group interview)

Women ex-combatants who also seek Western medical healing do so for none war related illnesses such as conceiving. A female traditional healer related an example.

---

138   The group interview was conducted in Shona in Harare at ZANU-PF headquarters on 18 February, 2005 then translated in to English.

" I would love to have a child. I would even want three eggs at once so that I have my three children at one go, then I forget about it... They said that I will never be able to conceive because there are fibroids in my ovaries and it is too late to remove the fibroids. When they took out the ovaries as well, they told me that they were sorry because I will never be able to have a child. If they had not removed the fibroids and the ovaries, I would probably have gone back to the traditional methods. Now that I no longer have ovaries, other healing methods that can help are more than welcome" (Female traditional healer 1)[139]

Different experiences of the war have resulted in the application of different healing processes. To this extent, ex-combatants and civilians have not utilised mental health services to a great deal partly because they do not believe in them. The Amani Trust (1997) notes that, there have not been the fully trained personnel to deal with post-traumatic stress disorders taking in to account cultural beliefs. As a result, there is very little statistical data to verify the psychological effects of their war experiences.

However, for any healing process to be helpful, it has to take in to account cultural understanding of the causes of physical and mental health problems being experienced by the individual.

6.13.1 Commemoration

Soon after independence, the Government constructed the Tomb of the Unknown Soldier in commemoration of all those who perished without being identified (The Jackson Advocate Newspaper, 5th October, 2002). In addition, the Heroes day was set as a holiday for honouring the memory of the combatants who perished during the struggle (The Jackson Advocate Newspaper, 5th October, 2002).

Governments of other countries have constructed memorials after coming out of conflicts. Winter (1995) looks at how cultural, social and artistic work after the Great War consoled the grieving in Europe after the carnage in the trenches. He observes that in England, France and Germany, rituals, painting, cinema, literature, poetry, and the building of memorials gained new power from their ability to mediate the enormous personal losses of 1914-1918.

The European Society of Traumatic Stress Studies (1998) noted that in Croatia, The Wall of Pain placed in Zagreb is in memory of the veterans of the patriotic war for independence against the Serbs. The Wall of Pain is a memorial patterned after the Vietnam Veteran Memorial Wall in Washington, DC (The European Society of Traumatic Stress Studies, 1998).

The author supports Winter's (1995) analysis that in commemoration, mourning individuals and communities, unrelated by blood, become one family as they offer each other support and consolation. In addition the author feels that rituals and commemoration memorials bring together those who are mourning and the experience itself of sharing the loss of their loved ones becomes a healing therapy. In Zimbabwe, the construction of the Tomb of the Unknown Soldier and the setting of the Heroes day as a holiday for honouring the memory of the combatants bring people who are not related together. In this sense they become one family as they all mourn and remember the loss of their loved ones.

---

139   Interview with traditional healer 1 was conducted in Shona in Harare at ZINATHA headquarters on 11 February 2005 and translated in to English

6.14 Findings

The study found out that women were deeply traumatised by the liberation struggle and different healing approaches have been applied in an attempt to heal the women's traumas.

6.14.1 Effectiveness of the healing approaches

Twenty-three years after the liberation struggle, the women - both ex-combatants and civilian - still exhibit symptoms of psychological distress. To this extent, it would appear that either the healing approaches adopted have not been able to cure the illnesses or that the treatment for psychological distress was sought much later when the women might have been exposed to additional social, political and economic difficulties.

Patel et al. (1997) have observed that factors that impact on psychological illnesses in Zimbabwe, include absolute poverty, limited public health services, widespread civil unrest and sex inequality. Patel et al. (1995) further note that psychological illnesses in Zimbabwe are common in women, and cause considerable disability, as most patients do not receive effective treatment due to lack of economic resources and other factors.

An increased vulnerability in women to develop psychiatric problems during war and civil violence was reported in similar studies. In London General practices during World War 2, a ratio of 2:1 (female to male) for neurotic illness was observed (Lewis, 1942). In Belfast, Northen Ireland, a ratio of 3:1 (female to male) was found for all psychiatric disorders and the stress of civil violence was the major or contributing factor in all patients (Lyons, 1979). In their study of psychological impact of war trauma on civilians, an international perspective, Krippner and McIntyre, (2003) have noted that trauma on civilians reveals a high level of social and economic hardships.

In this regard, a study on experiences of Namibian ex-fighters fifteen years after independence, LeBeau (2005) noted that social structural factors interact with psychological factors and, in turn, result in a perpetual state of psychological distress.

An observation made on the experiences of ex-soldiers twenty years after the Falklands War reveals that veterans continue to suffer psychological illnesses and more veterans have taken their own lives since the South Atlantic conflict ended than the number of servicemen killed in action (http://campaignfortruth.com/contact.htm, 2nd August, 2007).

In view of the psychological illnesses that patients bring for treatment, it may be useful to adopt the concept of trauma as an extended on-going process rather than as a single event. This idea includes understanding crisis or trauma as a cumulative process extended over time and space. Eyre (1998) notes that the concepts of recovery or rehabilitation in the latter stages of trauma need to be exercised in a way that looks beyond the first few months and years, in order to address the psychological distresses associated with social, legal, and political systems.

6.14.2 Children of traumatised parents

Among those suffering the long term health effects of wars are children of traumatised parents. Indeed one of the ex-combatants in this study revealed that her own children do not understand her. The children just say *"mamma watanga"* (mum has started again). In a study conducted among traumatised parents from the Holocaust and direct combat show that 80% of traumatised parents reported moderate to severe verbal violence towards their children; 26% of traumatised parents reported physical violence towards their children; 32% of traumatised parents reported not meeting their children's physical needs: 58% of traumatised parents reported not meeting their children's emotional needs (The European Society of Traumatic Stress Studies, 1998)

6.15 Challenges facing health providers in meeting women's health needs

Although traditional and western medicine have played an important part in attempting to meet the healing needs of the women traumatised by war, there appears to be challenges that health practitioners face.

6.15.1 Western medicine

A study done by Chikara and Manley (1991) on mental health in Zimbabwe showed that the country like many other developing countries, suffers from a shortage of trained mental health professionals. Any gains that might have been obtained by training more health workers have been undermined by the brain drain of professionals to other countries. Professionals such as doctors, nurses, social workers and family networks who could offer the healing support to the ex-combatants and civilians have migrated. Meldrum (2003) reports that more than 80 per cent of doctors, nurses and therapists who graduated from the University of Zimbabwe medical school since independence in 1980 have gone to work abroad, primarily in Britain, Australia, New Zealand, Canada and the United States.

To this end the psychological suffering of ex-combatants and civilians after the liberation struggle may not be due to any conscious neglect by the government or its representatives. It is more likely due to lack of mental health professionals with adequate knowledge about war- related trauma. These factors have a bearing on the effectiveness of healing processes given.

It took health professionals in the United States some time before recognising war-related psychological trauma in Vietnam veterans (Mason, 1990 and Matsakis, 1988). Many afflicted veterans had suffered without relief, making their lives and those of their families miserable and dysfunctional (Mason, 1990 and Matsakis, 1988). Many were not able to get and maintain adequate employment and many became homeless (Archibald and Tuddenham, 1965). Those with critical psychological distress may have been diagnosed as schizophrenics or manic-depressives, there being no appropriate diagnostic criteria to describe and validate their problems (Archibald and Tuddenham, 1965).

Shay's (1994) study of the experiences of American soldiers of the Vietnam War draws parallels with the experiences of Greek soldiers of the Trojan Wars. The study shows that 3 000 years after the Trojan Wars, traumatic experiences of war still affect human lives throughout recorded history. Shay's (1994) study suggests that although over time the diagnostic labels for the psychological disorders experienced by warriors as a result of battle have changed as the science of mental health has advanced and matured, the human suffering caused by wars has not.

To this extent, it has been noted that in most cases, post traumatic stress disorder is not curable but is treatable (Center for Disease Control, 1988; Kulka et al., 1990). Consequently, treatment involves the recognition of symptoms, their fluctuations, and the need to offer counselling and support (Center for Disease Control, 1988; Kulka et al., 1990).

6.15.2 Discriminatory policies

The discriminatory policies in Southern Africa including Zimbabwe led to a segregated health system in which the white minority enjoyed the best medical services while the black majority and particularly those in rural areas were catered for by health institutions characterised by poor facilities and inadequate resources (Freeman and Motsei, 1992; Karim et al., 1994). Although after independence blacks could now access the health institutions that belonged to whites only, costly western medical services were, and continue to be, inaccessible to the majority of the black population. When the blacks are able to fund western treatment, they find that the service provided does not meet their needs. To this extent ex-combatants and civilians have sought healing from traditional healers when western medicine has failed to heal them. Van der Geest et al. (1990); Van der Geest (1997); and Gilson et al. (1994) have criticised the quality of biomedical health services in Africa. These authors note that in contrast to traditional healers, staff in primary care clinics appear to show little concern and respect for their patients on the significance of cultural variations in concepts of sickness

6.15.3 Health concepts

Traditional medicine and biomedicine differ in their concept of the nature and causes of illness. Ndetei and Muhangi (1979) in their study of psychiatric illness in a rural setting in Kenya, observed that mental illnesses may be viewed in terms of magical, social, physical and religious causes, but rarely as diseases within the Western biomedical paradigm. In this sense the women ex-combatants and civilian women have tended to rely on traditional medicine because cultural health concepts alienate them from the western health care system. A Western psychiatry doctor working with Shona patients found that many of his patients in Zimbabwe held a faith in ancestor spirits. They would say, "My ancestor spirits are putting a hex on me or bewitching me". The psychiatry doctor noted that from a western perspective, "this sounds crazy and like a delusion in and of itself," (http://www.noevalleyvoice.com/2001/October/Lind.html, 11th June, 2006).

6.15.4 Traditional healing

Although traditional and western health systems have operated side-by-side in South Africa and Zimbabwe since the arrival of the Europeans, western healing enjoyed greater formal acceptance by colonial governments because it was seen to be based on scientific and rational knowledge. In contrast, traditional healing has been marginalised because the colonial perception was that it was based on mystical and magical religious beliefs (Freeman and Motsei, 1992). The mystery associated with the methods of acquiring knowledge of traditional healing was demonstrated by a Zimbabwean female-traditional healer when she described how she became a healer after crossing the crocodile infested Zambezi river whilst being possessed by a spirit.

"The journey was dangerous. Crossing the Zambezi escarpment, the eagles were my tour guide. I arrived at the Caborra Bassa Island and the Mozambicans said MuZimbabweano Muzimbabweano (look at that Zimbabwean, look at that Zimbabwean). I was now swimming and walking where I could not swim. I couldn't stop my legs from walking. I now settled at this Island, seeing hippopotamus bathing in the Zambezi river, eating mostly see food and leaves from the forest surrounding us. I would also do domestic duties such as pounding millet as there are no grinding mills there. At the end of my stay, I went back home and started healing using herbs that I never knew before and I had not been taught about herbs in Mozambique. The knowledge of herbs just came as soon as I arrived back in Zimbabwe from Mozambique" (Female traditional healer 1)[140].

---

140 Interview with traditional healer 1 was conducted in Shona in Harare at ZINATHA headquarters on 11 February 2005 and translated in to English

In this regard, Reynolds (1996) in her study on Traditional Healers and Childhood in Zimbabwe notes that children in her study believed that to become a traditional Healer (n'anga) one must be possessed by an ancestral or njuzu (maimed) spirit and taught about healing through dreams. Others believed that the ability is inherited or learnt from a n'anga or it can be bought.

Traditional healers in Tanzania are inducted in similar ways, through: inheritance within a family kinship; ancestor-spirits (*midzimu*), dreams, the experience of having an illness cured by traditional medicine and through a personal decision, followed by a period of apprenticeship (Gessler et al., 1995)

These traditional ways of acquiring healing methods appear to baffle practitioners of biomedicine who have acquired their knowledge through scientific means.

6.15.5 Colonial reinterpretation of the work of traditional healers

N'angas or vana chiremba are healers who use the knowledge of herbs, plants and 'throwing bones' to heal (Chavunduka, 1998). Chavunduka (1998) further notes that n'angas (*plural*) can also be possessed by healing spirits but as Jeater (2006) comments, in defining n'anga (*singular*) most western authors tended to downplay or disregard the spiritual aspects in a n'anga.

During the colonial era, the white population described n'angas as witchdoctors and bone throwers. "While the term 'witchdoctor ' at least gave some indication of the status and role of the diviner in the African communities, the term 'bone thrower' was a product of the white imagination. It lacked the implications of healing, knowledge of herbs and support in times of calamity, which formed the mainstay of the work of the n'anga or chiremba. It was a highly emotive term, suggesting barbarism, savagery and superstition" (Jeater, 2006, p.136).

Due to the confusion brought about by the colonial reinterpretation of what traditional healers do, many people in Zimbabwe including ex-combatants associate n'angas with witchcraft (*varoyi*). Since people cannot bewitch themselves, only others are responsible for someone's setback. To this extent, witchcraft accusations have several social functions that serve to expose problems within social relationships.

Thus religious traditional healers are the ones who gained respect and still do among the ex-combatants. Apart from the crucial roles that spirit mediums played in directing the liberation struggle, what draws ex-combatants and civilians to spirit mediums appear to be the way spirit mediums acquired healing knowledge – inheritance within a family kinship.

6.16.Traditional Religion and limitations

While traditional processes of healing have been recognised, it is also important to acknowledge their limits. Honwana (1998) notes that the extreme disruptions in terms of social change, political change, displacement and economic hardship have been important factors shaping and inhibiting healing processes. In communities where people were killed by their neighbours and families divided for long periods of time; where people can no longer muster the resources necessary to carry out ceremonies properly, and where the reputation of traditional leaders was compromised during the war, the effectiveness of customary remedies becomes questionable.

6.17 Coping strategies

How the patients (including family board members) appraise their situation or illness influenced both by environmental demands and individual beliefs and values are the primary determinants of how they cope.

In this sense the female traditional healer and the female patients tried to make sense of their problems, by helping and empathising with one another against the background of poverty and female subordination.

In a study of white displaced farmers in Zimbabwe, Knight (2006) notes that making meaning is a coping strategy that entails both a reappraisal and reinterpretation of not only the event but also the context of the event in a person's life.

Conclusion

Out of the ten ex-combatants and 2 civilians interviewed, one ex-combatant talked about physical wounds.

> *I got shot on my left leg and my arms one is shorter than the other one and I was left with some fragments which are still in my body but they have removed one of the bullets which was in my left leg in Zimbabwe (Female ex-combatat in the UK)[141].*

The rest of the ex-combatants and civilians talked about psychological wounds. Traditional healers also explained that they saw patients suffering from psychological wounds. It appears that more people are affected by psychological than physical wounds. To this end, Traditional, Christian and Western approaches have been employed towards healing the psychological wounds of ex-combatants and the civilians after the traumatic experiences of the liberation struggle in Zimbabwe.

Although ex-combatants and civilians have consulted western medicine, its use is only partial because many patients still consult with spirit mediums and n'angas after their hospitalisation to complete their treatment, and perhaps to determine why they became ill. In this regard where treatment is sought depends on the understanding and the patient's perception of the causes and nature of the illness.

At the time of this study, some women still exhibited signs of war traumas. However, religious traditional healers' rituals have contributed to the maintenance and restoration of well being in the community to others as explained,

> *The trouble of seeking help from the church is that the woman has to continuously go to church, when she gets tired, the problems resurface. We, the traditional healers perform rituals that will cure the person and the problems are solved for good. (Female traditional healer 1)[142]*

> *"I am aware that quite a number of patients who were treated and felt that they were healed came back to thank the healer" (Male professional G)[143]*

---

141   Interview was conducted in UK at the participant's house on 10 March 2006 in English and Shona and was translated in to English and quoted verbatim

142   Interview with traditional healer 1 was conducted in Shona in Harare at ZINATHA headquarters on 11 February 2005 and translated in to English

143   Interview was conducted in English at the participant's house on the 13th of February, 2005 and quoted verbatim

Treatment and prevention have focused upon the quality of human relationships and social interaction. To this extent, healers have provided their patients with moral and social guidelines to prevent them from experiencing social setbacks or catching the same illness again.

In this regard, the prevalence of customary healing rituals bear witness to the capacity of those affected by war to harness local cultural and institutional resourcefulness to address their problems (Honwana, 1997). In addition to the assistance that came from the Government through ZINATHA, people use means available to them to heal the social wounds of war and to restore stability in their communities. They do not wait for outsiders to come and meet their needs.

As western and traditional medicines represent very different conceptual frameworks to healing psychological wounds, sensitivity to the political, environmental, cultural and economic contexts is crucial to the success of collaborative interventions. In this respect, it is important to try to bridge the language and value divide between modern western and traditional medicine because people make use of both systems. A traditional healer points to the importance of collaborative healing.

> *"There is Western medicine, there are us n'angas (traditional healers) and there is vapostori (African Independent church prophets). All the methods serve their purposes. There is need for all of us to work together to give our patients the best. Even though our ways of helping the patients are different, what is required is respect for each other's methods and acceptance of a problem which is beyond each other's knowledge. Then the patient can be transferred to the healer who can help, be it a western doctor or n'anga or vapostori"* (Male traditional healer 3).[144]

6.19. Contribution of the study to healing

The study shows that in order to restore the women to wellbeing in a more meaningful way, there is need to use collective healing approaches, be they western or traditional or indeed a combination of both. In this regard findings of this study mirror those found in a study by Shaw (2002) in to refugees and rituals in Sierra Leone. Shaw's (2002) study indicates that local diviners may have as big a role to play as Western trauma therapists. This study provides a pointer to possible directions in which post-conflict research on healing might move. The study further shows that in addition to church healing, western and traditional healing may both be applied in some situations especially after understanding the differences between cultural and western health concepts and appreciating the contribution of both frameworks to the restoration of well being.

However, some traditional healers may find that patients who experience some healing at the initial stages will consult the traditional healers again as some war traumas may surface and resurface in varying order, intensity, and duration. Some American veterans who served in the Vietnam war more than three decades ago still experience post-traumatic stress disorders associated with flashbacks of the horrors of war (Center for Disease Control, 1988; Kulka et al., 1990). With life expectancy at 34 for women, researchers face challenges in obtaining information about the effectiveness of traditional healing in the long term.

---

144   Interview with traditional healer 3 was conducted in Shona in Harare at ZINATHA headquarters on 11 February 2005 and translated in to English

Chapter Seven: Conclusion

7.1 Introduction

This thesis argues that although women of Zimbabwe took up arms to fight alongside men to achieve freedom, they are not liberated because one of the elements in liberation is freedom to get health care. However after achieving independence the women ex-combatants have not received adequate healthcare from the government in order to heal the physical and psychological 'wounds' they suffered during the 1975 to 1990 war. Further, the government has not educated the nation about women ex-combatants in a culture that sees women primarily as mothers, wives and daughters, not fighters, leaving women ex-combatants unaccepted and traumatised. As a result the women were not able to fully enjoy the gains of the liberation struggle because any meaningful development of a nation depends on the health of its people and an understanding of what the women ex-combatants went through in order to achieve national independence. In recent years other economic, political and social issues such as the economic meltdown, the civil unrest, the aids pandemic and poverty have confused the picture.

7.2 The liberation struggle.

Rather than remaining victims of colonial conquest, men and women created their own history by learning that dignity and equality were more important than life and in this regard they risked their lives to achieve recognition of their humanity through the liberation struggle. The dignity, humanity and freedom that men and women sought through the revolutionary violence had health consequences, which they never thought about nor knew, at the beginning of the liberation struggle.

As the liberation struggle progressed the health of both male and female ex-combatants was affected by violence, hunger, diseases, lack of water, lack of sleep, the witnessing of dead bodies, and seeing people being killed. While the colonial Government and guerrillas killed each other, civilians were caught in the middle and they were killed too. Although the liberation struggle brought death, injury, disability, migraine - a type which they had never known existed - hiccups, *matekenya* - worms that ate flesh between toes or other closed parts of the body to both male and female ex-combatants - this study has revealed for the first time the range of unexplained and stress related illnesses – including *hurricanes* - a mysterious disease with no medical explanation - that women ex combatants in particular, suffered. Further, women suffered health effects associated with biological differences between women and men.

Women survived *madef* – cessation of menses, skin rashes, the brutality of rape, torture, sexual exploitation and unwanted pregnancies and became more vulnerable to health and mental health concerns than men were because women's bodies were employed as tools of war despite the sexual code that forbade rapes. However, there was difference of opinions between peasant women ex-combatants and the elite women ex-combatants regarding the different experiences in the camps. The peasant women ex-combatants apportioned blame between men and women towards the issue of rape as they argued that women needed to protect themselves. Peasant women do not appear to have taken in to account the concept of power over powerlessness when women were raped. The educated elite women found that their interests were in opposition to men's as they were bombed and given military training when more women, untrained to fight, had been killed.

Later women combatants were to find that they were traumatised through out the liberation struggle and in independent Zimbabwe because of the physical and psychological 'wounds', oppression and exploitation from the war, fellow comrades and ZANLA male leadership. These experiences were rooted in political and social relations. It appears that the injustices that women suffered were embedded in the Marxist theory that Lise Vogel (1983) describes and points to patriarchy as the main cause of oppression and exploitation of women. The oppression of women combatants then raises questions on the application and role of the Marxist-Leninist-Maoist ideology that ZANU had adopted at the beginning of the revolutionary struggle against the colonial settlers. While the same ideology was instrumental to the process of overthrowing the settlers, it also created a different class exploitation of women within the ZANU-ZANLA black movement based on gender and sex. However, there were times too when on one hand women oppressed and on the other helped each other. Class differences in women also contributed to the distresses experienced by other women especially when senior women organised younger girls to sleep with male commanders. On the other, it was the class of educated women that led to a successful rebellion against the practice of carrying war materials without being trained to fight. Thus, this study challenges Nhongo's findings that all women were treated the same irrespective of their back grounds as ZANU leadership had warned women who challenged gender issues that they risked official ostracism. After the rebellion some women combatants, including those of middle class origin, rose to the positions of commanders and led battalions.

In addition to the physical and psychological wounds, women ex-combatants' perception of the war is that it has disadvantaged them in terms of marriages, being able to conceive and have children, being unable to be good parents, being stigmatised and looked down upon – issues that have left the women in a perpetual distress.

In this thesis I have demonstrated that the traumas that women ex-combatants are experiencing arose from the difficulties women experienced when they were - crossing the rivers, displaced, faced with poor conditions in the camps that included rapes, hunger, diseases and lack of cotton pads for menstruation, given subordinate roles during the war based on gender discrimination and class exploitation.

7.3 Rape and fertility

Fellow comrades as well as senior commanders who were supposed to protect female combatants raped them. People that the women trusted abused and betrayed them.

The women ex-combatants believe that women who were raped became infertile and were not able to bear children later. In this sense, the women are suffering the war traumas of being raped during the liberation struggle and becoming infertile due to the sexual abuses they suffered.

In addition, forced unprotected sexual relations meant that women were further put at risk of contracting sexually transmitted diseases including HIV and yet the women are the ones who were regarded as loose and the carriers of the diseases. Indeed during the First World War working class women were perceived as polluting and as reservoirs of sexual infection (Davidson and Hall, 2001).

7.3.1 Rape and impunity

Rape has continued to affect women in Zimbabwe because men have not accepted that rapes took place during the liberation struggle. Men's refusal to accept the responsibility that comes with their actions appears to be rooted in the assumption that women are there to please men at whatever cost including their health. In this respect, the programmes to raise consciousness in women's health needs do not stop the sexual brutality against women that men appear to present as a natural fact of life. If the rapists discovered that their actions came with a price, perhaps women would be spared further sexual attacks and they would begin to concentrate on how to heal their war traumas and get involved in development programmes in order to rebuild their lives and that of the society.

7.3.2 Women's voices

Although women's voices are critical to their health needs most women who participated in the liberation struggle approached by the author were afraid to speak out publicly because they felt that sharing their war experiences would expose them to more violence. Their voices would become targets. Some women ex-combatants refused to acknowledge that they fought in the liberation struggle. These women could be somebody's wife, mother, nurse, work colleague or one's neighbour. The women have camouflaged themselves and may not be identified as ex-combatants because of fearing what might happen to them if they told the truth of their war experiences. What these women ex-combatants have done is to keep quiet about who they are. Once they were proud to be known that they were liberators of their nation and women but today they conceal that part of their identity leaving them psychologically ' bruised'. In this regard, the public space available to women shrinks, taking away whatever gains women thought they had achieved by fighting alongside men. In this respect women are left hopeless and helpless, a situation that triggers their war traumas and reminds the women that the freedom they thought they would get by joining the revolution never came. Instead what came was lack of support to address the health consequences of war.

The women living in silence afraid of mentioning what happened to them are carrying a 'heavy burden' of the liberation struggle as memories of the violence they experienced refuse to be banished. Those who talked about their war experiences reacted differently to emotions that inevitably surface during such sensitive topics. Some appeared to have lost their minds, others talked for a short duration unwilling to participate any further. Female ex-combatants feel forgotten for their roles during the struggle. The women explained that they have lost trust and faith in the leadership for which they sacrificed their lives and that of their children.

7.4 Witchcraft accusations and the impact on the health of women

The colonial Government's tactics of discrediting the effectiveness of African religion by poisoning food, water, and clothes and by causing disappearances had psychological traumas on women. Rather than questioning the ability of African religion to protect and advise the guerrillas, women became the scapegoat.

Guerrillas blamed women for having caused the deaths of other guerrillas when the guerrillas got killed by soldiers or died from eating poisoned food and drinking poisoned water and when husbands or children disappeared during the liberation struggle. Women were accused of having caused these misfortunes through witchcraft since in the African religion there is no event that takes place in a vacuum. Most of the women accused of witchcraft were killed by the guerrillas. The psychological trauma of witchcraft accusations affected the well being of the women and their families. In this respect, the societal attitudes over women have not only affected the women's position in society but their health as well.

7.5 The Long term physical and psychological wounds

While some women experienced irregular menstrual cycles the other health problems the women are experiencing now include the psychological disturbances such as nightmares, depression, stigma, illness and difficulty in coping with the war experiences. Torture and rape have stripped the women's bodies and 'souls' and replaced security and confidence with fear and shame.

The consequences of rape affect not only the victims, but also their families and society long after the conflict ends. Raping women increases the likelihood of reproductive health problems including unwanted pregnancies and responsibilities. Further babies born as a result of rape are constant reminders of a painful period and happiness that babies should bring turn to despair. Thus while physical scarring can heal, given time, psychological scars last a long time.

As the ex-combatants reflect on their war experiences, they feel that they were abused at every opportunity. The initial excitement of being able to do something about the oppression they were experiencing at home and the reality that awaited them after independence are like two parallels. The health problems that women are experiencing now make them regret having gone to war and they suggest that other ways of solving disputes should be sought.

7.5.1 Traumas of displacement and loss

Both female ex-combatants and civilian women suffered traumas of displacement. The destruction of the civilian homes, assets and the creation of the protected villages meant that the African pattern of living was destroyed and the very social fabric so important to the African women was destroyed. This work supports the observation made by CCPJZ (1999) that the disruption of life impacted on the health of the women whose lives are guided by the African norms contained in an African home. The disruption of the lives of women ex –combatants can be likened to that seen in refugees from many countries where people have been displaced by wars. The refugees often experience a double effect of trauma - up to one-third of refugees report an experience of torture - as well as displacement and dislocation from the culture and community that usually supports them (Reeler et al., 2001). To this extent, the disruptions to the social support systems in times of war create a situation of "on-going stress", and some Southern African workers now talk about the "continuous stress syndrome" (Straker, 1992).

The destruction of civilian homes, harvested grains and the burning of field crops can be likened to what Daneel (1998) termed an invasion of the inner soul of those who had grown up and had their livelihoods depended on them. The Government's inclination to give priority to political liberation an attitude of 'first sort out politics and then the other issues' failed to realise that the quality of the women's lives was interwoven with their belongings which were lost during the liberation struggle. Parkinson (1993) notes that the relationship between loss and trauma is similar to the stress reactions produced by traumatic reactions of bereavement and grief. This is because experiencing traumatic incidents means loss and loss is an inevitable consequence of human life. In this regard, loss impacted women in terms of physical, psychological, social, sexual and spiritual functioning, and was thus related to the subsequent health and well being of the individual. In terms of the social functioning, loss also impacted family systems and disrupted normal social relationships, thus potentially disintegrating social support networks. In this regard Payne et al. (2000) note that it is common for people to experience overwhelming feelings of isolation following a loss, even when surrounded by others. To this extent, women ex-combatants further felt isolated when they were not accepted in to civilian life and civilian women displayed emotions of anger for having been forgotten.

Payne et al. (2000) note that following the isolation are emotions of anger and hostility. The anger, hostility and loss, may be expressed more generally towards an 'unfair God' (Payne et al., 2000).

7. 5.2 Traumatic events and sense of control

The traumatic events destroyed the women's fundamental assumptions about safety of the world, the positive value of the self, and the meaningful order of creation. It takes a long time to rebuild an inner foundation of basic trust when people have encountered human evil in a frightening form such as in the liberation struggle. The women knew some of the perpetrators and Janoff-Bulman (1985) observes that when the perpetrators are neighbours and former friends, faith to humanity is challenged. During the liberation struggle, the people who were fellow comrades in arms and people who were known to the women were suddenly raping them, and promises of a free Zimbabwe by political leaders were never fulfilled. People whom they never dreamed would behave in such a way turned on the women or let them down. Agger and Mimica's (1996) study on betrayals in war times point out that betrayals such as these, threaten one's core beliefs and lead to an existential crisis and a loss of trust in humanity. They reported an intense sense of betrayal in their study of two thousand women in psychosocial programmes at the end of the Bosnia Herzegovina and Croatia war.

7.6 Women ex-combatants and integration

Women ex-combatants felt isolated when they were not accepted in to civilian life. Payne et al. (2000) note that following the isolation are emotions of anger and hostility. The anger, hostility and loss, may be expressed more generally towards an 'unfair God' (Payne et al., 2000). In this regard women are suffering from the chronic stress described by McLean and Link (1994) as strains that derive from societal responses to characteristics of a person that include her as a class of person such as sexism. In this regard women ex-combatants are classified as unnatural females because of male roles they performed during the liberation struggle. Classifying women ex-combatants as unnatural could be a result of men fearing that after the liberation struggle, women if left to do so, would occupy their positions of authority which they had always enjoyed in the traditional religion. These views were observed in Britain when the Amalgamated Society of Engineers (ASE), signed an agreement with the Government that all women dilutees would be forced out at the end of World War 1 as part of the return to the status quo (Woollacott, 1994).

After the liberation struggle, the return to the status quo also meant the expectation that women would start bearing children. There are women ex-combatants who are living with the stigma attached to barren women by the African religion. Although men can also be infertile, it is only the women who are stigmatised.

Infertility and the violent behaviour in women ex-combatants became barriers in being accepted. To this extent the violent behaviour demanded by wars is in conflict with the socially constructed gendered expectations of "femaleness", norms and socialisation patterns. Thus the image of woman as the mother, wife and the goddess of peace, retains its power in spite of women's active military involvement because it symbolises qualities that fend off the barbarism implicit in war (Higonnet et al., 1987). Because of the nurturing instinct in women, femininity has the possibility of restoring peace. However the societal expectations, combined with war traumas, have left the women with perpetual psychological illnesses that prevent them from working towards peace restoration and their own development. Payne, et al. (2000) observe that when neither resistance nor escape is possible, the human system of self-defense becomes overwhelmed and disorganised – a situation that leads to helplessness. Van der Kolk (1987) notes that helplessness shares many features with depression and the affected people often develop chronic stress

Thus in addition to war traumas, women also suffer from societal gender views, expectations and betrayal. In this regard the health of each woman ex-combatant is a combination of war traumas, a degree of choice and chance filtered through complex meanings of the Shona culture of which she is a part and the significant influences within it. Avison and Gotlib (1994); Chesney and Rosenman (1983); Payne et al. (2000); Sapolsky (1994) observe that social and psychological sources of trauma influence health outcomes. To this extent whichever healing therapies are adopted in the transition from war to peacetime, they must also address the psychosocial effects of war on women ex-combatants because the trauma and pain have afflicted not only individuals but also their families. As the trauma and pain became widespread and ongoing, they affected entire communities. In this regard 'healing' goes beyond the alleviation of individual traumas'. It includes the mending of the social divisions, which exist both within and between communities. To this extent, healing processes must be supported, not only because it is the right thing to do, but also because in the midst of the suffering that women endure during and after conflicts, women continue to hold their families and communities together.

Despite what they have experienced, many women ex-combatants expressed the wish to have their physical and psychological wounds healed in order to rebuild their lives and contribute to peace initiatives. The women have recognised that war is not the solution to problems and that the well being of people can not be achieved through violence or humiliation of one another. In this regard, women are showing that suffering can be transformed into a force that would build a more secure future for humanity and that they also want to be shapers of their own health, development and peace processes in their country. With help from others, the healing of the traumatic wounds and the grieving process of all the losses can be facilitated and the rebuilding of the shattered lives can begin. How quickly one is able to rebuild the practical realities in life, such as one's house, livestock, getting a job, settling down in marriages, getting children to schools, accessibility to health centres and the possibility of feeling safe and accepted will greatly influence the healing process.

7.7 Healing processes

Winter (1995) in his study about commemoration as a healing process after the First World War notes that the one experience shared by survivors of war regardless of socio-economic status, educational attainment, or political tendency, is that of bereavement. To this extent, women from all classes - the ex-combatants and the civilians, who were caught up in the middle, have turned to western or traditional religion for healing. They have also turned to churches. Although traditional religion, western biomedicine and Christianity have played an important part in supporting ex-combatants and civilians, they face challenges in meeting the health needs of the women.

7.7.1 African religion

This research has shown that the psychological traumas of the liberation struggle are linked to the power and anger of the spirits of the dead who were wrongfully killed or not accorded proper burial rites. The bitter spirits are considered harmful to their killers and passers-by. Thus cleansing and purification rituals have played an important part towards healing of individuals, families and reintegrating the communities. However African religion still regards women as minors to the extent that they have no control over their health needs without the authority of male representatives. A female n'anga highlights how the restrictive measures in the Shona culture have led women to come out with alternative ways to meet their health needs by breaking the rule; the rule of being represented by males. Female traditional healers have sought guidance direct from ancestral spirits on how to help female sufferers without male representation. What now threaten the female traditional healers to continuously provide healing to women are economic hardships. The female traditional healers have to look for other means to support themselves because the women they heal are not able to pay for the health treatment they receive, as they are poor.

7.7.2 Biomedicine

Although women ex-combatants and civilian women have made use of Western medicine, they have found out that it does not fully meet their health needs because in the tradition, an illness is not an individual affair. To this extent, Western models have been criticised for their strict considerations of the person as a self-contained entity, an individual completely independent of others (Brackken et al., 1995). In this way, many challenges are raised when research on trauma and posttraumatic experiences have to be done with traumatised people from societies where the individual is conceived as part of an extended living and a dead family, special group, or community. In addition, the traumatic experiences are not strictly confined to their overwhelming impact on the individual psyche. With few doubts a broader conceptualisation of trauma is needed in which loss or disintegration of cultural beliefs and values should be considered as traumatic experience too (Igreja et al., 1999).

7.7.3 Christianity

When traditional religion and western biomedicine are not able to meet the health needs of the women, they have turned to Christianity. More women than men consult faith healers. Thompson (1978) notes that men assign to religion the function of legitimising their own life pattern and situation in the world. However After independence other ex-combatants have blamed Christianity because the perception is that from the colonial era up to the present, it has continued to distort the meaning of traditional healing, called it a pagan religion and yet during the struggle African religion played an important part. To this extent Christianity has left some patients confused and given Western healing approach legitimacy over the African religion.

Whichever healing approach one takes, indicates that ex-combatants are living with traumatic experiences of the liberation struggle which carry with them pain that affects not only the bodies, but the 'hearts and minds' of those who suffered.

7.8 Contribution of the study to the understanding of war trauma

The liberation struggle has left women suffering from long term health issues. Many women who are not married have attributed these circumstances to the social stigmas attached to women ex-combatants.

Research done on women and healing in post conflict nations may include but are not limited to the selected countries. Studies conducted in Sudan show that women from the North and the South took the initiative to come together across ethnic and religious divides to talk about healing and building peace (UNIFEM, 2002). In Ghana women refugees from Liberia learned construction skills through a United Nations Development Fund for Women (UNIFEM)-supported schemes. In South Africa the Truth and Reconciliation Commission was established as a step towards ending impunity (UNIFEM, 2002).

In the former Yugoslavia the medical practitioners have utilised community integration as a healing process to empower women and help them adapt to the new social context (Gutlove and Thompson 2003). Women were engaged with volunteer action and being active and helping others contributed to the restoration of worthiness in the women (Gutlove and Thompson 2003).

In Rwanda work done in the aftermath of the genocide included discussions in small groups about experiences of the conflict. Lectures were also conducted to help victims understand why the genocide occurred, what effects these types of experiences could have on individuals and communities, and how healing could be achieved (Staub, 2000). Surveys conducted two months after the treatment indicated that trauma scores were lower in the group treated through integrated community programmes than trauma scores in the control group (Kester, 2001).The treatment group also exhibited a willingness to forgive perpetrators, provided they acknowledged what they had done.

While these initiatives can be extended and adopted to assist women achieve well being in Algeria, Mozambique, Guinea-Bisau and Cape Verde, Angola and Namibia where women have fought in liberation struggles and experienced war traumas similar to those experienced by women in Zimbabwe, the same initiatives can not be applied to Zimbabwe. This is because Zimbabwe is now a closed country from the outside world due to the political climate presently prevailing in that country. In this respect, the necessary financial and technical support needed for rehabilitation and other health development processes are withheld by the countries in a position to do so. Although African religion and traditional healing help the women to some extent, these have their limitations. Most family members who could provide social networks have migrated.

The contribution of this study to the world of knowledge is its findings about the illnesses and traumas that women ex-combatants experienced during and after independence. Further where women's voices about their war traumas have been heard in other post conflict countries, healing has been facilitated. In Zimbabwe details of rape traumas in women ex-combatants have not been acknowledged and accepted by the Government in order to facilitate healing processes. This has meant that women have been afraid to reveal the full extent of rape abuses that took place during the liberation struggle. Although trauma cannot be erased, providing the space for the women to be heard in a safe environment can give the women a feeling that they have control over their lives again and can contribute to psychological healing and social reconstruction.

Further, both ex-combatants and civilians have not been taught about war traumas in order to rehabilitate ex-combatants in particular female ex-combatants. Rehabilitation programmes are tailored towards an understanding of what war traumas are and elimination of stigma attached to female ex-combatants.

For Zimbabwe to heal, women need to reveal the full depth of their experiences, first to themselves and then to the nation that should understand the universal and culturally specific ways that war traumas are experienced and processed by individuals, families and the culture. In this respect where western knowledge and practices are applicable, they should be used to complement, rather than replace, established social and cultural healing (Wessells, 11th October 2007, www.child-soldiers.org/resources/psychosocial). Thus Western practitioners can learn from traditional healers who understand that in the traditional culture, when one is ill, she suffers with the whole family. This awareness could be incorporated in the medical provision given to the sufferers. An interface between biomedicine approaches and traditional approaches could be more helpful. Religious healing - Christian and traditional - in Zimbabwe becomes an important integral part of the healing processes because it promotes holistic 'healing' through the concepts of forgiveness and reconciliation.

In addition the Government ought to take responsibility of what happened to the women during the liberation struggle. Unless the full extent of the women's war traumas is recognised, Zimbabwe will remain a traumatised nation.

Women who shared their war experiences did so in the hope that their war traumas would be understood and their health needs would be addressed. The women also wanted their sacrifices and contributions to be recognised and acknowledged as an important part of the history of the liberation struggle.

Further research may look at the health impact of war traumas on the children of ex-combatants and civilian women traumatised by events of the liberation struggle. This becomes an important study when one considers that children are the nation's future leaders.

Bibliography

Sources are listed in the following order:
* Literature
* On-line sources
* Theses
* Newspaper articles
* Organisations

Adebayo A. (Ed.) (1999) Comprehending and Mastering African Conflicts, The search for Sustainable Peace and Good Governance, Zed Books London.

Afshar, H. (1993) Women in the middle East, Macmillan Press.

Agger, I. and Mimica, J. (1996) 'Psychosocial assistance to victims of war in Bosnia and Herzegovina and Croatia, an evaluation' Women in Emergencies, European Community Humanitarian Office (ECHO) Brussels.

Alexander, J. (1996) 'Things Fall Apart, the Centre Can Hold: Processes of post-war political change in Zimbabwe's rural areas', in Bhebe, N. and Rangers, T. (eds) Society in Zimbabwe's Liberation War, James Currey, Oxford.

Alexander, J., McGregor, J., and Ranger, T. (2000) Violence and Memory: One Hundred Years in the 'Dark Forests' of Matabeleland. Heinemann, Portsmouth.

Allcock, J. B. et al. (1998) Conflict in the Former Yugoslavia , Published by ABC Clio, California.

Altheide, D. (1996) Qualitative Media Analysis, Sage Publications, Inc.

Amani Trust (1997) 'Survivors of Torture in Mount Darwin District, Mashonaland Central', Report prepared by the Amani Trust, Harare.

Aranha, J. (2002) Traditional Dwellings and Settlements Working Paper Series 2002-2003, Colonial Hybridity, Vol. 143, pp. 23 - 47, Berkeley, CA.

Archibald, H. C. and Tuddenham, R. D. (1965) Principles of Preventive Psychiatry, Basic Books, New York.

Arendt, H. (1969) On Violence, New York: Harcourt, Brace and World.Arksey, H. and Knghit, P. (1999) Interviewing for social Scientists, Sage Publications, London.

Avison,W.R., and Gotlib,I.H. (1994) Stress and mental health. Contemporary issues and prospects for the future, Plenum Press New York.

Bailey, K.D.(1994) Methods of Social Research, Published by the Free Press, New York.

Baker, H. (1977) Cecil Rhodes: the man and his dream, published by Books of Rhodesia, Bulawayo.

Baker, M.W. and Gaskell, G. (2000) Qualitative Researching with Text, Image, and Sound, Sage Publications.

Baker, T.L. (1994) Doing Social Research (2nd Edn.), New York: McGraw-Hill Inc.

Ball, M. S. and Smith, G.W.H. (1992) Analyzing Visual Data, Qualitative Research Methods, Series 24, Newbury Park, CA: Sage Banister, P., Burman, E., Parker, I., Taylor, T. and Tindall, C. (1999) Qualitative methods in psychology: A research guide, Buckingham: Open University Press.

Barbalet, J.M. (1985) "Power and Resistance", The British Journal of Sociology, 36 (4): 531-548.

Barry, U. (1986) Lifting the Lid: Handbook of Facts and Information on Ireland, Attic Press, Dublin.

Barnes, B. (1988) The Elements of Social Theory, UCL Press.

Bell, J. (1999) Doing Your Research Project, Open University Press. Buckingham.

Belle, D. (1982) Lives in Stress: Women and Depression, Sage Publications.

Bhebe, N. and Ranger, T. (Eds.) (1995) Soldiers in Zimbabwe's Liberation War, Volume One, James Currey, London.

Bhebe, N. and Ranger, T. (Eds.) (1996) Soldiers in Zimbabwe's Liberation War, Volume Two, University of Zimbabwe Publications.

Bhebe, N. (1999) ZAPU and ZANU Guerrilla Warfare and the Evangelical Lutheran Church in Zimbabwe, Mambo Press, Harare.

Bingham, A. (2005) "The British popular press and venereal disease during the Second World War", Historical Journal, 48 (4): 1055-76.

Blake, R. (1978) A History of Rhodesia, Alfred Knopf, New York.

Bourdillon, M. F. C. (1984/5) Religious symbols and political change. Zambezia, 12: 39-54.

Boehmer, E. (1998) The White Man's Burden, Oxford University Press.

Bowling, A. (1977) Research Methods in Health, Open University Press.

Boyden, J., (1994) 'Children's Experience of Conflict Related Emergencies: Some Implications for Relief Policy and Practice' Disasters 18 (3).

Boyden, J. and Gibbs, S. (1997) Children of War: Responses to Psycho-Social Distress in Cambodia', The United Nations Research Institute for Social Development, Geneva.

Bracken, P., Giller, J. & Summerfield, D. (1995) Psychological Responses to War and Atrocity; The Limitations of Current Concepts, Social Science and Medicine, Vol. 40, No. 8,1073-1082.

Bracken, P. & Petty, C. (1998) Rethinking the Trauma of War, Free Association Press, New York.

Braham, R. L. (1988) The Politics of Genocide: The Holocaust in Hungary, Syracuse University Press, New York

Brannen, J. (1988) "The Study of Sensitive Subjects", Sociological Review, 36 (3): 552-63.

Brayborn, G. and Summerfield, P. (1987) Out of the Cage, published by Rourtledge and Kegan Paul. Ltd.

Braybon, G. (1981) Women Workers in the First World War: The British Experience, Croom Helm, London.

Bremmer et al. (1992) "Dissociation and posttraumatic stress disorder in Vietnam combat veterans" American journal of psychiatry, 149:328-332.

Brickhill, J. (1995) 'Making peace with the past: War victims and the work of the Mafela Trust' in N. Bhebe and T. Ranger (eds.) Soldiers in Zimbabwe's Liberation War, Vol.I (Harare, University of Zimbabwe Publications). Plenum Press, New York.

Brown, G. (1997) Oral Marketing Research with Black Women, Sage Publications, California.

Bruner, J. (1986) Reflexivity and Narratives in Action Research, Colombia Press.

Buckley, T. and Gottlieb, A. (1988) Blood Magic, University of California Press.

Bulhan, H. A., (1985) Frantz Fanon and the psychology of oppression, Plenum Press, New York.

Burke, P. (1992) History and Social Theory, Published by Polity Press in association with Blackwell Publishers.

Burman, E. (1994). 'Innocents Abroad: Western Fantasies of Childhood and Iconography of Emergencies' Disasters Vol. 18, No. 3.

Bystydzienski, J. M. and Sekhon, J. (Eds) (1999) Democratization and Women's Grassroots Movements, Indiana State University Press, Bloomington.

Cabrera, M. (2002) 'Living and Surviving In A Multiply Wounded Country', A paper presented to Womankind, London.

Canive, J. M. and Castillo, D. (1997) "Hispanic Veterans Diagnosed with PTSD: Assessment and Treatment Issues", NCP Clinical Quarterly 7(1): 12-15.

Chavunduka, G. L. (1998) The Professionalisation Of Traditional Medicine In Zimbabwe, Jongwe Printing and Publishing Company, Harare.

Chavuduka, G.L. (1999) Christianity, African Religion and African Medicine, a paper presented at The World Council of Churches, Harare.

Chesney, M.A. and Rosenman, R.H. (1983) Specificity in stress models from Type A behaviour , John Wiley & Sons, New York.

Cheater, A. and Gaidzanwa, R (1996) "Citizenship in Neo-patrilineal States: Gender and Mobility in Southern Africa", Journal of Southern African Studies 22 (2): 189-200.

Chikara, F and Manley, M.R.S. (1991) "Psychiatry in Zimbabwe", Journal of in Hospital and Community Psychiatry, 42 (9): 943-947.

Chingono, H.(1999) Ian Smith and UDI, A written paper, Centre for Defence Studies, University of Zimbabwe.

Chung, F. (1989) "Education with production before and after independence'
211-224 in Turmoil and Tenaci, Banana, C. S. (Ed.), The College Press, Ltd, Harare.

Cliff, T. (1984) Class Struggle and Women's Liberation. London, Blackwell.

Cock, J. (1992) Women and War in South Africa, London: Open Letters.

Cohn, N. (1993) Europe's Inner Demons: An Inquiry Inspired by the Great Witch Hunt, Pimlico, New York.

Connelly, F. et al. (1984) My Country is the Whole World, Pandora Press, London.

Connelly, F.M. and Clandinin, D.J. (1990) "Stories of Experience and
Narrative Inquiry", Educational Researcher, 19 (5), 2-14.

Coote, A. and Campbell, B. (1982) Sweet Freedom: The Struggle For Women's Liberation, Pan Books, Ltd, London.

Cosslett, T., Easton A. and Summerfield, P. (Eds.) (1996) Women, Power, and Resistance, Open University Press.

Cotterill, P. (1992) "Interviewing Women: Issues of Friendship, Vulnerability, and Power." Women's Studies International Forum, 15: 593-606.

Cowans, J. (1998) "Visions of The Postwar: The Politics of Memory and Expectation in 1940's France", History and memory Journal, 10.

Creswell, J. W. (1994) Research Design: Qualitative and Quantitative Approaches. SAGE, Thousand Oaks, CA.

Crotty, M. (1998) The Foundations of Social Research, Sage Publications, London.

Daneel, M.L., 1990. Exorcism as a means of combating wizardry: liberation or enslavement?, Missionalia, 18 (1): 220-247.

Daneel, I. (1998) African Earthkeepers in Interfaith Mission in Earth Care, (1), Unisa Press, Pretoria.

Davies, M. (1983) Third World-Second Sex: Women's Struggles and
National Liberation, Zed Books, London.

Davies, M. (1994), Women and Violence, Published by Zed Books

Davidson R ad Hall L.A. (Eds.) (2001) Sex, sin and suffering: venereal disease and European society since 1870. Routledge, London.

Des Pres, T. (1976) The Survivor: An Anatomy of Life in the Death Camps, Oxford University Press.

DePrince, A.P. (2001) Trauma and posttraumatic responses: An examination of fear and betrayal, University of Oregon Press.

De Vaus, D.A. (1993) Surveys in Social Research (3rd edn.), London: UCL Press.

Dey, I. (1993) Qualitative Data Analysis: A User Friendly Guide For Social Scientist, Routledge , London.

Denzin, N. K. (1989) 3rd edn The Research Act, Prentice Hall, New Jersey.

Denzin, N. K., and Lincoln, Y. S. (1994) A Handbook of qualitative research. Thousand Oaks, Sage Publications, California.

Denzin, K. and Lincoln, Y.S. (Eds.) (1998), Strategies of Qualitative Inquiry, Sage Publications, California.

Denzin, K. and Lincoln, Y.S. (1998) Collecting and Interpreting Qualitative Material, Sage Publications, California.

Denzin, K. and Lincoln, Y.S. (Eds.) (2000) A Handbook of Qualitative Research (2nd edition) Thousand Oaks, Sage Publications, Inc.

Diamond, H. (1999) Women and the Second World War in France 1939-1948, Pearson Education limited, Harlow.

Dombrowski, N.A. (1999) Women and War in the Twentieth Century, Garland Publishing, Inc.

Doyal, L. (1995), What Makes Women Sick, Macmillan Press Ltd.

Duchen, C. and Bandhauer-Schoffmann, I. (eds) (2000) When The War Was Over, Leicester University Press.

ECOSOC (Economic and Social Council of the United Nations), (2005) 'Combating impunity' Report on Human Rights.

Eisenberg, L. (1977) Disease and Illness: Distinctions between Professional and Popular Ideas of Sickness. Culture, Medicine and Psychiatry 1:7-21.

Enloe, C. (1983) The Militarization of Women's Lives, Pluto Press, London.

Enloe, C, (2000) Maneuvers: The International Politics of Militarizing Women's Lives, University of California Press, Berkeley, CA.

Eyre, A. (1998) More than PTSD: Proactive responses among disaster survivors, The Australasian Journal of Disaster and Trauma Studies, (2): 2-11.

Foucault, M. (1994) Power: Essential Works of Foucault 1954-1984 Vol.3 (edited by James Faubion), New Press, New York.

Fanon, Frantz (1967a) Black Skin, White Masks, Published by Grove, New York.

Fanon, (1967c) Toward the African Revolution, Published by Grove, New York.

Fanon, F. (1968) The Wretched of the Earth, Published by Grove, New York

Firestone, S. (1979) The Dialectic of Sex, The Women's Press.

Fletcher, R. (2001) Post-Colonial Fragments: Representations of Abortion in Irish Law and Politics, The Journal of law and Society, 28 (4): 568-589.

Frankfort-Nachmias, C. and Nachmias, D. (1996) Study Guide for Research Methods in the Social Sciences, St. Martin's Press, New York.

Frankel, E., Frankel, J., Khlevniuk, O. (Eds.) (1992) Revolution in Russia: Reassessment of 1917, Cambridge University Press.

Frankfort-Nachmias, C. and Nachmias, D. (1996) Research Methods in the Social Sciences, 5th Edition, Arnold Publications, London.

Fraser, T.G. and Keith, J. (Eds.) (1993) Men, Women and War, Dublin, Lilliput Press, Dublin.

Freeman, M. and Motsei, M. (1992) Planning health care in South Africa: is there a role for traditional healers? Social Science and Medicine, 34:1183-1190.

French, M. (1992) The War Against Women, Hamish, Hamilton Ltd, London.

Gaidzanwa, R. (1992) Bourgeois Theories of gender and Feminism, SAPES Books, Harare.

Gann, L. (1981) The Struggle for Zimbabwe, New York: Praeger Publishers, New York.

Gaskell, G. (2000) Qualitative Researching, Sage Publications

Gaventa, J. (1980) Power and Powerlessness: Quiescence and rebellion in an Appalachian valley, University of Illinois Press, Chicago.

Gelfand, M. (1977) The Traditional Medical Practitioner in Zimbabwe, Mambo Press, Gweru.

Gessler, M. C., Msuya, D. E., Nkunya, M. H. (1995) Traditional healers; traditional medicine; Tanzania, Journal of Ethnopharmacology, (48): 145 -160.

Gilbert, M. (1994) The First World War: A Complete History. Henry Holt, New York.

Gilligan, C. (1982) In a Different Voice: Psychological Theory and Women's Development, Cambridge University Press.

Gilligan, J. (1996) Violence: Our Deadly Epidemic and Its Causes,
Grosset/Putnam books, New York.

Gilson, L., Alilio, M. and Heggenhaugen, K. (1994) Community satisfaction with primary health care services: an evaluation undertaken in the Morogoro region of Tanzania, Social Science and Medicine, (39): 767.

Glaser BG, Strauss AL. (1967) The discovery of grounded theory, Hawthorne, Aldine, New York.

Goldthorpe, J.H. (1969) The affluent worker in the class structure, Cambridge University Press.

Goverde, H., Cerny P. G., Haugaard M., Lentner H. (eds.) (2000) Power in Contemporary Politics, London, Sage.

Green BL, Friedman MJ and de Jong JTVM, (eds.) (2003) Trauma interventions in war and peace: prevention, practice and policy, Kluwer/Plenum, New York.

Green, B. L. (1990) 'Defining trauma: Terminology and generic stressor dimensions' Journal of Applied Social Psychology, (20):1632-1642.

Green, E. and Honwana, A. (1999) "Indigenous healing of war-affected children in Africa" Paper for the World Bank.

Goverde, H. et al. (eds.) (2000) Power in Contemporary Politics:Theories, Practices and Globalisations, Sage Publications.

Guba, E. and Lincoln, Y. (1985) Naturalistic Inquiry, Sage, New York.

Gundani, P. H. (2001) Church, Media, and Healing: A Case Study from
Zimbabwe, Published by Word and World Theology for Christian Ministry, Minnesota.

Gutlove, P. and Thompson, G. (Eds) (2003) Psychosocial Healing: A Guide for Practitioners Based on programs of the Medical Network for Social Reconstruction in the former Yugoslavia, Institute for Resource and Security Studies, Cambridge, Massachusetts.

Hallencreutz C.F.and Palmberg, M. (eds.) (1991) Religion and Politics in Southern Africa, Published by Scandinavian Institute of African Studies, Uppsala.

Hamilton, R. (1978) The Liberation Of Women; A study Of Patriarchy and Capitalism, George Allen & Unwin Publishers, Ltd.

Hammersley, M. (1992) Social Research: Philosophy, Politics and Practice, Sage, London.

Hammersley, M. (1995), The Politics of Social Research, Sage Publications, Ltd, London.

Hammersley, M. and Gomm, R. (1997) Bias in social research, Sociological Research Online, 2 (1).

Hanmer, J. and Maynard, J. (!987) Women, Violence And Social Control, Published by Macmillan Academic And Professional Ltd, London.

Hartley, J, (1994) Hearts Undefeated, Published by Virago Press.

Hartman, J. E. and Messer-Davidow, E. (1991) Academic knowledge and Social Change; in (En) Gendering Knowledge; Feminists in Academic. University Of Tennssee Press.

Hartmann, H. (1982) Capitalism, patriarchy and job segregation by sex, Schocken, New York.

Hawkesworth, M.E. (1999), The continuum Publishing Company, New York.

Hayes, S. (1995) Christian responses to witchcraft and sorcery, The journal of Missionalia, 23 (3): 339-354.

Hayes, B., Coomans, D., and Bradley, B. (1994). Perinatal dysphoria: Recognition and management at three sites in Australia, Public Health Research Development Committee.

Hays, N. (1977) "UDI-A Political Strategy", a written paper on UDI, University of Zimbabwe, Centre for Defence Studies.

Hearn, J. and Collins, D.L. (Eds). (1996) Violences of Men: How Men Talk about and How Agencies Respond to Men's Violence to Women, Sage Publications.

Hegel, G.W.F. (1966) The Phenomenology of Mind, Allen and Unwin, London.

Hennessy, P. (1992) Never Again: Britain 1945-51, Penguin.

Herman, J. (1992) Trauma and Recovery: The Aftermath of Violence-from Domestic Abuse to Political Terror, Basic Books, Harper Collins Publishers, Inc.

Higgins, L. A. and Silver, B. R. (1991) Rape and Representation, Columbia University Press.

Higonnet et al., eds. (1987) Behind the Lines: Gender and the Two World Wars, Yale University Press, New Haven and London.

Holloway, I. (1997) Basic Concepts for Qualitative Research, Oxford: Blackwell Science.

Honwana, A. (1997) "Sealing the Past, Facing the Future: Trauma Healing in Mozambique," in Accord no.3. Conciliation Resources, London.

Honwana, A. (1999) "The Collective Body: Challenging western concepts of trauma and healing", Track Two, 8 (1).

Howard, M. and Paret, P. (1984) Clausewitz, Carl von on war, Princeton University Press.

Huberman, A.M. and Miles, M. (1998) Qualitative Inquiry, Sage, Thousand Oaks, CA.

Hubers, J. (1991) Feminists Methods, Sage Publications, London.

Humbaraci, A. and Munchnik, N. (1974) Portugal's Wars, Joseph Okpaku Publishing company, Inc. New York.

Hungwe, C. (2003) Liberty or Incarceration: A study of the Lives of Elderly People in an Old People's Home, unpublished Masters' Thesis submitted to the Department of Sociology, University of Zimbabwe.

Hutchinson, S. A., Wilson, M. E., & Wilson, H. S (1994) "Benefits of participating in research interviews", IMAGE: Journal of Nursing Scholarship, 26: 161–164.

Igreja, V., Schreuder, B., and Kleijn, W. (1999) The cultural dimension of war traumas in central Mozambique: The case of Gorongosa, Transcultural Mental Health On-Line.

Igreja, V., Schreuder, B., and Kleijn, W. (2001) The cultural dimension of war traumas in central Mozambique: The case of Gorongosa, Psychiatry On-Line.

Inglis, R. (1989) The Children's War, published by William Collins Sons &Co.

Jacobs, S. (1999) Traumatic grief: Diagnosis, treatment and prevention, Published by Brunner and Mazel, New York.

Janoff-Bulman, R. (1985) "The Aftermath of Victimization: Rebuilding Shattered Assumptions," Trauma and Its Wake, Brunner/Mazel, New York.

Jeater, D. (2000) "No place for a woman: Gwelo town, Southern Rhodesia, 1894-1920", Journal of South African Studies, (26): 29-42.

Jeater, D. Law Language And Science: The Invention of the "Native Mind" in Southern Rhodesia, 1890-1930, Heinemann, Portsmouth.

Janoff, B. (1985) Trauma and its wake, Brunner Mazel, New York.

Jirira, O. (1995) "Gender, Politics and Democracy", SAFERE: Southern African Feminist Review, 1 (2): 1–29.

Johnson, J. M. (2002) "Sex, Race, Gender and Power: Southern Rhodesia"
Journal of Women's History, 14 (1): 174-182.

Jong, E. (1987) A Lesser Life, Published by Michael Joseph Ltd, London.

Joseph, S. et al. (Eds.), (1997) Understanding post-traumatic stress: A psychosocial perspective on PTSD and treatment, Wiley, New York.

Joyce, P. (1989) Religions in South Africa, Published by Struik, Cape Town.

Karim, A., Zibuqu-Page, S.S. and Arendse, R. (1994) Bridging the gap: Potential for a health care partnership between African traditional healers and biomedical personnel in South Africa, Medical Association of South Africa, Johannesburg.

Kawachi I. and Kennedy B.P. (1997) The relationship of income inequality to mortality - does the choice of indicator matter? Social Science and Medicine. (45): 1121-7.

Keats, D (200) Interviewing a practical guide for students and professionals Open University Press, Buckingham.

Kesby M. (1996) "Arenas for control, terrains of gender contestation: guerrilla struggle and counter-insurgency warfare in Zimbabwe 1972-80", Journal of Southern African Studies (22): 561-584.

Kester. J.D.(2001). From eyewitness testimony to health care to post-genocide healing Successes and Surprises in the Application of Psychological Science, Journal of American Psychological Society (14): 6.

Kinzie, J. D., Fredrickson, R. H., Ben, R., Fleck, J., and Karls, W. (1984) 'Posttraumatic Stress Disorder Among Survivors of Cambodian concentration Camps' American Journal of Psychiatry, 141 (5): 645-650.

Kitchen, M. (2000) Europe Between the Wars, Longman, New York.

Knight, Z. (2006) 'Trauma and Beyond Trauma of Political Displacement' The Australian Journal of Displacement, 2006 (1).

Kriger, N. (1992) Zimbabwe's Guerrilla War: Peasant Voices, Cambridge University Press.

Krippner, S., & McIntyre, T. (Eds.). (2003)The psychological impact of war trauma on civilians: An international perspective, Praeger, Westport, Connecticut.Kubatana network alliance, (2005) Electoral Systems and Gender Quotas in Southern Africa ,Unpublished Conference paper.

Kubatana network alliance, (2005) Electoral Systems and Gender Quotas in Southern Africa, Unpublished Conference paper.

Kulka, R.A., Schlenger, J.A., Fairbank, R.L., Hough, R.L., Jordan, B.K., Marmar, C.R., and Weiss, D.S. (1990) Trauma and the Vietnam war generation: Report of findings from the national Vietnam veterans readjustment study, Brunner/Mazel, New York.

Kvale, S. (1996) Interviews, An Introduction to Qualitative Research, Sage Publications, London.

Laclau, E. and Mouffe, C. (1985) Hegemony and Socialist Strategy: Towards a Radical Democratic Politics, Published by Verso.

Lan, D. (1985) Guns and Rain, Guerrillas and Spirit Mediums in Zimbabwe, James Curry, London.

Langan, M. and Day, L. (1992) Women, Oppression and Social Work: Issues in Anti-Discriminatory Practice, Routledge Publishers.

Lapchick, E and Urdang, S. (1982) Opression and Resistance: The Struggle of Women in Southern Africa, Greenwood Press, Westport.

LeBeau, D (2005) Experiences of Namibian Ex-Fighters, Peace Centre Research Report.

Lee, R. M. and Renzetti, C. (1993) Doing Research on Sensitive Topics, Newbury Park, CA: Sage Publications.

Lee, R.M. (1993), Doing Research On Sensitive Topics, Sage Publications, London.

Lees, S. (1997) Carnal Knowledge: Rape on Trial, Penguin, Harmondsworth.

Levine-Clark, M. "Engendering Relief: Women, Ablebodiness, and the New Poor Law in Victorian England." Journal of Women's History 11 (4): 107.

Lewis, A. (1942) "Incidence of neurosis in England under war conditions",
Lancet, (2): 175-183.

Lewis, J. (1992). Women in Britain since 1945, Blackwell, London.

Liebling, H. J. and Shah (2001) "Researching Sensitive topics: Investigation of the sexual abuse of women in Uganda and girls in Tanzania" Law Social Justice and Global Development, (LGD) electronic law journal (1).

Lifshitz, F. (1998) "The politics of Historiography: The Memory of Bishops in Eleventh-Century Rouen", History and Memory Journal, (10).

Lyons, A. (1979) Civil violence-the psychological aspects, Journal of
Psychosomatic Research, (23): 373–393.

Maanen J. (1983) Qualitative Methodology, Sage Publications.

Macksoud, M., Dyregrov, A., and Raundalen, M. (1993) Children and mothers in War: An Outcome Study of a Psychosocial Program, Child Development, 72 (4): 1214–1230.

Mahamba, I. (1986) Woman in Struggle, Zimfep, Harare.

Malloy, P.F., Fairbank, J.A., and Keane, T.M. (1983) "Validation of a multimethod assessment of post traumatic stress disorder in Vietnam veterans" J Consult Clinical Psychology, (51): 4-21.

Malakpa, S.W.G. (1994) "The role of special education and rehabilitation in post-war resettlement and reconstruction: the case of Liberia" Liberian Studies Journal, (XIX): 1

Maraire, J.N. (1996) Zenzele: A Letter to my Daughter , Weidenfeld and Nicolson, London.

Mararike, CG. (1999) Survival Strategies in Rural Zimbabwe: The Role of Assets, Indigenous Knowledge, and Organisations. Mond Books, Harare.

Marks, D.F. et al. (2000) Health psychology: theory, research & practice. Sage Publications, London.

Marshall, C. and Rossman, G.B. (1989) Designing Qualitative research, Sage Publications, California.

Marshall, C. and Rossman, G.B. (1999) Designing Qualitative Research, Sage Publications, London.

Marshall, L. (2004) Militarism and Violence against Women: A Feminist Peace Network Journal, Vol. 17 no. 4.

Marshall, P. (1997) Research Methods, How to Design And Conduct A Successful Project, Plymouth: How To Books.

Martin, D. and Johnson, P. (1981) The Struggle for Zimbabwe: The Chimurenga War, Zimbabwe Publishing House.

Marwick, A. (1977) Women at War, 1914-1918, Fontana Paperbacks.

Mason, J (1996) Qualitative researching, Sage Publications, London.

Mason, P.H. (1990) Recovering from the war: A woman's guide to helping your Vietnam vet, your family, and yourself, Penguin, New York.

Matsakis, A. (1988) Vietnam Wives: Women and children suffering with veterans suffering from post-traumatic stress disorder, Woodbine, Washington, DC.

May, T.(1993) Social Research, Open University Press, Buckingham.

Maxwell, D. J. (1993) Local Politics and the War of Liberation in North-East Zimbabwe Journal of Southern African Studies, 19 (3).

Mbiti, J. (1989) African Religions and Philosophy, Heinemann Educational Publishers, Oxford.

MacCurtain, M. and O Corrain, D. (1979) Women In Irish Society: The Historical Dimensions, Greenwood Press, Westport.

McFadden, P. (2001) "Political Power: The Challenges of Sexuality, Patriarchy and Globalization in Africa", Seminar Paper hosted by the Mauritius Women's Movement (MLF) and the Workers Education Association (LPT), Port Louis, Mauritius.

McFadden, P. (2002) "Becoming Post Colonial, African Women changing the meaning of citizenship", Seminar Paper presented at Queens University Canada.

McFarlane, A. and de Girolamo, G. (1996) "The nature of traumatic stressors and the epidemology of posttraumatic reactions" in van der Kolk et al., (Eds.) Traumatic Stress: 129-154. New York: Guilford Press.?

McLaughlin, J. (1996) On the Frontline: Catholic Missions in Zimbabwe's Liberation War, Baobab Books, Harare.

McLean, D.E.and Link, B.G. (1994) Unravelling complexity: Strategies to refine concepts, measures, and research designs in the study of life events and mental health. In W.R. Avison and I.H. Gotlib. (eds.) Stress and mental health: Contemporary issues and prospects for the future, Plenum Press, New York.

McNeill, M. (1960) The Life and Times of Mary Ann McCracken: A Belfast Panorama, Blackstaff Press, Belfast.

Meldrum, A. (2003) The brain drain has badly hit Zimbabwe's fragile health service, The Observer, 10th August.

Melrose, M. (2002) Labour Pains: Some Considerations On The Difficulties Of Researching Juvenile Prostitution: International Journal Of Social Research Methodology, 5 (4)

Melrose, M. (1999) Word from the street: the perils and pains for researching begging in H Dean (ed.) Begging Questions: Street level economic activity and social policy failure. Polity Press.

Miles, M. (994) Qualitative Data Analysis, Sage Publications, Newbury park.

Mitchell, S. (1996) Daily Life in Victorian England. Greenwood, Westport.

Moch, S.D. and Gates, M.F. (2000) The Researcher experience in Qualitative Research, Sage Publications, California.

Moorcraft, P.L. (1990) African Nemesis, Published by Brasse (UK) Ltd.

Moore-King, B. (1988) White Man, Black War, Baobab Books, Harare.

Morse J. M. (1994), Critical issues in qualitative research methods. Thousand Oaks, CA: Sage publications.

Moser, C.A. and Kalton, G. (1983) Survey Methods in Social Investigation, Published by Ashgate Ltd Aldershot, Hampshire.

Mugo, M. G. (2000) Gender Issues- Women in National Liberation Movements. Seminar Series, Southern African Regional Institute Of Police Studies, Harare.

Mukonyora, I, (1999) Women and Ecology in Shona Religion, University of Zimbabwe, Harare.

Mullings, L. (1997) On our own terms : race, class, and gender in the lives of African American women, Routledge, New York.

Mupinda, M. (1997) "Loss and grief among the Shona: the Meaning of Disappearances", Legal Forum, (9): 41-49.

Mungazi, D. (1996) The mind of Black Africa, Praeger Publishers, London.

Mupfudza, R. (2004) Bloodshed is a sin against the Earth and the Creator, The Daily Mirror, 17th Nov.

Musemwa, M. 1996. "The Ambiguities of Democracy: The Demobilisation of the Zimbabwean ex-combatants and the Ordeal of Rehabilitation 1980 -- 1993" in Cilliers, J. Dismissed: Demobilisation and Rehabilitation of Former Combatants in Africa.

Musengezi, C. and Staunton, I. (2003) A Tragedy of lives: Women in prison in Zimbabwe, Weaver Press, Harare.

Musisi, S. (2005) War and mental health in Africa, Masson, Milan.

National centre for PTSD (2005) Centre for the Study of Traumatic Stress: A Guide to understanding posttraumatic stress disorder and acute stress disorder, Washington DC.

Ndetei, D. M. & Muhangi, J. (1979) The prevalence and clinical presentation of psychiatric illness in a rural setting in Kenya, British Journal of Psychiatry, (135): 269 –272.

Neuman, W. L., (2000) Social Research Methods; Quantitative and Qualitative Approaches, 4th edn. Boston, MA: Allyn and Bacon.

Newman, E. (1997) Survey research Methods, California: Sage Publications.

Newell, R. (1994) Interviewing Skills for Nurses and Other Health Care Professionals, Routledge, London.

Nhongo-Simbanegavi, J. (2000) For Better or Worse: Women and ZANLA in Zimbabwe's Liberation Struggle, Weaver Press, Harare.

Northrup, C. (1994) Women's Bodies, Women's Wisdom: Creating Physical and Emotional Health and Healing, Bantam Books, New York.

Nyangoni, W. (1978) African Nationalism in Zimbabwe, University Press of America, Washington DC.

Nzenza, S. (1988) Zimbabwean Woman - My Own story, Karia Press.

Obelkevich, J., Lyndal Roper, and Raphael S. (Eds.) (1987) Disciplines of Faith, Studies in Religion, Politics, and Patriarchy, Routledge and Kegan Paul Ltd.

Omaar, R. and de Waal, Alex. (Eds.) (1995) Rwanda: Not So Innocent When Women Become Killers, African Rights, London.

O'Toole, L. L. and Schiffman, J.R. (1997), Gender Violence: Inter discipline Perspective, New York University Press.

Oxfam, (2003) "Women's Land Rights in Southern and Eastern Africa", Sarpn Journal.

Patel, V., Gwanzura, F.and Simunyu, E.(1995) The explanatory models and phenomenology of common mental disorder in Harare, Zimbabwe, Psychological Medicine, (25): 1191 –1199.

Patel, V., Todd, C. and Winston, M. (1997) Common mental disorders in primary care in Harare, Zimbabwe: associations and risk factors, British Journal of Psychiatry, (171): 60 –64.

Parkinson, F. (1993) Post-trauma stress, Sheldon Press, London.

Payne, S., Horn, S., and Relf, M. (2000) Loss and bereavement, Buckingham: Open University Press.

Polit, D.F., Beck, C.T. and Hungler, B.P., (2001), Nursing Research: Principles and Methods, Lippincott, Philadelphia.

Preston-Shoot, M, Roberts, G. and Vernon, S. (2001) Values In Social Work Law: Strained Relations Or Sustaining relationships, Journal Of Social Welfare And Family, 23 (1).

Punch, M. (1986) The Politics and Ethics of Fieldwork, Sage Publications, Beverly Hills.

Pugh, M. (1992) Women and the women's movement in Britain 1914-1959, Macmillan, Basingstoke.

Raeburn, M. (1978) Black Fire! Accounts Of The Guerrilla War In Rhodesia, Julian Friedman Publishers Ltd, London.

Rai, S. M., Lievesley, G. (Eds.) (1996) Women and the State: International Perspectives, Taylor and Francis, London.

Raine, N. V. (1999) After Silence, Published by Virago, London

Ranger, T. (1967) Revolt in Southern Rhodesia 1896-97: A Study in African Resistance, Heinemman, London.

Ranger, T. and Alexander, J. (1998) Competition and Integration in the Religious History of North-Western Zimbabwe, Journal of Religion in Africa, (28): 3-31.

Ranger, T. (1999) Voices from the Rocks: Nature, Culture and History in the Matopos Mountains, University of Indiana Press, Bloomington.

Reardon, T. (1993) Women and Peace, Suny Press, New York.

Reeler, A. P., and Mupinda, M. (1996) "Investigation into the sequelae of Torture and Organised Violence amongst Zimbabwean War Veterans", Legal Forum, (8): 12-27.

Reeler, A.P., Mbape,P., Matshona,J., Mhetura,J., and Hlatywayo, E. (2001) "The prevalence and nature of disorders due to torture in Mashonaland Central", Torture, (11): 4-9.

Reid-Daly, R. (2001) Pamwe Chete: The Legend of the Selous Scouts, Covos-Day Books.

Reinharz, S. (1992) Feminist Methods in Social Research, Newbury Park, CA: Sage.

Reissman, C. K. (1993) Narrative analysis, Newbury Park, Sage, California.

Reynolds, P. (1996) Traditional Healers and childhood in Zimbabwe, Ohio University press.

Reiter, A. (2000) Narrating the Holocaust, Continuum International Publishing group.

Richter M. M. (Ed) (2001) Immigrant Groups from Southeastern Europe in Trieste. In N. Švob Đokic, Redefining Cultural Identities, Culturelink, Institute for International Relations, Zagreb.

Ribbens, J. and Edwards R. (1998) Feminist Dilemmas in Qualitative Research, Sage Publications, London.

Richards, K., Pillay, Y., Mazodze, O., Govere, A.S. (2000) "The Impact of Colonial Culture in apartheid South Africa and Rhodesia on Identity Development: An African Perspectives", Paper published by North Carolina A and T State University.

Robson, C. (1993) Real World Research, Blackwell Publishers (Ltd), Oxford.

Rogel, C. (1998)The Break up of Yugoslavia And The War In Bosnia, Greenwood Press, Inc. Westport.

Roncaglia, I. (2003, December) "Analysing recorded interviews: Making sense of Oral History", Conference Report,

Rossi, P.H., and Freeman, H. E. (1993) Evaluation, A systematic Approach, Thousand Oaks, CA: Sage Publications, Inc.

Roth, S. et al. (1990) 'Victimisation history and victim assailant relationship as factors in recovery from sexual assault' Journal of Traumatic Stress, 3(1), 169-180.

Rossiter, A. (1990) Granting Civil Rights to the Foetus in Ireland - A Victory to Christian Fundamentalists Worldwide: Women Against Fundamentalisms (1): 8-10.

Rowbotham, S. (1973) Hidden from History, Pluto Press, London.

Sandelowski, M. (1994) "We are the stories we tell: Narrative knowing in economic geography" The Professional Geographer, (43)

Sapolsky, R.M. (1994) Why zebras don't get ulcers: A guide to stress, stress-related diseases, and coping, WH Freeman and Company, New York.

Saywell, S. (1985) Women In War, Grapevine Publishers.

Schlebusch, L. (1990) Clinical health psychology: A behavioural medicine perspective, Southern publishers, Johannesburg.

Schmidt, E. (1992) Peasants, Traders and Wives. Shona women in the history of Zimbabwe, 1870-1939, James Currey, London.

Schoenberger, E. (1991) The corporate interview as a research method in economic geography, The Professional Geographer , 43 (2):180-189.

Schwandt, T.A. (1997) Qualitative Inquiry. Thousand Oaks, CA: Sage.

Seidman, G.W. (1984) Women in Zimbabwe: Post Independence Struggles; Feminist Studies, 10 (3).

Seidman, I. (1998) Interviewing as qualitative research: A guide for Researchers in Education and Social Sciences, New York: Teachers College Press.

Shakespeare, P., Atkinson, D., French, s., (Eds.) (1993) Reflecting on Research Practice, Open University Press, Buckingham.

Shaw, R.(2002) Memories of the Slave Trade: ritual and the historical imagination in Sierra Leone, University of Chicago Press.

Shay, J. (1994) Achilles in Vietnam: Combat Trauma and the Undoing of Character, Atheneum, New York.

Shoko, T. (2006) My Bones Shall Rise Again, Paper on War Veterans, Spirits And Land, University of Zimbabwe.

Sieber, J. E. and Stanely, B. (1988) "Ethical and Professional Dimensions of Socially Sensitive Research", Psychologist, 43 (1).

Silverman, D. (1999) Doing Qualitative Research: A Practical Handbook, Sage: London.

Sinclair, I. (1996) 'She was the flame they could never put out': A film transcript based on the role of women and the struggles for the independence, Zim Media Productions.

Smith, B. (1986) The War's Long Shadow, Published by Andre Deutsch Limited.

Somnier, E., and Genefke, I. K. (1986). "Psychotherapy for Victims of Torture" British Journal of Psychiatry, (149): 323-329.

Spielberger, C.D. (1979) Anxiety: Current trends in theory and research, New York: Academic Press.

Spradley (1979) Participant Observation, Harcourt, College Press.

Stanton, C. E. (1898) The Woman's Bible, European Publishing Company, New York.

Staub, E. (2000) Genocide and mass killings: Origin, prevention, healing, and Reconciliation, Political Psychology, (21): 367-382.

Staunton, I (1990) Mothers of the Revolution: The Experiences of Thirty Zimbabwean Women, James Currey, London.

Stephens, W. (2002) Demon Lovers: Witchcraft, Sex, and the Crisis of Belief, University of Chicago Press, Chicago.

Straker, G. (1992) "The continuous traumatic stress syndrome: the single therapeutic interview", Psychology in Society, (8): 48-78.

Summerfield, D. (2000) "Childhood, war, refugeedom and 'trauma': Three core questions for mental health professionals", Transcultural Psychiatry, 37 (3): 417-433.Summerfield, D. (1995) Beyond trauma: Cultural and societal dynamics, Plenum Press, New York, 1995.

Sumerfield, P. (1989) Women Workers In The Second World War, Routledge, London.

Taber, R. (1970) The War Of The Flea, Paladin publishers.

Terraine, J. (1970) Impacts of War 1914 and 1918, Hitchinson and co.

Thompson, K. (1978) Man's Religious Quest: Quest and questioning, The Open University Press.

Thompson, P. (1988) The Voice of the Past: Oral History, Oxford/New York.

Truman, C. et al. (2000), Research And Inequality, UCL Press, London.

Turner, K. and Phan, T. (1998) Even the Women Must Fight: Memories of War from North Vietnam, John Wiley and Sons, New York.

Turshen, M. (2002) "Algerian Women in the liberation struggle and the civil war: from active participants to passive victims?" Social Research: An

International Quarterly of Social Sciences, 69 (3): 889-911.

Turshen, M. and Twagiramariya, C. (Eds.) (1998) What Women Can Do in War Time, Zed Books, London and New York.

Urdang, S. (1989) And Still They Dance, Published by New York University Press.

Van der Kolk, B.A. (1987) Psychological trauma. American Psychiatric Press Inc. Washington.

Thompson, P. (1988) The voices of the Past: Oral History, Oxford University Press.

Van der Geest, S., Speckmann, J. D. and Streefland, P. H. (1990) Primary health care in a multi-level perspective: towards a research agenda, Social Science and Medicine, (30):1025 –1034.

Van der Geest, S (1997) Is there a role for traditional medicine in basic health services in Africa? A plea for a community perspective, Tropical Medicine and International Health, 2 (9): 903-911.

Van, Maanenn J. (1983) Qualitative Methodology, Sage Publications.

Van Rensburg, H.C.J. & Marts, A. (1982). Profile of disease and health care in South Africa, Published by Academia, Pretoria.

Vogel, L. (1983) Marxism and the Oppression of Women: Toward a Unitary Theory, Rutgers University Press, New Brunswick, New Jersey.

Waite, G. (2000) 'Traditional Medicine and the Quest for National Identity' in Zimbabwe, in Zambezia, 25 (2).

Wanyeki, L (2003) Women and Land in Africa: Culture, Religion, and Realizing Women's Rights, Zed Books Ltd., London.

Ward, M. (1983) Unmanageable Revolutionaries: Women and Irish Nationalism, Pluto Press, London.

Waterhouse, R. (1996) Mozambique Rising From the Ashes, published by Oxfam, Oxford.

Weber, M. (1978) Economy and Society: An Outline of Interpretive Sociology, in Fischoff et al. University of California Press. Berkeley, California.

Webner, R. (1999) Tears of the Dead, James Currey, London.

Weisbord, A. (1974) Perspective for the Portuguese Revolution, From the magazine La Parola del Popolo May-June 1974.

Weiss, R. (1986) The Women of Zimbabwe, Kesho Publications, London.

Weiss, R. (1995), Learning from Strangers, The Free Press, New York.

Westad, O.A. (2005) The Global Cold War: Third World Interventions and the Making of Our Times, Cambridge University Press.

Wiles, R., Charles, V., Crow, G. and Heath, S. (2004) Informed consent and the research process, a paper presented at the ESRC Research Festival at the university of Oxford.

Windle, P. (1995) "The ecology of grief ", BioScience, (42): 363-366

Windrich, E. (1978) Britain and the Politics of Rhodesian Independence, Africana Publishing Company, New York.

White, A.M. (2003) All the Men are Fighting for Freedom, All the Women are Mourning Their Men, But Some of Us Carried Guns: Fanon's Psychological Perspectives on War and African Women Combatants, Boston Consortium on Gender, Security and Human Rights, Working Paper No. 106, Pennsylvania State University.

Winter, J. (1995) Sites of Memory, Sites of mourning: The Great War in European Cultural History, Cambridge University Press.

Woollacott, A. (1994) On Her Their Lives Depend: Munitions Workers in the Great War, University of California Press, Berkeley and Los Angeles.

Young, I. M. (1990) Justice and the Politics of Difference, Princeton: Princeton University Press.

Zimbabwe African National Union Patriotic Front – ZANU PF (2005) The Importance of the National Anthem and Flag, Department of Information and Publicity, Harare.

Zimbabwe Women Writers (2000), Women of Resilience: The Voices of
Women's Ex-combatants, Zimbabwe women writers, Harare.

Ziyambi, N. (1997) The Battle of the Mind: International New Media Elements of the New Religious
Political Right in Zimbabwe, University of Oslo, Oslo.

On line sources

On line: BBC News of The World on Witchcraft, 12th August 2006, http://news.bbc.co.uk/2/hi/
africa/5141406.stm.

O line: religion and ethics, 30th August 2005, http//www.bbc.co.uk/religion/religions/paganism/
subdivisions/wicca.shtml -

http://web.odu.edu/webroot/instr/AL/smoorti.nsf/pages/reflections

On line: Betrayal in Freyd, J.J. (2005) What is a Betrayal Trauma? What is Betrayal Trauma Theory?
17th July 2007,

http://dynamic.uoregon.edu/~jjf/defineBT.html.

On line: British Educational Research Ethics, 10th September 2003,
www.bera.ac.uk.

On line:Chiwome, E. and Mguni, Z. 2003. "The Discourse on Zimbabwean Women in the War
of Liberation and the Land Reform Programme: Myth and Reality", 17th July 2005, http://www.
gwsafrica.org/knowledge/zifikele.

On line: Complementary healing in Wessells, M. (2007) Trauma, culture and community: Getting
beyond dichotomies, 11th October 2007,

(www.child-soldiers.org/resources/psychosocial).

On line: Data analysis of interview transcripts, 15th January 2006,
http://www.coe.uga/html

On line: Data Analysis of interview transcripts, 15th January, 2006 http://web.odu.edu/webroot/
instr/AL/smoorti.nsf/pages/reflections

On line: Declaration on the Elimination of Violence Against Women: General Assembly resolution
48/104 of 20 December 1993, 12th June, 2005, www.ohchr.org/english/law/eliminationvaw.htm

On line: Dullar Omar, South Africa's Minister of Justice discusses the Truth and Reconcilliation
Commission, 8th April 1997.

On line: Ethics, Bioethics Journal (15): 341-344, Cambridge University Press, 15th December 2006,
http://journals.cambridge.org/

On line, Ethics, Bioethics Journal (15): 381-391, Cambridge University Press, 15th December 2006,
http://journals.cambridge.org/.

On line: Gender relations of power are maintained through a set of institutional and cultural
practices, 7th January 2007,

http://interconnected.org/matt/archive/musings/Gender.html.

On line: Health effects of TNT, 20th January 2008
http://www.atsdr.cdc.gov/toxprofiles/tp80-c5.pdf.

On line: More Falklands veterans have committed suicide, 2nd August 2007,, http://campaignfortruth.
com/contact.htm.

On Line: National Health Service, Health Assessment Indictors, 17th July 2007, www.bedshealth.
nhs.uk.

On line: Narrative inquiry-making history of the past, 11th November, 2005,
http//barthes.ens/Mansfield

On line: Self Dialogue, Identity and Narration', 11th November 2005, http//barthes.ens/ Mansfield.

On line: Stop Violence Fact sheets, 5th August, 2005
www.amnestyusa.org/stopviolence/factsheets/armedconflict.html

On line: Sudan: rape as a weapon of war in Darfur, 5th August 2005.
www.amnestyusa.org/stopviolence/factsheets/armedconflict.html

On line: The German Minister's apology to the Namibians, 13th November 2005, http://www.africa.no/Detailed/6694.html.

On line: What Paul Linde Learned from His African Patients, 11th June 2006, http://www.noevalleyvoice.com/2001/October/Lind.html.

Theses

Lan, D. (1983) "Making history: Spirit Mediums and the Guerrilla War in Dande Area of Zimbabwe", PhD thesis, London School of Economics.

Nhongo-Simbanegavi, J. (1997) ", Zimbabwean Women In the Liberation Struggle: ZANLA And Its Legacy, 1972-1985", PhD thesis, University of Oxford.

O'Gorman, E. (1999) "Gender, resistance, and Zimbabwe's liberation struggle", PhD thesis, University of Cambridge.

Shah, A. (2002) "South Asians Muslims Adjusting to British Citizemship", PhD thesis, University of Luton,

Newspaper articles

The Financial Gazette, 10th April 1997, Female guerrillas threaten to expose the rapists.

The Herald, 10th April 1997 (Zimbabwean National Newspaper), Discourse on Gender and War.

The Herald, May 10, 2006 (Zimbabwean National Newspaper), Witchcraft Act Amendment Hailed.

The Jackson Advocate Newspaper, 5th October 2002, Meeting challenges in this new century.

The Independent, 26th November 2006, Dead by 34: How Aids and starvation condemn Zimbabwe's women to early grave.

The International Herald Tribune, 24th October 2007, UN issues warning on violence against women in post-conflict countries.

The New York Times, 17th January 1917, Munitions Plant Blast.

The Zimbabwe solidarity newsletter, 3rd February 2005, Experience of women recruits in the ZANLA forces.

Organisations

The American Psychiatric Association Diagnostic and statistical manual of mental disorders (1981) Causes of Secondary amenorrhea, American Psychiatric Association, Washington DC.

The American Psychiatric Association Diagnostic and statistical manual of mental disorders (1987) War traumas, American Psychiatric Association Washington DC.

The American Psychiatric Association Diagnostic and statistical manual of mental disorders (2000) War traumas, American Psychiatric Association Washington DC.

The Barrow Neurological Institute (2003) Post Traumatic Stress, New York.

The Catholic Commission for Justice and Peace in Zimbabwe (1997) Breaking The Silence: a Report on the Disturbances in Matebeleland and the Midlands, Published by CCJPZ, Harare.

The Catholic Commission for Justice and Peace in Zimbabwe (1976), The Man In The Middle: torture, resettlement and Eviction and Civil War in Rhodesia, Published by CCJPZ, Harare.

The Center for Disease Control Vietnam Experience Study (1988) "Health status of Vietnam veterans: Psychosocial characteristics", Journal of the American Medical Association, 259: 2701-7.

The European Society of Traumatic Stress Studies (1998) First international conference on psycho-social consequences of war, Dubrovnik, Republic of Croatia.

The International Conference of The Red Cross, Women and War, Geneva, 59th Annual Session of the United Nations Commission on Human Rights. Agenda item 12 - 11 April 2003.

The United Nations Children Fund Report (1994) Rights and Rehabilitation, Harare.

The United Nations Children's Fund (1986), African Crisis: The Human Dimension of Political Conflict, United Nations, New York.

The United Nations Development Fund for women (2000), Women War Peace and violence against women, United Nations, New York.

The United Nations High Commissioner for Human Rights, (2004) Remedy and Reparation for Victims of Violations of International Human Rights and Humanitarian Law, United Nations Resolution, Geneva.

The World Council of churches (1998) Ecumenical Decade of Churches in Solidarity with Women, Ecumenical Decade Festival, Belvedere Technical Teachers College, Harare, Zimbabwe.

The World Health Organization report (1948) Violence and Health, International Health Conference, New York.

The World Health Organisation report (1994) Health and Development Issues, Harare.

The World Health Organisation Report (1997) Psychosocial Needs of Children in Armed Conflict and Displacement , Geneva.

The World Health Organization report (2001) Mental health: new understanding, new hope, Geneva, Switzerland.

The World Health Organization report (2002) Traditional Medicines, Washington.

The World Health Organization report (2005) Resolution on health action in crises and disasters, Geneva.

The Zimbabwe Human Rights NGO Forum (2000) Organised violence and Torture during the liberation struggle, Special Report.

The Zimbabwe Human Rights NGO Forum (2001) Gender and Constitutional Issues: A Special Report 2 by the Research Unit.